The Good Thing About Mortar Shells

Choosing Love Over Fear

When love beckons to you, follow him,
Though his ways are hard and steep.
And when his wings enfold you yield to him,
Though the sword hidden among his pinions may wound you.
–Khalil Gibran

Jennifer van Wyck

Published by Van Wyck Consulting, August 2020
ISBN: 9781777339807

Editor: Maz Loton
Typeset: Greg Salisbury
Book Cover Design: George B Stevens

DISCLAIMER: This book is a self-help guide intended to offer information on how to live an exceptional life. It is not intended in any way to replace other professional health care or mental health advice, but to support it. If you should feel any strong emotions that you are having difficulty managing, please seek professional help. Readers of this publication agree that neither Jennifer van Wyck, nor her publisher will be held responsible or liable for damages that may be alleged as resulting directly or indirectly from the use of this publication. Neither the publisher nor the author can be held accountable for the information provided by, or actions resulting from, accessing these resources.

"The good thing about mortar shells is they make holes in all the walls and so the birds can make nests." That is what I had said while sitting on the roof of our compound in Syria. I was there during the civil war, at the time when the world was trying to deal with the influx of Syrian refugees trying to escape where I had made my new home. I lounged on the roof of our guesthouse, trying to get some needed fresh air and sunlight. As I was talking with my family, the birds were chirping cheerfully in the background. My dad had commented on how surprised he was to hear the sound of birds. Then we had a heartfelt conversation about how yes, war exists, but love always overcomes. He was so moved by what I had said that he later emailed me and said I needed to make this quote the title of my future book. I dedicate this book to both my parents that have been so supportive of my choices.

Acknowledgments

To my teacher and twin flame, Cora van Wyck and her soul mate and my father Gerald van Wyck. Thank you for birthing me, trusting me, pushing me and preparing me for the world. Mom thank you especially for constantly reminding me of the path of love and alerting me if you think I'm getting off track. You both are the most incredible parents I could wish for.

To my Mentors and spiritual teachers, Alyson Jones and Diane Raphael. You both have nurtured and supported me on this career path and spiritual path. I cannot express my gratitude for everything you have done.

To all my clients! It is beyond incredible to be able to witness your courage and vulnerability and strength. You face your fears and gain new insights and teach me new things every day. You force me to clarify my concepts and create techniques so that you can experience the truth of your own knowing. I am continually humbled and inspired by you.

To my brothers Thomas and Christopher/Max, thank you for challenging me and calling me out and teaching me and supporting me. I have been shaped and continue to learn and grow from you both. I would not be me without you!

To all my friends who have patiently and compassionately supported me through the years. Pierre, Lorentza, Krystal, Constance, Marie Noelle, Fatih, Mari, Charlie, Olga, Julie, Jodi, Azaria, Cedric, Sam, and Jessie. You comfort me when I'm struggling and remind me about love. You have philosophical conversations until all hours of the night. You put up with my repetitive dad jokes and let loose and enjoy the silly little things of life with me. You celebrate my joy as if it was your own. I couldn't ask for better friends.

Oma and Opa yes cat, you are constantly in my thoughts and your unwavering support, prayers and lovely emails are such a gift.

To Julie Salisbury my publisher and editor for helping me make something coherent out of all the ideas, theories and techniques that were floating around in my brain. Your calm phone calls and guidance in this emotional and vulnerable process was a life raft in stormy seas. I could not have done this without you.

To Holly Chadwick, thank you so much for your support in the promotion of my book. Your expertise is essential in ensuring this book lands in the hands of those that need to read it.

To all the humanitarians who jeopardize their personal and physical life for the betterment of others, your courage and passion is awe inspiring and it is a pleasure to work alongside such caring, intelligent, and bighearted people.

To all the people who I have crossed paths with that have changed my life profoundly, the young man who yelled at me, the bus driver who smiled, the young woman who didn't give me change and the hundreds of others who I believe are angels on earth and have given me an invaluable gift, I am so incredibly grateful for the gifts you have given me.

To my ex-husband. You are a wonderful human and it was a pleasure to share nine years of life together. You taught me unconditional love for which I will be eternally grateful.

Contents

Introduction

When I was 16, I almost checked myself into an insane asylum. I was quite sure that I needed to be put in a straitjacket and left in a padded room. I even went as far as to confide my fears to my mom, telling her I was convinced that I was certifiably crazy and that I was perilously close to completely losing my mind.

It turned out I was going through an existential crisis, my first of now three. I was also struggling with generalized anxiety disorder, which I'd had since I was a small child. But I had never been diagnosed, so I had no idea what was going on until almost 10 years later. Additionally, I was a highly sensitive empath, so all of these sensations felt 10 times worse than for someone less sensitive. I felt like I was literally losing my mind—ergo, the insane asylum.

If you have ever felt like there was something wrong with you or that stress is consuming your life, if you feel anxious or heartbroken, lonely or afraid that you're on the wrong path, then there is a reason you are reading this book right now. Fear has consumed so many lives. It is our natural default to avoid and look out for things we're afraid of. But there is another entirely different way of living.

Instead of the path of fear, we can choose the way of love.

Choosing love over fear doesn't mean ignoring fear, or pretending that fear or shitty things in the world don't exist. In fact, it's just the opposite; if we are to make a choice, that means we know and acknowledge the existence of the things we need to choose between, in this case, love and fear. Choosing love means seeing fear, seeing pain, seeing destruction and wanting something different: choosing love.

This book is made up of four parts. The first three parts address different kinds of fear: the more we look at fear and understand it, the more impossible it is for it to control us. The last part discusses love: what it is and how we can choose it in every moment.

As I write this book, I'm in confinement in France. The Pandemic is happening right now, and yes, I'm one of those who used it to write a book. I can't help but feel that the universe has conspired against me somehow, knowing that I would continue to put off writing this (as I have for the past six years) unless I was given no other choice. But now, I'm finally attempting to put my experiences into words; my experience of being a human, a humanitarian, and a psychotherapist, and continually striving to choose love over fear.

This book is a culmination of my life lessons until now. I'm not very old, nearly 40, yet I have lived life fully. I have truly looked death in the face. I have walked across fire and sailed across an ocean. I have worked as a humanitarian in some of the toughest places in the world, assisting struggling communities after losing everything because of disease, war or natural disaster. I have received a Meritorious Service Medal from the Canadian government for the work I did during the Ebola outbreak. I have just finished spending two years in Syria working in areas previously controlled by ISIS. But most important is that as a psychotherapist where I have delved into the depths of my soul. By exploring the universe that is yourself, and by facing those evil, dark, hideous and monstrous places that hide in all of us with compassion, that is when we can finally achieve true happiness.

I am still on this journey of choosing love. I still struggle with fear and the belief that I'm inadequate. I've avoided writing this book because I'm so scared of the responsibility that writing a book has and how it forces me to shine my light, something that I have regularly shied away from. As I write these words, I have a brutal head cold, and usually, when I get sick, it's my body's way of telling me to take time for myself, but this time the message is one of fear. My body is telling me, "Don't write this. Who are you to write a book? Who cares what you have to say? You're taking on too much. You can't do this." I am listening to these thoughts and asking for the fear under them to be healed, and I'm going ahead and writing anyway.

I'm not writing this book because I'm perfect, but because I know I have to write it. Perhaps people might look at my life and feel sorry for me: I'm in the process of a divorce, I've been quarantined alone for the last two months, I've lost two jobs because of the pandemic, and I have no idea about what will happen in the future. In the last couple of years, my life has crumbled around me. No, I'm not wealthy or successful, yet I do have something that many people spend their entire lives trying to find: I have a deep sense of love and joy. At this moment, my heart is singing; it is expanding so much that my chest can't contain it. Now I can see joy and beauty everywhere. My heart radiates love and warmth, and I can't help but think I am the luckiest person in the world!

One of my goals of writing this book is to show how it's possible to go from anxiety and fear to happiness and love, regardless of outer circumstances. I was born an anxious little girl who hid in the world of intellect. But then I was catapulted into the realm of emotions, ironically through my study of quantum physics, which I integrated into my master's thesis. Then I was pushed to my limits and forced to learn how to harness my huge heart. So now, I am immersed in love and fulfillment, even when I'm surrounded by disaster and suffering.

I believe that you can find happiness regardless of where you live or in what situation you find yourself. Although our life circumstances can undoubtedly limit our choices, I still believe happiness is possible (although more difficult) in the direst situations. I genuinely hope that my small life will offer you the insight, techniques, and perhaps the inspiration to dare to find happiness in your own life. I will use my own bumbling life as an example of what has and hasn't worked, and then also give concrete, practical ways that I have used with hundreds of others so that you too can experience joy and healing, and expand from lessons on your own journey.

In this book, we will look fear in the face together. We will understand the different types of fear: external, learned, and internal. We will see how they impact your life, and then I will give you techniques of how you can heal these fears. Lastly, we will look at what it means to choose love, how you can choose love in every moment, and how you can fill your life with happiness and joy. I hope you will get an intellectual knowledge of how to find happiness and also a knowing in your heart by incorporating the techniques and exercises. How often do we know in our head that something is terrible, but we do it anyway? But when you know something in your heart, you can't help but change. You are about to embark on a powerful journey. It's not easy, but it is the most important journey of your life.

The messages, techniques and worldview contained in this book are just my paths. There are hundreds of roads, and if you don't resonate with my guidance, then there is nothing wrong with you; it just means there's a different path for you. I'll still see you at the top of the mountain because all of us will get there no matter which way we choose. Some of us might take a little longer, or perhaps take the more tortured path, but all routes are perfect.

I know love in such a beautiful and deeply meaningful way, and it infuses the cells of my body and shines out of my soul, and I cannot possibly ask for a better gift. My most profound wish is that you experience this as well, on whatever path you choose to take.

Keep connected to Love

Choosing love over fear requires companionship and support. I want to do all I can to assist you on this journey. Below are some ways you can stay connected to love.

www.vanwyckconsulting.com
Go to my website and find free meditations, tools, interviews and information on how to delve into this journey deeper.

#thegoodthingaboutmortarshells
Share your stories of choosing love over fear! Give inspiration and feel the love using #thegoodthingaboutmortarshells

Grounding
Throughout this book I refer to grounding which is foundational for everything we do. Download my free grounding meditation at www.vanwyckconsulting.com and feel yourself more in control, more peaceful and more purposeful in 21 days.

Part 1

External Fears

And think not you can direct the course of love, for love, if it finds you worthy, directs your course.
Love has no other desire but to fulfil itself.
Khalil Gibran

Chapter 1
External Fears

In the year 2001, the country of Zimbabwe was going through a terrible crisis. The dictator, Robert Mugabe, was systemically killing Caucasian settlers and appropriating their land. Naturally, as a wisp of a girl who was often mistaken for a child—even though I was the wise old age of 20—I decided I needed to go there. At the airport, my father offered me 5,000 Canadian dollars (double my savings) not to go.

The biggest challenges were before I even boarded the plane. Grappling with doubt and choosing love. I want to tell you my story, the indecision along with the adventure.

It was a while ago, and so my memory is fuzzy on how it all unfolded. But I know that I had decided to backpack with two girlfriends of mine through South Africa, Namibia, Botswana, Zambia, Malawi, Mozambique and Zimbabwe. I also KNEW that this was something I had to do. I had a distinct feeling that this trip would change my life, and although I was right, I was completely wrong about how I was going to accomplish it.

Listening to other people's fears

My poor father. I was his little girl, and little did he know that I was experiencing my first *knowing* form of intuition. He didn't know that I felt I had no choice but to listen to my heart. Of course, my trip terrified him.

After trying to use the regular routes of logic and wise parental advice, he escalated his tactics. I started getting asked to go for coffee by his friends who had fled South Africa, and they would tell me their horror stories involving death and rape. Simultaneously, my dad sent me news reports of all the horrible atrocities that were going on there. I became increasingly petrified.

But the beautiful gift of being born with high levels of anxiety is that I was used to being scared. In fact, I was always afraid. It forced me to learn at a young age that if I ever wanted to leave my house, then I couldn't let fear influence my decisions. Still, I wasn't only terrified about what would happen in Southern Africa, I was also petrified of what my dad would think of me, and of him being angry with me for disobeying him. Although my mom was silent, I didn't want to disappoint her either, or for both of them to think I was stupid. The fear of what others will think of us is often the scariest fear of all.

But when I know, I really just know, down to the cells of my body. I believe that we always have a choice in life, even if circumstances reduce the choices available to us. I know I could have chosen not to follow my intuition, but that option didn't feel possible to me; it would have felt wrong in every part of my being. Not only was I was scared of disappointing my parents, but I was also frightened and quite convinced that I would probably die in Africa, but I still felt I had to go.

Now I feel lucky that I have such a strong sense of knowing, but back then, I didn't feel lucky. I was consumed with guilt and torn between my knowing and my parents' certainty that I should stay.

Who am I to know better than them? Why is it so important that I go if I'm probably going to die? What is the right thing to do? It took extreme willpower to not give in to their fears. But even at that age, I knew that the "right" thing was to follow my intuition. I have found that as the years have progressed, I will have a knowing that I need to do something, and then that knowing will go away, and I have to trust that I still have to do that same thing even though I can't feel it anymore. Thankfully, in this first instance of experiencing knowing, the feeling stayed with me, which allowed me to get through what happened next.

I remember my dad taking me aside in our house. I remember he was nervous, and I knew whatever he would say to me came from his heart. He prefaced the conversation with the fact that as my father, he needed to do everything he could to make sure I was safe. He paused, and then he said for his own conscience that he then had to tell me that if I insisted on going on this trip, if I continued to ignore the information and signs showing me how dangerous this trip would be, if I refused to take care of my life and was stubborn about putting my life in danger, then he, as my father, had no choice but to kick me out of the family.

My heart stopped.

We are a very close family. He didn't actually say kick me out of the family. Rather, if I left, "I couldn't come back to this home and that he couldn't continue to have me as a daughter," because it was too painful for him.

It's funny how time slows down when you need it to. It gave me the chance to understand, at that moment, he loved me so much that he felt he needed to do this. My heart went out to him. I took a deep breath and told him I understood. I told him that I loved him so much and that I'm sorry it had come to this, but that I still needed to go to Africa. However, I respected what he felt he needed to do.

And to my wonderful dad's credit, he immediately back-pedalled.

He said hurriedly that he couldn't really kick me out of the family, and then something along the lines of, "Why I was so stubborn?" and "Why did I feel like I had to go so much?!" We hugged, and from then on, our relationship changed. I was no longer his little girl, and he was no longer my godlike father, but we were equals who could share our problems and listen to each other's theories on life. Like all things, this shift was a subtle change in our relationship that I couldn't put into words until a couple of years later.

Why did I have to go to Africa?

Nothing major happened on that trip; no life-changing events. It was a fantastic trip, and we saw all the Big Five wild animals. We made friends with many people, and countless strangers invited us to their houses and shared the little food they had with us. We drank this disgusting homemade yogurt alcoholic drink that makes you want to throw up. We went to "bush parties." We lived out of a tent for four months. We hitchhiked across Southern Africa, got stranded multiple times, and hitched a ride on the back of a small pickup with 20 other people all squished together holding on to nothing but each other. We got kicked out of numerous bars because we were with friends of a different race from us. We had to bribe the police so they would stop beating up our friend. We defended our lives, frantically banging pots and waving large sticks of fire against a herd of elephants trying to stampede our small camp, while simultaneously a massive bush fire closed in on us. We laughed, we cried, we communed with nature, and we made lots of friends.

It was a fantastic trip.

But I remember getting back home and being disappointed. It was a great trip, but nothing that spoke to my soul. It was a phenomenal vacation, but not a life-changing adventure. It wasn't something that seemed to justify the feeling I had that I absolutely must go there.

Why did I have that knowing? Why had I felt like I needed to move heaven and earth to go on that trip? It's incredible how intuition can lead you down a road, and you think you know the destination, but then it turns out to be something you hadn't even known existed—and way better than you expected.

They say hindsight is 20/20. Looking back now, I realized that I hadn't even known intuition was a thing, I certainly didn't fully understand it. This whole experience opened up my eyes to that part of life that subtly exists: everywhere. I learned that I could follow my heart even against my parent's wishes at a time when my parents were my whole world. It showed me I had the strength to overcome other people's fears, and that I was made of some strong stuff below my soft surface. It opened up the possibility that I had my own path, separate from anyone else's. Despite the conflict it had created with my parents, this showed them, in ways that words couldn't, that I had my destiny. It transformed our relationship and evolved it into a deep friendship. What's more, it showed them that their fears aren't necessarily true or accurate. Can you imagine if I would have listened to my father? Perhaps I would never have become a humanitarian. How tragic would that have been?

The second lesson I learned happened a few months after returning from Southern Africa. An opportunity to go on a similar trip had just landed on my lap. That's when I realized that I am a strong person. I can make things happen, that if I just relax and let things flow, the perfect situations will unfold. I don't need to force things. I shouldn't push things. I can trust in the universe that life unfolds as it needs to.

It was the need to learn these lessons that gave me my secure knowing, not the fact that there was some treasure buried in Africa somewhere. Isn't life strange how it plays out?! All of that heartache, all of that fear, when the lesson was that I have the answers inside of me and the universe is holding me and will do things for me if I just listen.

So why share all of this with you? It's because I want to highlight how intuition works. Why I'm grateful I've followed it in my life, and what I've learned from my experiences so that perhaps you can learn them faster and with less pain than how I discovered them. Not being controlled by external fear transformed my dad and I's relationship for the better and taught me that the universe would take care of me. But I couldn't have overcome my parents' fear if I hadn't paid attention to my intuition and if I didn't respectfully ask my dad to let me live my life. Intuition, healthy boundaries, and overcoming external fears are all so interconnected. That is what I learned, really learned in the depths of my heart.

External fears

As a humanitarian, I am constantly surrounded by fear. I often go to the heart of places that everyone else is trying to escape. How can I do this? I often get this question from friends and acquaintances, and they don't even know that I have struggled with anxiety my whole life, or that I'm a highly sensitive empath. The short answer is that I choose love over fear, and the longer answer you will find in the pages of this book. But like any good story, before we can get to the good part, the happy ending or in this case choosing love, we need to go through the struggle, the swamp, we need to overcome the villain. Except fear is not the villain, it is merely a road sign that says, "Love is needed here!" So, before we can drive full speed down the freeway of love (I'm so cheesy), we need to stop and fill in the potholes, we need to acknowledge fear, give it compassion, and heal it.

I have tried to avoid fear an embarrassing amount of times, and it's a lesson I need to learn repeatedly. I never wanted to see the pain. As a highly sensitive empath, I feel SO MUCH, and the pain of the world and the pain of loved ones was the worst type of pain because it made me feel so helpless. I would have done anything to take the pain away from those around me. As a child, I used to pray that I could suffer instead of everyone else. Seeing everyone in pain was so overwhelming that I couldn't handle it. So, I hid in my brain; I focused only on the logical and rational. I slowly shut down my heart and numbed myself, so although this meant I could no longer feel joy, at least it reduced the pain. I fell into a five-year depression.

Now, however, I know the immense healing power that just witnessing others' suffering can have. After more than a decade working as a humanitarian and a psychotherapist, I have learned that we can't just skip the uncomfortable bits. Not only does it not work, but these are the bits that are the key to finding true happiness for ourselves, our communities and our planet. Although this book is all about choosing love, the first step of our journey together is to understand fear.

It is only by facing our fear that we can heal it.

There is no other way around it. I have tried and looked and tried again. We have to face our fear. It is only in facing our fears that we can understand them. We will start by focusing on external fears.

External fears are everywhere; they continuously surround us. But what exactly are they? External fears are fears outside of you. They are the fears of your friends and family, of your society, they are the fears of all others that have nothing to do with you but that we often take on without even realizing it. External fears are fears whose roots are outside of us. Perhaps it's the fear of our parents worry that we won't be successful, or the headlines in the news that warn us of the next disaster. External fear was my father thinking I would die in Africa.

The thing about external fears is that they aren't our reactions; they aren't our fears or even our emotions. They are someone else's. Perhaps this other person wants us to take on their concerns, or maybe because we love and respect the other person, we begin to take on their fears, but they didn't start in us. Because they aren't our fears, there is not a message that we need to learn from them. Other people's worries are still a road sign that "Love is needed here!" but it's not for our road. That doesn't mean we don't treat these fears with love and compassion, but I am warning you that if external fears distract us, we will get lost on our journey. Or worse, we'll buy into the external fear of our loved ones and support them in giving that area hate and avoidance instead of the love it is requesting. Other people's worries are misleading and are the unnecessary baggage we are carrying. They not only inhibit and diminish our life, but also the lives of those we love most. We can always handle our own emotions, but when we take on other people's, that's when we feel overwhelmed, and that's what we can't handle.

We can know when we take on external fears as our own because we'll have feelings of being trapped or restless. Or if we've taken on these fears as a way to take the burden off someone else, we will often feel overwhelmed and hopeless. These are the main clues that external fears are inhibiting your life. Do you feel trapped or restless? Are you feeling overwhelmed or lost? If so, then pay extra attention.

What's most important to know about all fear is that the more you ignore it, avoid it, or pretend it doesn't exist, the bigger it will grow. This is truth. If we are going to choose love, then we need to look fear in the face, and Part 1 is all about looking directly at external fears, understanding the effect of external fears, and in so doing, helping those you love most overcome their anxieties.

External fears are powerful, and that's me writing from having grown up in a society that encourages us to be independent. I can't even imagine how powerful they must be in a collectivist culture or where you are ingrained with the idea that your most significant responsibility is to take care of others. But although they are powerful, external fears teach us two incredible things: they teach us to know our own intuition, and they teach us healthy boundaries.

Intuition

All of us have our own journey that we must travel. This journey includes life lessons that we need to learn, as well as how we can best assist those around us. When we complete our journey, we become one with love, and our completion is what truly helps heal humanity. We are all going to achieve the mission, we will all get to the top of the mountain, it's just that some of us might choose paths with more suffering, or we might get lost and take longer to get there. Intuition is our internal compass; it is what tells us which path we need to take. It is what ensures that we learn the lessons we need to learn, and it is what gets us to the top of the mountain the quickest and with the least amount of suffering.

Many of us have heard of intuition and those gut feelings that people do or don't listen to. Intuition is your soul whispering to you; it's your map through life. It's the road signs that tell you when you're going the wrong way or that there is a big curve coming up, but don't worry, if you miss a turn, there will be an opportunity to take another turn up ahead. The road might not be as pleasant, but perhaps that road is the only road that will help you understand something important. In short, there are no mistakes. My intention for this book is not to make you feel guilty, or that there is something wrong with you. Instead, it is my goal to reduce the suffering in your life, to help you see the signs to turn at before you pass them and to fill your life with more joy and happiness. Regardless of what you choose, I know that you will succeed and complete your journey. Without a doubt, I know this, which leads me to the different ways that your intuition might talk to you.

I have found that intuition can communicate in four main ways: knowing, seeing, hearing and feeling. Usually, when we are just beginning to listen to our intuition, we will only notice one or two of the ways that intuition might speak to us. However, as you get more adept at hearing your intuition, you may find that it speaks to you in all four of the ways. Understanding how your intuition communicates to you is crucial because it will help you know what to look out for; intuition can be hard to hear and even harder to trust. Not trusting our intuition can lead to a world of pain as I'm confident many of you reading this have experienced. Once we know how our intuition communicates to us, it is much easier to follow.

The four ways of intuition

Knowing

As you have probably figured out, the first way that intuition communicated with me was through knowing. Knowing is perhaps the most annoying way of how our intuition speaks to us. How do you explain to others or even yourself that you just know? How do you know? How do you know you're not wrong? You can't possibly know that! These are all the thoughts that go through my head. All I can ever say to people asking me is that I just know. I have an entirely irrational certainty, and that's it. There is nothing tangible about knowing. Knowing is just a knowing that you have to do something. It doesn't feel or look like anything, it just IS, and (you can ask all my friends and family) when I get this knowing there is no other choice for me but to follow it. Once I have this knowing there is no going back, I will do whatever this knowing says. I know this sounds a bit lemming-like, but remember this is my intuition, it's my roadmap, and it's not going to tell me to jump off a cliff unless that is for my highest good. I can trust it wholly and utterly.

Sometimes following my intuition does feel like jumping off a cliff, except instead of seeing what's beneath me, I'm jumping into an abyss. It's absolutely terrifying, and I have so many doubts. BUT every time I've leapt, my life has gotten exponentially better in ways that I couldn't have imagined for myself. Whether it's through healing meaningful relationships, experiencing and facing profound lessons, or genuinely being able to contribute to the good of the world, every time I took a leap and then looked back, I would never change to go back to how things were.

I've only experienced the battle ram of knowing 5-7 times in my life; writing this book is the latest example. I've found that there seems to be a pattern now of how it works. I'll start with a strong sense of knowing down to my bones, and that usually lasts for a month or so, or at least until I take action to follow it, but then once I start to follow it, the feeling will evaporate. Then I'm left with feelings of doubt. Did I really feel that? Is it still true? Am I supposed to continue? What if I'm not supposed to do that anymore? Now that I've figured out the pattern, I know to expect this period of nothingness and keep moving forward with what I used to know to be true. This nothingness will last until I've done what my intuition asked of me, and then I'll be filled with a profound sense of peace, of rightness, the feeling that I'm precisely where I'm supposed to be. To me, these feelings are priceless and make anything, ever, worthwhile.

Knowing is the least subtle of how intuition communicates to me, and it seems to be the form my intuition takes when I REALLY need to do something. Unfortunately, when I really need to do something, it is often considered a bit dramatic, dangerous, or crazy, so my friends and family would argue and try to convince me to let go of this insane notion. I realize that I didn't just look stupid to them but also selfish, stubborn, or even callous. Some told me I didn't care about their fears or concerns and took it as a sign that I didn't care about them, which was heart-wrenching! I tried to explain why, but many people simply won't get it, and you won't have rebuttals to their very logical and valid concerns. However, I have been lucky that my family has always forgiven me for following this knowing, and now they are even supportive or at least don't try to stop me when I have it. I have lost some friends, but these have been replenished with new friends that support me in being the best version of me possible. The real gift of knowing is that it's not subtle. It's easy to identify the external fears that are trying to control you, and knowing's brute force helps us stay on our path and not wander off. Have you ever experienced this knowing? How would you describe it? Did you follow it? What happened?

Seeing

The more you listen and pay attention to your intuition, the more all four ways of communication will show up. After my first powerful experience of knowing, I suddenly became aware of the concept of intuition, something I hadn't known or thought about before. I noticed that my intuition also communicated with me more subtly through images or pictures. In this way, your intuition might show you an image, or a movie, or a symbol in your mind, especially through dreams. I began noticing themes in my dreams, including past dreams, and I started being able to lucid dream, controlling them so that I could finally resolve some recurring nightmares I had. I sometimes have intense dreams that I know have an essential message for me.

I've also had powerful meditations where I'll have visions. I had one meditation where I saw a vision of a double helix coming up my spine and then giant wings spreading out of my shoulders. I didn't know what this meant, and so when I googled it, I found out that this image represents kundalini activation, which then helped me make sense of the physical sensations I was suffering from since this meditation. Many cultures believe that there is powerful energy at the base of your spine, lying dormant. Kundalini activation is when that energy awakens and moves up your spine with such force that it can have several very uncomfortable physical reactions, especially if you have energetic blocks that inhibit this force of energy. It's kind of like a geyser exploding. Some of the physical sensations can last for weeks or even months. The way your body reacts depends a lot on how much you've spiritually prepared for the activation. It felt as if my whole body was shaking for weeks, and my hands were shaking so much that it was hard to hold things. It also felt like extreme anxiety on overload, and I had lost my appetite. It can also feel like you're losing your mind. It is not a common experience, and many people meditate for a long time to prepare their bodies for this activation. An enlightened spiritual teacher can activate you, or you can get activated spontaneously like I was. Once your kundalini energy is activated, you have a lot more power. Therefore, you need to be very aware of your thoughts because it's easy to manifest them. You also have to be very aware of any energetic blocks you have in your body and make sure to clear them.

Shortly after I had this vision, I received a necklace with giant wings. It was perfect. When I have an experience of a particularly powerful image, I try to wear a piece of jewellery that resembles that image so that I can always remind myself of the experience and why it happened.

This form of intuition might also come through flashes of images. They usually aren't solid, more like a cloudy image that is only in your mind rather than through sight, and this is another way I recognize my intuition has something it wants me to know. I find this often happens when I work, and there is something that I need to focus on or include in the work I'm doing for others, either with my clients or in my humanitarian work.

Similar to this is when I use my intuition in the form of visualizations. The brain can't tell the difference between what it imagines and what is real, and using visualizations is a fantastic way to capitalize on this to create healing in the conscious and subconscious mind. As I lead my clients through visualizations, I will ask them what they see, and then we will work with those images to decipher the message they need to hear. It is a profound and powerful experience, and I'm always so humbled by the process. It can be challenging for my clients because they worry they're not doing it right, but it's impossible to do it wrong as long as you relax and work with whatever comes up, not overthinking the process. Specific images or archetypes can have a deep symbolism that can span cultures.

Carl Jung has done fascinating work on archetypes, and I sometimes use these archetypal images in the visualizations I guide people through. For example, in the grounding process, which is being present in your body in the present moment, my clients will often prefer the image of a tree. I will guide them to imagine themselves becoming like a tree and growing roots deep into the ground. Grounding creates a deep sense of peace and relaxation, a quiet power and a gentle strength. Notice if some archetypal images resonate with you, perhaps an animal or a symbol or a plant, and research what that image means. There might be a message for you there.

I have also witnessed my clients physically heal themselves by going into their pain and describing what they see. We then work together to untangle and unravel the message that the pain or illness has, and once that has been communicated, then the pain or disease can disappear. However, it's important to note that the goal of this process is not healing but understanding the illness or the pain; healing is often just a by-product.

If you think images are the most potent way your intuition communicates to you, then perhaps start keeping a dream journal, or notice what images stand out in your mind. Are there some images that are particularly important to you? Why? Also, look into guided visualizations and use them to give yourself emotional and perhaps physical healing.

Hearing

The third way your intuition can speak to you is through sound. It could be in the form of hearing a single word, or a phrase, or even a noise that gets your attention, and you're not sure what it is, but it makes you stop and focus. Sometimes it might be a song on the radio that you keep on hearing. For me, it often comes in the form of a single word, and as with all signs of intuition, I'm never sure if I heard it in my mind or if someone said something, and I just can't see who spoke it. Sometimes it sounds quite loud, although it can often be as soft as a whisper.

When I was in Amman, Jordan, which was the first time I had been in the Middle East, I had been attracted to the symbol of the All-Seeing Eye, which is one eye usually with a blue iris. I had just bought a necklace with a pendant of this and was putting it on when I heard a "click" in my mind. I then knew that there was something about this piece of jewellery that I needed to pay attention to. Six months later, I got a job offer to work in Syria. I was still wearing the necklace, and it gave me confirmation that I needed to go to the Middle East, even though that had never been a place I was interested in working. I am so grateful that I accepted that opportunity. Understanding the incredible cultures there and being able to advocate and work for women's rights in communities controlled by ISIS was heart-expanding, to say the least.

When I first tried to increase my intuition, I found that it was always accompanied by doubt! But it's that word, or that sound, or that phrase—and you DID hear it, you just don't know how or who said it—that is intuition.

Feeling

The final way that intuition can communicate to us is through feeling, which can be either in the form of emotions or physical sensations. This type is associated with "gut feelings" or a feeling in your heart.

Feeling is a strong intuition for me, and I use it all the time in my work. I can feel other people's emotions in my own body so if they give me permission then I can know what emotion they are feeling and where in their body they are keeping it, without them having to say anything (it sometimes freaks my clients out at first, but they get used to it). Using my feeling intuition is useful in my work because we can quickly get down to the heart of an issue. We often give all our energy to talking about one thing when it's something entirely different that is upsetting us.

As a highly sensitive empath (HSE), you might naturally have this gift, although if you don't know how to manage it, then it will feel like a curse. As an HSE, you can pick up other people's emotions, and they start to feel like your own, which can get confusing because then you can't figure why you are feeling that emotion. Another way to think of this is to think about empathy. Intuition through feeling is empathy, and HSEs have this but on steroids. Sensitivity is a true gift, but only if you learn healthy boundaries. Once you do, you can help people process their emotions without taking them on yourself, and just the simple act of empathy can have a massive healing impact.

Though, it is not just feeling other people's emotions that is a form of intuition; you might also feel their physical pain. Physical sensation in my body is how I identify what to focus on in my client. I'll feel physical pain in a particular part of my body, or sometimes I might feel like it's difficult to breathe or like there is a rock in my gut. I'm more and more starting to appreciate the body and the wonderful way it communicates important messages to us from our high self, God, the universe—or whatever you would like to call it. I believe the body is temporary, like a meat sack that we wear. But this meat sack has a special kind of wisdom and is something that we need to take care of and pay attention to. I'm mentioning this only because my whole life I have had resistance to being in my body. This entire world of bodily knowledge through feeling intuition is opening up to me, even though my feeling intuition has been one of my more definite forms of intuition. Sometimes I get overwhelmed with all the information available to us, but at this moment, I'm quite excited about it.

Some tools you can use to strengthen your intuition

Awareness

The more you are aware of how your intuition communicates with you, and the sentiment it has when it does so, the more you'll be able to trust what it says. A Course in Miracles says that your ego always speaks first and loudest. So, don't listen to that voice. Instead, be aware of how your intuition speaks to you (knowing, seeing, hearing, or feeling) and pay attention to those senses. Intuition can often be confused by overthinking your fears or other people's concerns, and something you think might be your intuition is the opposite. Your intuition will have a particular attribute, just like you can recognize your friend's voices. You can understand the quality of your intuition once you spend time getting to know it. When you think you've heard it communicate with you, you can use the following tools to double-check.

Visualization

This is a meditation that one of my teachers taught to me that can help with making decisions.

1. Sit quietly and start with taking three deep breaths. Ground yourself by imagining tree roots coming out of your feet into the ground beneath you. (For a free audio of this grounding go to my website at www.vanwyckconsulting.com.)
2. Visualize at most four closed doors in front of you. Behind each door is an option you are trying to get clarity around. Have one door for each option. For example, if you're trying to decide if you should accept a job then behind door one

imagine your life if you took this job, then behind door two, imagine your life if you didn't take this job.

3. Open the first door, step inside, and notice how you feel, what you see, or however your intuition speaks to you. Notice what it is like. Is it a pleasant experience? Is it a neutral one or an uncomfortable one? Do the same for the other doors.
4. Notice which door you experience as being the loveliest. Then gently come back into the room. The door that you enjoyed the most is the decision you should take.

Meditation

It is always best to take some time for yourself and just be quiet to hear intuition. Listen, feel the different emotions you have at this moment, label them, and ask what your heart wants you to do. Be aware that you need to take time to understand what your heart is feeling before you will be able to get any wisdom or guidance from it. Empathize with your heart first and feel the different emotions it has before you ask for any message that it might have for you.

Journaling

If visualization or meditation is not your thing, then you can also practise through journaling. Journaling often helps to untangle the jumble of thoughts and emotions that are tumbling inside of you. Write down all the thoughts and feelings that you have and then ask yourself any questions you need clarity around. Write down the first thing that enters your head and continue writing until you have more clarity. Seeing things down on paper and writing everything inside your mind can help you better understand yourself.

The tools described here just outline the different roads you can go down. Unfortunately, there is not space to go into each of the following tools. However, they will give you a direction of what you can learn about more in-depth should you be interested.

Muscle testing

Muscle testing works on the premise that when you are in line with yourself and your highest good, you have internal strength. This strength collapses when you are not in line. There are various ways to muscle test from holding out your arm and having someone pushing it down to holding up your fingers and pushing them down. The specifics of muscle testing are intricate, but if this interests you, then do some research on how to learn how to do this. Be aware that with all muscle testing, you need to do some self-clearing and ego clearing before you can begin. If the teacher doesn't mention this, find another teacher.

A Pendulum

A pendulum is similar to muscle testing. Instead of resistance, your pendulum will move in different patterns that mean specific things. I learned how to use a pendulum right before I went to Haiti, and it has been handy. Although please note that if you use something like this, you need to take time to clear yourself, connect to your higher self and then ensure that your ego is under 4% otherwise you can get skewed answers. Also, I've found that with a pendulum, it might give me answers that are incorrect but are what I need to hear at the moment to make a decision in the right direction. Again, many online courses can teach you how to use a pendulum but be picky with whom you choose to follow. This field is unregulated, and some people don't know what they are doing.

I find we often listen to other people's fears because we don't have trust in our inner knowledge. We are afraid that we are making a mistake, so we listen to what other people tell us. But it's impossible to make a mistake, and listening to other people's fears just deters us from our path.

I don't know what would have happened if I had not followed my intuition. But even if I had messed up and ignored it, I think that another opportunity to learn the same lesson would have presented itself. Perhaps with a more prominent sign, so the universe could ensure that I would listen. That's why I don't think there are any wrong turns, there are just opportunities that we miss, and so perhaps more suffering needs to enter our lives so that we are more likely to see the signs.

That is why intuition is so important, and going with what you feel is best. Don't let your mind make things too convoluted. You don't need to second-guess yourself continuously.

Pay attention and listen

This chapter is just a basic introduction to intuition. However, I think the way intuition communicates with us is often not covered when you study it, so I hope it has helped support you to more clearly identify when your intuition is speaking and trust in it a little more. The vital thing to know is that once you start focusing on it, paying attention to it and listening to it, it will get stronger and stronger and will feel less like a guessing game. Intuition is essential if you want to follow a life of fulfillment and find happiness; it is the only roadmap to happiness.

Boundaries and intuition

Boundaries and intuition are fundamental concepts to keep in mind when facing external fears. In the following chapters, I will share examples of when I've had strong intuition in my life, and I was able to follow that over and above external fears, or the fears of my loved ones. It could sound selfish, and perhaps it is, you'll have to judge for yourself. All I can say is that I'm so grateful and feel so blessed that I was able to follow my intuition and have my life unfold precisely as it did.

Remembering the four ways that intuition can communicate with us will help identify your intuition and your or someone else's fears. Once you start to trust your intuition, you can figure out what external fears you've picked up, and once you can do that, you can take off the extra baggage you are carrying. Life is tough enough; we don't need to carry a piano on our backs as we travel up the mountain. Knowing what fears are yours and not yours will make your life infinitely easier. Your intuition is how you know what you need to do. It's how you know that you are on the right path, and what route you need to take. However, you can still let external fears lead you astray if you don't have healthy boundaries. That is why before we can go more in-depth into external fears, we first need to discuss healthy boundaries.

Chapter 2
Healthy Boundaries

Boundaries

Boundaries are vital for healthy relationships and to not take on other's external fears. So, I need to preface this by stating that I was born, raised, and educated in a very individualistic culture, and that completely colours my perspective on boundaries. Individualistic cultures are the western-style cultures where we are taught to be independent and separate from others. In contrast, collectivist cultures are cultures that believe in a very interwoven family and extended family system. Examples of individualistic cultures are North America and Europe, while collectivist cultures are more Asian, African and South American. There is no better culture; instead, they are just very different value systems.

I have worked and lived in many collectivist cultures, and with my shallow understanding, I still believe that what I'm going to write here is valid. But it is you that has to use your intuition (do you see what I did there?) to discern if what I say resonates or works in your life.

What are boundaries? Well, if you've worked with me, then you'll know about the garden metaphor that I continually refer to over and over again. The garden metaphor is the idea that you are some sort of plant, let's say a cactus, which means you like lots of sunshine, lots of sand, maybe some lizard poo for food and just a little water. We've all heard of the golden rule: "Do unto others as you would have them do unto you," but contrary to public opinion, this is a recipe for disaster. Say, for instance, your partner is a rose, that means they like cooler weather, lots of water, some partial sun, they need to be pruned at certain times of the year, and they like fertile soil. If you treat them how you want to be treated, you'll take away their shade and water, bring them to a place way too hot for them and feed them lizard poo that makes them want to throw up. Your rose partner will suffer and die unless they intervene with your treatment, and the same goes for if they take care of you.

Hollywood teaches us that the best romantic relationship is where you take care of your partner (you go into their garden), and they take care of you (they go into your garden). But here, the BEST-case scenario is both of you are barely alive. Can you imagine treating a rose like a cactus or a cactus like a rose?

The problem with life is that NO ONE KNOWS WHAT YOU NEED. We so wish this wasn't true, we all dream of someone who can truly and wonderfully take care of us, ideally through the ability to read our mind. We crave this immensely, and we put all our attention on what others do or don't do for us, to the point where we don't even know how to take care of ourselves. In non-violent communication, the whole premise is that people don't actually know what they want. So, our job through the way we communicate is to help them clarify what they want, and our responsibility is to define what we want and then make a clear request.

I know this is easier said than done. People want us, no, demand us to go into their gardens. When my now ex-husband had moved to Vancouver to be with me, he signed up for a graduate certificate in English. He was from the French part of Canada and so didn't feel very confident in his English skills. When he signed up, I told him I hate editing, and so if he has to write papers, then he needs to factor in that I'm not going to do the editing for him. So, of course, I end up editing all his papers. BUT I had one week when I was absolutely swamped with clients, and I was launching an online program, and I knew that I had to practise what I preach and so I told him that I needed to take care of my garden this week and really couldn't edit his paper. He was furious with me. He gave me the cold shoulder for two weeks, and it was hell. I hate it when people are mad at me, and I wanted to screw my garden and just edit his paper, which would have been easier on my heart…in the short term. But I knew that was just me falling into the trap of going into his garden to ease my own anxiety (and his). I found a friend who could edit his paper, but he was too embarrassed, so he handed it in unedited. Finally, after two weeks, he got over it and was no longer upset. Then he got his paper back, and he received an A.

If I hadn't stayed in my garden, he would never have known that he didn't need me, that he was smart enough. Although those two weeks were tough, it changed the nature of our relationship subtly; we became more balanced, more like equals. It was painful, but it was worth it, and I'm so glad, even now that I stayed in my garden, and he was too.

Healthy boundaries are knowing ourselves, knowing what we need, and then taking the time to know other people, understand their needs, and then perhaps help them meet those needs themselves. We have to realize that no matter how hard we try or wish or pray, no one can fulfill our needs, and we can't meet other people's needs. We need to take responsibility for ourselves before we can support our loved ones. You've probably heard it before, but I'm going to repeat it: you need to put the oxygen mask on yourself before you put it on others.

Healthy boundaries

Healthy boundaries include knowing what your stuff is and what's not. Often, we will see someone we love in pain or hurting, so we try to take on that pain to help them (aren't we so nice?). Still, how I see it is that we haven't actually helped them, because we haven't helped them heal the root of their pain and so even though you did indeed take the burden off them, they will grow it back in a matter of days if not hours, and now you've just doubled the amount of that suffering that's in the world (not so nice). This also means that by taking off their burden, we haven't supported them in facing the root of their problem. We have enabled them to continue putting this burden on others as a short-term fix, instead of encouraging them to work on healing themselves. Although both parties often do this subconsciously, it can be a detrimental pattern. And although taking on other people's pain is done with the best intentions, it leads to damaging results. We can be supportive of others, but we can't walk the path for them. It is not helpful, on any level, to take on other people's pain.

I see this happen over and over, and I have a technique of when I'm working with my clients to identify this because we can always handle what life gives us. But we can't manage what life gives us plus the stuff we take on from others. If you ever feel overwhelmed with an emotion or something feels too big to handle, it's probably because you took on stuff that isn't yours, so you need to separate that out. To do this, imagine the sun is shining a beautiful beam of light on it and evaporating it. You can find a recording of how to do this on my website.

Taking responsibility for other people's reactions

The core theme of healthy boundaries is that we cannot blame others for our emotions, and similarly, we are not responsible for other people's emotions. Now I know that could sound cold or harsh but hear me out. There are literally millions of ways we can react to the same event; in fact, there are as many ways of responding to an event as there are people who experienced the event. We are all a unique galaxy of values and experiences, personality traits and DNA sequences, and so we all will have different emotions or reactions to an experience. We have to own that. We have to take responsibility for our reactions if we are ever going to take the driver's seat in our life.

We can't blame others for our reactions to an experience because how come everyone didn't react in the same way? Now before you blow me off as not understanding how horrible some experiences are, remember that I have lived in war zones, I have seen and heard of some of the most awful things happening on the planet right now. Of course, some experiences can inspire a common reaction; for example, being raped almost universally inspires the person raped to feel like it was their fault. However, the fact that it's their fault is ridiculous, as anyone who works in this sector will know. AND, that person is now responsible for how they are going to respond: are they going to stay in shame, or are they going to give themselves love?

We can't control what happens to us, but we can always choose what we do. If we blame others for our reactions, then we are essentially giving them our power. We're saying my pain is your fault, and so unless you fix it, I will have this pain for the rest of my life. I refuse to accept this. My pain was inspired by what someone else has done, but I'm not going to let them continue to ruin the rest of my life, and so I'm going to take control of my healing regardless of what they do or don't do.

This goes both ways. Yes, I am always responsible for my actions, but I can't predict (although I often try) how someone will react to the various things I might do, and I'm also not responsible for where they take it from there. If I'm aware of the pain I've inspired in someone else, I can assist them in their healing journey. However, I can only support them if they, 1) communicate to me that I have caused them pain, or else I might not even know, and 2) tell me what they need from me to assist them in their healing. Apologizing and asking for forgiveness can often go a long way in helping them heal, but only if they forgive. Again, what they choose to do or not do is out of our control.

I used to be so worried that I wasn't taking responsibility for my own actions that I would take responsibility for everyone else's actions. If someone was sad, I would think and blame myself for making them that way. I would constantly go over conversations I had with people to make sure I didn't say anything that might have hurt their feelings. I can't tell you the countless times I would call people and apologize for something I said that I thought offended them. In reality, however, they had no idea what I was talking about and didn't even notice the comment I had been obsessing over (this is also a highly sensitive empath thing). The point is, I took responsibility for everyone's emotions and reactions, and I let that control and influence what I did or didn't do. That, dear reader, is not taking 100% responsibility: that is taking 200% responsibility. I will never forget the moment I learned this with such clarity that I honestly think it must have been an angel that came down to teach me this lesson.

I was walking along a busy shopping street in Vancouver one Saturday morning. I was a little hungover, and I was mostly keeping to myself as I walked. As I was walking, a young guy came up beside me and told me that I had a nice jacket. I thanked him, smiled, was very polite, and kept on walking. I went into a store, and he followed me in. I was puttering around looking at magazines when he came up to me and asked me, "Hey, how would you like to make a million dollars?" Again, I was polite. I smiled at him and thought about it for a second, and then I said, "You know what? I don't think I would. I'm really…" He cut me off and started yelling and waving his hands, "What do you mean you don't want a million dollars??! Are you fucking crazy???! Who the FUCK doesn't want a million dollars??!!!" And at that moment, even though he was yelling at me in a store and making a big scene that would typically really embarrass me, a light bulb literally went off in my head (seeing intuition), and I finally got it! There is no way I could have been more polite or kind to this guy. His reaction had NOTHING to do with me! I couldn't believe it. I finally deeply understood that I couldn't hold myself accountable for his reaction; it was all him! I had no idea what caused it or why, and it wasn't my business.

I don't know what happened after that. After he finished yelling, I think he must have left the store in a huff, but I know I must have looked foolish with my dazed look and a grin plastered over my face. It was such a profound understanding of a question I had been contemplating for years, and to this day, I really do think he was an angel, and I'm profoundly grateful for that experience. That experience has stayed with me for over two decades. Although the nuances of how we can best assist others are still something I'm learning, this experience has been a foundational lesson in my life. We are 100% responsible for our reactions, and others are 100% responsible for their reactions.

Much like intuition, the theme of healthy boundaries is a vast topic that we are just dipping our toe into. But for the sake of external fears, we must remember the garden analogy, and that we can't, no matter how hard we try, fulfill other people's needs, and it's impossible for them to fulfill ours. Instead, the best way to be there for others is to take care of our own heart first and foremost, and then we can meet people at the fence between our garden and theirs.

Healthy relationships

Healthy relationships are relationships that encourage both people to be the best version of themselves. They are mutually encouraging, loving, and involve healthy boundaries where both parties take responsibility for their role in the relationships and ownership for their actions within the relationships. We will come back to the concept of healthy relationships repeatedly throughout this book since human relationships are fundamental in learning and healing ourselves. One aspect of healthy relationships includes making requests of others rather than demands.

Requests versus demands

It is through listening to our intuition and remembering our pure magnificence that we can overcome external fears and have healthy relationships. External fears aren't just scary things outside of us. It's not only others trying to put their worries on us, but it's also us trying to control our surroundings in an interpersonal way that means trying to control others. We see this in the difference between demands and requests. In the book "Non-Violent Communication," Marshall Rosenberg describes requests as gifts because they involve us being vulnerable with others and honestly sharing what we would like.

However, demands are a form of external fear. They are actions that others give us that we need to follow. If we don't obey demands, then we will be punished, or if the person doesn't follow our demand, then we will punish them. Demands come from a place of fear because when we are making a demand, we aren't entirely honest with ourselves; we aren't asking for what we truly need. Instead, we are asking for something from someone else, which will prove something to us. For example, if I ask a friend to hang out with me on a specific day, and they say they are busy, and then I get upset, I then made a demand. There was only one acceptable answer that they could give me. But why would I get angry that they can't hang out? What if it was because they had a work deadline, or another engagement, or a million other understandable reasons? I would be upset because I am making that rejection mean something, perhaps I'm interpreting it as they don't like me, or I'm not important, or I'm no fun. It could be anything, and it's my responsibility to understand what it is, and instead of making a demand, make a request that meets that need. My demand to hang out was actually a need for connection, or affection, or companionship. When I put my demands on others, I'm not taking the time to look honestly at what my needs are and instead put it on others to do whatever I say so that I feel better. Often, even when people do fulfill our demands, it still doesn't meet the underlying need, and so doesn't quite make us feel better, and so we start making more and more demands. Instead, we need to understand our underlying needs, and then we can make a request from that place.

Requests come out of a place of love. They come from the knowledge that we are already complete. We will not be ruined or destroyed if others don't comply. Requests are us communicating our needs and desires and just that. They are genuine questions, where there is no punishment or malice if the person can't fulfill the request. It just means perhaps we need to ask in a different way, a different time, or to a different person. To use the same example, if I had truly requested to hang out with my friend, then I would do so with the understanding that I would like to have companionship or connection with someone, and if they can't, then I'm completely ok with it. Perhaps I'll ask if there's a different time that works for them, or I'll ask a different friend to hang out so that I'm still getting my need for companionship met. If I feel that my friend doesn't like me because they never seem to want to hang out with me, but they do with others, then I can have an honest conversation with that friend to see if this is accurate. So often, we can make assumptions about why others do something, and these assumptions are based on our own fears and are not the reason at all.

Requests are letting go of the answer we might get, accepting the response we receive and having the underlying knowledge that we will be fine if we don't get what we want. Using requests instead of demands is a way that we can avoid falling into the trap of external fears within our personal relationships. Because we are free to be ourselves, we don't have to do certain behaviours to make someone happy, and therefore we don't need to take on the fears of our friends to make them happy. Requests and demands are related to having healthy boundaries, where we are taking responsibility for our own happiness and not putting it on others to fulfill.

No wrong path

You know when you are at a fork in the road, and you decide to take a particular path? And, while you're on that path, you worry that perhaps it was the wrong one, and maybe you should turn back and go down the other way? I had the rare opportunity to get a glimpse into the life I could have had if I had taken a different path. It is such a profound gift to know that even when I react rashly, the choices I make are exactly what I need at that time. I found this lesson invaluable in terms of listening to my intuition. So often we try to make a perfect choice, we work so hard that we end up not making any choice and life passes us by. Choose! Take hold of life! Trust and leap. There is no way you can mess up.

When I was 17, I moved to Scotland to work as a chambermaid in a castle. In true fairy-tale fashion, I fell in love within a couple of months. The man was a musician, just like my dad, and I was smitten. He was my first true love, and I twisted myself into all sorts of pretzels to please him. We decided that we were going to get married that summer and run away to an island without telling anyone. But no matter how much I changed myself, I always managed to upset him.

It went on for months like this; me trying my best to be everything he ever wanted or needed and him being hurt by things I would do or say. I was demoralized and exhausted, and so one night, I decided, screw this! I was just going to be myself.

I made this decision while he was making me dinner, and I said something without triple-checking if it was ok to say it. To my horror, my boyfriend blew up at me. He started yelling at me about how insensitive I was. He told me he was going to take me home right now. Then once we were in the car and I was trying to explain myself so that he wouldn't be angry, he interrupted me and said he would drop me on the side of the highway if I said another word. So, I cried silently.

The next day he called me to apologize, but it was too late. I had been struck with how much I couldn't be myself, and I knew I could no longer be in a relationship where I had no voice. Still shaken with the prospect of being abandoned on the side of the road, I quit my job and left the country a week later.

I was utterly heartbroken. Food tasted like sand, and I felt lost without my now ex-boyfriend. Life had no meaning; I was never going to love someone as much as I had loved him. Why did I leave so quickly? What would have happened if I had forgiven him? For YEARS, I questioned whether I had done the right thing.

Five years later, I was visiting a friend in Scotland, and we randomly stumbled across my ex-boyfriend with his now-wife. He seemed rattled and excused himself right away while I spent some time talking to his wife. She was lovely and so kind. She was great for him and entirely unlike anything I could be.

It was fantastic.

A massive weight lifted off my shoulders. I could finally see what my life would have been like if I had stayed and taken the other path when I was at that fork in the road. I would have been her if I had stayed, and I did not want to be her.

Although I had left rashly, looking back, it's obvious to see that it was an unhealthy relationship. Still, it took the fear of being stranded in the middle of nowhere at night (at a time when cell phones weren't standard) to realize that this relationship wasn't right for either of us. If you don't listen to the whispers of your intuition, then they will grow louder until you can't ignore them. Even so, I was torn and confused if I was right to leave, but meeting his wife allowed me to see that it WAS the right decision. It was the universe telling me that I can trust how life unfolds, I can trust the choices I make. The universe is taking care of me, and I can relax. It was another layer of learning not to worry so much. I can't fuck up my life, no matter how much I fear that I have.

Whatever path you choose is the path you needed to choose. Stop worrying about "what ifs." If something is supposed to happen, then it will, if you weren't supposed to do something, you won't. Yes, sometimes we choose more difficult paths, but that just means we need to learn the hard way. Personally, I try to learn things when the universe only whispers suggestions to me. Still, sometimes I need everything to be stripped away before I'm willing to change or let go. When things are stripped away, it's not as a punishment. Sometimes it just needs to happen so that our heart has more room to grow. Pain in life is inevitable, but suffering is voluntary. We create suffering when we judge ourselves or others for why things happened.

If I had judged my father for threatening to kick me out of the family, then I would have created a lot of suffering. Thankfully instead, I was able to understand, respect and have compassion for him. Which then allowed him to have compassion for me. If we take on and obey other people's fears, our life will get smaller and smaller, and so will our hearts. By understanding other people's concerns, but not taking them on, we can have compassion and perhaps forgiveness for them. At the same time, we can still fulfill our purpose in life.

Chapter 3
Knowing I Had To Go To Haiti

In 2010, a massive earthquake struck Haiti. After it happened, I was angry. I wasn't even righteously angry, so there isn't a redeeming quality about it.

I was angry because subconsciously, I knew there was a connection from me to the earthquake, and I didn't like it. I didn't want to hear about the earthquake. I hated that everyone was talking about it. I tried to pretend that it hadn't happened. I was annoyed that people weren't going along with what I wanted.

It sounds callous, I know, and it was quite out of character for me; I usually would feel all the pain of the world to an overwhelming degree. That's what alerted me that something was up. This big tragedy had happened, almost 300,000 people had died in the span of a few days, there was constant news coverage and fundraising concerts, and yet my primary reaction was one of anger. How strange!

At this time, I was part of a small group of people who practised energy work on each other. When the Haiti earthquake came up in one of our meetings, I felt the swell of anger rise inside me. It was such a visceral reaction that I knew it was something I could no longer avoid, and I needed to look at it. I set aside some time to delve into the anger. The moment I did this, the knowing struck me. I knew I had to go to Haiti.

Through this experience, I have realized that if I have anger and resistance, it means my intuition is trying to tell me something. It alerts me that there is something vital that I need to look at, but I'm avoiding it.

That small group of energy workers ended up forming a small organization where we focused on what we could do to assist in the aftermath of the earthquake. We raised money and created a plan of programs we could implement to best assist. I ended up being the one focal person that went down to Haiti for a year. But as usual, getting there was difficult.

Timing

Another pattern I've noticed when my intuition tells me I need to do something is that it seems like everything opens up for me to do that thing for a brief moment. Then once I start, the universe swings in the other direction. It's as if I have to overcome hurdle after hurdle to complete what the universe wanted me to do in the first place.

When the earthquake happened, I was just finishing my master's in counselling psychology. I was completing my thesis defence on how quantum physics relates to psychotherapy. Thesis defences are very stressful. My dissertation was my first foray into integrating energy work into my professional life, and I was petrified. I had never felt so vulnerable in my life, which is probably why I made sure to include all the research possible. Previously, I had been very secretive about my studies and practice of energy work. I had an unrealistic fear that if people knew I did this, they would hang me for a witch. I was emotionally stretched to my max. Then add to that the tension with my boyfriend.

I had been with a wonderful man for three years. At that point, we had assumed we would get married, but he had recently taken a job long-distance, and it was tough on our relationship. Although he knew that I always wanted to work in disasters, he was agitated when I told him I wanted to go to Haiti for a year. He said he felt like I was helping everyone else but him. The tension was bubbling under the surface for months. A week before my thesis defence, he gave me an ultimatum; I could either choose Haiti or him.

This is another example of external fears. My boyfriend wasn't afraid of what would happen to me in Haiti. Rather, he was fearful that I was going to abandon him. I tried my best to explain to him and show him that it wasn't a case of choosing Haiti over him. I didn't love Haiti more and him second best; I loved him and myself equally. I needed to follow my heart. I believe that love is abundant; just because we love one thing doesn't mean we have less love for something else. It's just the opposite when you genuinely love something; it creates even more love in your life.

We already know that there is nothing that can stop me once I *know*, and it remained true even in the face of someone I loved with all my heart and wanted to spend the rest of my life with. If I have to choose between my intuition, what I feel is part of my life purpose, and my happiness, I will always select purpose, although now I know they are the same.

It crushed my heart to not give up Haiti for him. We broke up a week before my defence, and I was a complete mess. I was sobbing uncontrollably. I had to shut off my emotions completely to get through one of the most stressful ordeals of my life: defending my thesis. But then, as I was defending my thesis, I received several calls. It turns out one of my good friends had seriously been injured while I was defending. So, I went from my defence to the hospital. I can't describe how lost I felt. How could I leave when people needed me? My now ex-boyfriend accused me of being incredibly selfish for going, and he was right. Who was I to leave when there were people that needed me at home?

Following your intuition isn't about anyone else. It's about following your sole purpose. It's about fulfilling the reason you are here. I can look around anywhere and see ways in which I can assist, but some aren't my path. I could have been a nurse or a garbage collector or a sandwich maker. All those paths are needed, but they aren't my path. If I try to force myself into that expectation, I will make myself unhappy and thereby spread unhappiness and perhaps bitterness to those around me.

Thankfully, my friend recovered. But at this point, I was emotionally numb. Although my heart was shattered; I had the support of my family and friends. I no longer felt the *knowing* that I had to go to Haiti, but I decided to trust and follow through with going anyway. It was under these circumstances and with all these misgivings and guilt that I went.

It was the best decision I could have made.

Haiti

Haiti, oh, Haiti! It has more culture in its pinky than any other country I've been to. It is a cauldron of chaos and music and yearning and death and hopelessness and courage and resistance and strength. There was nothing that could have prepared me for Haiti.

I lived there for one year exactly to the day because I had given my word to stay for a year, but I should have left after eight months. Haiti is a lot to handle, and if you can't relax into the flow and the chaos, then it will eat you up and spit you out. When you follow your intuition, your life doesn't become easier. More vibrant, more joyful, and more filled with love? Yes, but not easier.

When I arrived in Haiti, my mind was blown open. I felt so strongly that I had finally found my purpose! Here I was helping people who were some of the most vulnerable people in the world. I was conducting groups and incorporating visualizations that used energetic techniques, and the results were nothing short of miraculous!

I was working directly with people who had gone through so much. People who had lost everything, been sold by their parents only to become sex slaves, had all their relatives die in the earthquake and then be gang-raped, been trapped in the rubble for a week before being rescued; you name it I heard it. The disclosures were so horrendous that when I worked out of the hospital, I had to change translators every two hours because they couldn't continue. I had to set aside time every day to assist my translators in dealing with the things they heard. I always say that I hear the worst of humanity, and I also witness the best of humanity. But this was my first real direct experience with complete and utter misery and suffering.

The voodoo prophet

There's this thought in the humanitarian world that it is better to start psychosocial support after all the basic needs have been addressed. There is a lot of sense in this; no one wants to talk about emotions when they're starving or don't have shelter. Therefore, mental health professionals don't usually arrive until a few months after a crisis. But, after the earthquake, there were so many people in need and so much chaos. So even when I arrived almost eight months after the quake, many camp inhabitants were still struggling to meet their basic needs.

I worked semi-successfully to connect them with some essential services. However, I also found that without psychosocial support, they couldn't even make use of these resources. For example, many people were so scared or depressed that they couldn't leave their tiny 2-person tent, let alone go to food distributions, or try to get a job. So, I focused on what I knew best, and I led psychosocial groups.

I led about 15 groups a week on various topics, ranging from stress management to dealing with trauma to mediation between warring camp leaders. I led groups for adolescent girls, gang leaders, and everyone in between. We would meet weekly and talk about their struggles and what they could do to improve them. I would give some psychoeducation on what stress is or whatever the topic for that week was. We would talk about voodoo and how they could protect themselves against it, and then we would do visualizations. Because the suffering was so immense, it seemed that most people would express their pain in the form of psychosomatic illnesses. They would have medical ailments that weren't caused by anything wrong physically. Because there was little to no medical care available, the groups I led helped people deal with their psychosomatic symptoms, as well as find the courage to leave their tents and start putting their lives back together.

I taught them how to ground themselves, deal with stress, protect themselves energetically (since they were scared of voodoo curses), and connect with the universe to have more energy and healing in their lives. I had stumbled across visualizations through my thesis work. I had been utterly amazed by the results they could produce, especially since they cost nothing and are as limitless as one's imagination.

They thought I was a prophet.

Miracles can happen

After a couple of weeks of doing groups, people who couldn't walk were able to walk again. One person regained sight in their one eye. Many said they no longer had "hypertension" (which was the common illness that everyone said they suffered from). People's headaches and migraines were gone, their stomach aches or "ulcers" disappeared, and they could eat again. It was overwhelming, yet I didn't entirely pay attention to all the results because there was so much misery, suffering, and hopelessness that I didn't have time to stop and appreciate any of the successes. That is one of the reasons why I crawled out of Haiti. But their adoration started getting out of hand. People began to have visions of me confronting their enemy for them. Or having dreams of me coming down from heaven saying to the Prime Minister, "You can't forget the children!" I had to work repeatedly with them, telling them they were healing themselves, that they were the ones doing all these incredible changes.

My whole goal was to empower them, and yet they wanted to give me all the power. It seems to be human nature; I've felt it myself. It's so much easier to blame others for our suffering and depend on others for our healing. It was a constant struggle for me not to accept the power they wanted to give me. I decided to train a group of 15 women to lead groups themselves. Then under my supervision, they led groups in pairs in other camps and were also able to see incredible results. They became leaders and took what I taught and made it better. Ashamedly, I must admit that there was a part of me that wanted to accept the glory they were trying to bestow on me. But along with glory comes responsibility, and I think there was a part of me that took on that responsibility, which led to my total breakdown.

The right amount of caring

I talked about the garden metaphor in Chapter 2. This metaphor is a big one and has many layers of understanding. We need to keep in our own garden and not invite others into our garden to take care of us, not long-term. Do you guilt people or demand that people come into your garden and take care of you "if they really love you"? Do you give away your power and think they are the ones that need to make you happy? Make sure that you know how to love and take care of yourself first before asking others to assist. This sounds much easier than it is. So often in life, we spend so much time focusing on others or blaming others that we don't know what we want or need, or how to take care of our heart. It's so essential that you learn to nourish yourself. Only once you are happy and healthy yourself can you then truly be there for others in a healthy and supportive way. Make sure your plant is flourishing before you go to meet people at the fence.

The same goes in regard to helping other people. We must respect that they know how to take care of themselves best; don't accept their power or take responsibility for their happiness. If you try to do all their emotional work for them, they will get weaker and weaker and will never learn how to nourish and love themselves. No matter how much you love someone, it will never be enough; they have to learn how to love themselves. Giving them respect and staying out of their garden can be one of the most powerful ways to assist others.

Sometimes, actually drawing a garden can be helpful. Start by drawing the plant that represents you, and then write down the things that nourish you; perhaps they are ways to build your self-love or self-care strategies. You can draw someone else's plant too if you need the reminder that you can't fulfill them, and they can't satisfy you. Putting up this picture somewhere can remind you to stay in your garden and not ask others to come into your garden, but instead meet each other at the fence.

Creating boundaries energetically

I used these techniques in Haiti when a big windstorm was coming, and people were worried about the tents they were living in.

I've also used them when I used to work in a rough part of Vancouver. One day, I was on my way to work where I provided free counselling to homeless people. As I was walking, I saw an aggressive man coming toward me really quickly. He was scowling and looked like he was going to hit me. I automatically used the following technique, and he suddenly stopped mid-stride, spun on his heel and then walked away from me.

1. Take a few deep breaths to ground yourself. This isn't essential, but it can help you concentrate better when you're first trying this out.
2. Imagine a beautiful light blue bubble that goes all the way around you like a giant egg. Imagine that it's about 1 m away from your skin.
3. You can make this bubble thicker or thinner, depending on what you need. The thicker you make the bubble, the less information you will get about the world. The thinner it is, the more perceptive you will be.

Blue is the colour of protection. This bubble blocks negative energy from getting to you but still allows positive energy to come through. If you want to be unnoticeable to others, then you can imagine the outer layer of this bubble is covered in liquid mercury. This creates a reflective layer over the top and will reflect any of the energy people send to you. That's what I did when the man looked like he was going to attack me. I like to think he saw his reflection and scared himself away. I often find myself in dangerous situations, and I use this technique all the time. So far, it's always worked!

I will usually give my clients three techniques to protect themselves. The blue bubble is the most popular, but some also like the following two techniques:

- Imagine a pink layer of light about 3 cm thick covering all of your skin and protecting you from anything coming towards you.
- Imagine that four guards are protecting you at all times, one in front and behind and one on both sides. These guards can take the form of any object that represents safety to you. They could be anything from roses to pets to ancient Chinese soldiers.

Play around with the three options and see which one you prefer. Perhaps you like to use different ones for different situations or have another idea you want to try. Have fun with them, play around, and see what works best for you.

Healthy relationships

By reading this book and examples from my life, you will understand the difference between your fear and someone else's. Knowing yourself helps you distinguish between what's yours and what's not. I often find that my clients are holding emotions or beliefs that aren't actually theirs. It's ubiquitous to internalize your parent's values or beliefs, and it's possible to take on a stranger's mood if you are a sensitive person. Having a therapist or someone who can help you detangle what's yours and what isn't is incredibly useful. If something ever feels like it's too much or that no matter how hard you try, you can't seem to process whatever it is, then most likely, it's because you are carrying someone else's stuff. When I was young, I used to dream of taking on the burdens of the world, though I soon learned that this is detrimental. We can always handle and move through our own emotions; it's when we carry other people's that we get stuck.

I like to think of the world as an organism. When we take on other people's emotions, we aren't getting to the root of why they have that emotion. We might take the burden off them for a while, but because the source is not healed, they will eventually just regrow that burden, sometimes within a couple of hours. Meanwhile, you are now carrying that burden, so you've just doubled the burden in the world because you have it, and they've grown it back. I know we want to help, and taking on people's burdens might seem like we are helping in the short term, but in the long run, you are making your life more difficult and increasing the amount of pain in the world, which isn't helping them at all.

Helping others with their pain

One of the simplest, yet most powerful ways to help others with their pain is with the following technique. This technique is very potent and is extremely helpful; don't underestimate its strength! It doesn't involve physical activity, but this technique can transform and transmute suffering, all while being respectful and seeing the divine in others. This technique can be done with a person, as I'll show here. It can also be done with an animal or even an event.

1. To begin, focus on someone you would like to assist.
2. Really see that person, see how they are struggling. Really see them, witness them, witness their struggle.
3. See the strength and beauty in them as they've struggled with their burden. See how far they've come, how brave or resourceful they are. Really try to respect them and their journey.
4. Send this person love. If you want, you can imagine a cord going from your heart to their heart, and you are sending love through that cord.

Love can be sent and felt regardless of space and time, so even if it's something you're reading about, an art exhibition, or something you've seen on the news, sending love is incredibly powerful and helpful and benefits the world. If it's a loved one or someone you're interacting with, also send them love and communicate to them that you see their pain. If you want to, you can also ask them if there is anything you can do for them or anything they need from you. (We often have to feel like we're being useful or doing something, so that's why I'm adding that last part, more for you than them.) The most crucial part is witnessing, understanding and sending love while having faith that they are strong enough and capable enough to get through this.

Some philosophers believe that there is no such thing as real altruism, and I tend to agree. It was a gift beyond words to serve some of the most suffering people in the world. I know I helped save dozens of lives, if not hundreds during that year in Haiti, and I improved thousands of lives beyond that. Yet I still feel like I was the one who gained the most. When you listen to your intuition, everybody wins. When you give, you get so much more back. But the key here is that you have to offer from the right place, you have to give when your heart asks you. Although I went through a difficult time in my life before I left for Haiti, the support of my friends and family gave me so much strength. Knowing that I was following the call of my heart and doing what I needed to do vastly improved my life and many others. When we assist others, we assist ourselves and vice versa. When you follow your intuition, there is no loser; everybody wins.

Maybe your heart isn't as dramatic as mine and doesn't ask you to go into the middle of disasters, but that doesn't mean you have any less impact on the world. You never know the chain of events your heart sets in motion. I have been profoundly touched by the smile from a bus driver who really loved his job. People think I'm an unusually good person for being a humanitarian, but it's not true. I'm merely following my heart. I feel that so much, if not all, of the world's suffering and pain, can be healed if we all just followed our hearts. Can you see how others have benefited when you followed your intuition? Your heart?

If I hadn't gone to Haiti, I wouldn't have been able to serve thousands and thousands of people, and I wouldn't have met one beautiful soul that was to become my husband. A man that I loved with all my heart, and although we are currently getting divorced, he is a man I spent more than eight magnificent years with. I am profoundly grateful that sometimes my intuition is like a sledgehammer.

Chapter 4
Ebola

Not being controlled by external fears is about knowing your intuition, what you need to do, and having healthy boundaries between your true self and the fear surrounding you. But as you do this, you will be confronted with deeper layers of external fear, such as our compulsive desire to control everything around us. External fear includes the fear of change and fear of the unpredictable nature of everything outside of us. In fact, this is at the root of all external fear; this is why we try to influence others, and others try to control us. We are convinced that if we can command everything outside of us, we will feel safe and secure. Overcoming external fear is understanding that controlling our environment is not only impossible but detrimental.

The niggling

Although I am deeply glad that I followed my intuition and went to Haiti, I was a total wreck when I got back. I had post-traumatic stress disorder (PTSD). I had witnessed some violent murders and deaths and kept getting flashbacks of them. I was drowning in guilt for leaving Haiti, and my physical health was in shambles after getting typhoid. I had almost destroyed myself trying to control Haiti.

I spent two years healing. I delved deep into myself and hired several talented professionals to help me recover. I had also started my own business at this time, which had grown to be very successful, but I was beginning to get a feeling. I was getting restless, I had been burned by my time in Haiti, and yet my intuition was starting to give me subtle signs that I needed to get back into "the field." I had a feeling that something big was going to happen, but I didn't know what it was. I was restless and feeling this sense of claustrophobia. I yearned for freedom, but I felt guilty. My mentor had done so much for me and was the reason my business was so successful. I felt so bad just leaving it all. My husband, Francois, was also nervous about becoming a humanitarian again; he wanted us to enjoy and be content with our life in Vancouver.

On August 24th Francois and I went to an ayahuasca healing ceremony. He cleared some trauma from Haiti and made an inner agreement that he was open to becoming a humanitarian again. On August 26th, news of the Ebola outbreak came to Vancouver and became headline news. On August 31st, he left to join the relief efforts in West Africa.

Francois leaves for Ebola aid work

Francois's deployment was bittersweet; I was scared, like the rest of the world, that he might die. But I was also extremely certain, finally knowingly certain that I would join him in the response. I was so proud that he was facing his fear and going.

Did I mention that I was certain I was going to join him?

At this point in my life, my poor parents and friends have given up trying to stop me from doing something that I know I have to do. But Ebola pushed the limits. It's just a distant memory for most of you, but I will never forget the pandemonium that Ebola caused. I remember the fear, the constant headlines, the pack of journalists following a nurse as she went for a bike ride after returning from assisting in the crisis. No one knew anything about Ebola but that it had a 60-70% fatality rate with no known treatment. I get it. But still, the fearmongering was excessive. Even with my emotional clearing techniques, I wasn't sure I would survive if I went. But even the fear of death can't stop me if I know. I knew what external fears were, and I wasn't going to let them control me. I'd done this many times already; I knew I had to go. The kicker was that I couldn't get there, no matter how much I tried.

Frustration at not being deployed

I had a job interview that I completely bombed, and I didn't get the job. I applied for job after job, and I heard nothing back. It was like my applications were going into a black hole. I missed Francois terribly, my heart was aching, but mostly, I was paralyzed with the frustration that I should be there right now! I should be helping! No one wants to go there. There is a shortage of aid workers because everyone is refusing to go. There are so many people dying. Why am I not there? Why am I not there??!

Months went by, and my world crashed around me. I spiralled into a depression, and still, no one would hire me, just silence. Francois was so busy he couldn't talk to me as much, I had lost my private practice, and still, I was stuck in Vancouver. I had to move into my parents' house because I was running out of money. I'm used to being able to move mountains to reach my goal, but no matter how hard I tried to make this happen, my life just kept getting worse and worse. Why wasn't the world cooperating?!

Letting go

I'm not sure about you, but there is a certain type of hell when you know something, but you don't know it. Limbo, for me, is worse than the most disastrous news you could give me. At least with bad news, you can make a plan to deal with it, you can organize your life to adjust to it. But how do you adjust to maybe? You can't. Why did I have this knowing that I had to work in Ebola if I couldn't go work in the Ebola response?? I felt so out of control and so useless and so alone.

Here is a journal entry from that time.

October 29th, 2014
A couple of days ago, I bused for two hours to take care of [my spiritual teacher] Dianne. I wasn't really taking care of her. I was serving her and helping her move furniture around and put up pictures. I really needed to do it because she was the one who reminded me of myself so that I made a decision out of love and not fear, and for that, I'm so incredibly grateful!!! I told her how I'm so ready to go to West Africa. That I will literally do ANYTHING that the universe wants me too.
She told me that I AM the universe. I don't need to give up control or lament the fact that the universe isn't doing XYZ but that I am it already.
So yesterday I spent an hour meditating and I got in touch with that part of me that is the universe. I felt the expansiveness of it: the love, the potential, the bliss.
Well, today is a different story. There is no potentiality. There is no meaning. There is just selling my belongings, writing a report, and trying to keep my life together... My mom just came in as I was writing this, and I started crying. And she said that I have to let go. And I know she's right. I have to let go of everything, of the belief that I have that I'm supposed to change the world, I have to let go of going to Liberia, or being reunited with Francois, or thinking that I know what's best. But how do I reconcile this with me being the universe? If I let go, then who's running this thing? If I'm the universe, then who else do I trust?

If I tune in, then I feel like I am the universe, and I am also blindfolded from it. As my mom was talking, I had the image of me letting go of the life ring, of me floating out into the middle of the ocean. Only then can a whale swim under me and lift me up, take me for a ride. Only then are miracles able to happen.
But fuck, I don't want to let go of the life ring! But if I die, I die, at this point (and I'm sorry I don't mean to be so dramatic) but at this point dying wouldn't be worse than this. I've never been afraid to die. But I am so afraid not to fulfill my purpose, to not live up to my potential. That is probably my biggest fear. But if anything has been a theme, then making decisions out of love, not fear, would be it. I have to love myself even as I'm puttering away here selling pots and pans and trying to get these bloody bookcases off my hands.
Fuck.

Intuition is all very well and good, but I also have to have boundaries with the world, with life. I can't meddle in everything. I'm not a puppet master. I can't control a single thing except how I react to everything outside of me. I have to let the fuck go. I needed to learn how to let go of control. By this time, I had learned not to let external fears control me, but I hadn't learned to stop trying to control my life. I can have an intuition about something, but I can't control how that something acts. I can tell my clients things that I see, but I can't make them change their behaviour. I can know that I need to assist with Ebola, and I can get ready to do that, and then I need to lean into the unknowing and trust that it will all unfold because it will. I didn't have to make my life hell for that four months-that-felt-like-eternity, but I did, and only because I didn't trust, I didn't surrender; I didn't let go.

November 22nd
I'm writing in you, of course, because I'm struggling, there's nothing like a little bit of pain to motivate you to do cathartic journaling. I've

> been continuing my Course in Miracles study, and I'm trying to keep to the concepts of abundance and letting go of ego and letting go of my attachments to my illusions, but I'm really struggling. A couple of lessons ago the lesson was "I want the peace of God," and holy fucking shit do I EVER want the peace of God. But then when I really go deep and meditate, it is hard to give up my ideas of what would bring me happiness (my illusions). For example, I want to make a big change in the world, I really really want to contribute to making people happier, I want to make sure my life is maximized, and most of all I think I want purpose, and yet I need to give this up to find the peace of God? Am I supposed to give these up? Honestly, it all seems so difficult and impossible! How do I just trust? How do I give up my purpose and meaning in life? Even though I KNOW that this is what I must do. Why do I have this feeling? For what purpose? What is the point of all this? Is God even real? Are my talents in intuition even real? Is it all just bull fucking shit? It feels impossible to let go of my giant bumbling interfering ego. I know the answer is simple and maybe I'll look back over these words and get frustrated because I just need to let go, not that complicated, not that hard. Still, I'm scared that I can't, and I feel like I can't, or maybe I can for a moment, but then I pick it right back up again.

I wish I could tell you a secret way to let go, but it's as simple as it sounds, although we make it difficult and complicated for ourselves. We really need to simply let go. I have come up with some visualizations to help with this that I'll share with you later.

This time in my life was not the first time that I had learned the dire importance of letting go. When I was 16, I almost died. It was acceptance and letting go that saved me, well, that and perhaps a miracle.

I was on a high school ski trip. We had gone to Whistler, and I was with all my guy friends. It was mid-afternoon, so all of us were getting tired, but we wanted to check out this one double black diamond run. As we made our way from the chairlift to the run, we passed a sign that said, "Warning don't fall you won't be able to stop." I remember chuckling. Why would someone put a sign like that up? Who falls on purpose?

We get to the top of the run, and as I look down, I can't even see the hill, I can only see the tops of the moguls. I anxiously remember the sign and take a deep breath as I plunge off the side.

I'm barely in control as I ski down only a few metres, and I completely freak out, all the guys are already making their way down. I'm one of the last ones still standing there, and I panic about being left behind. My mind automatically reverts to when I was learning how to ski. Whenever it was too steep for us, we just took off our skis and walked down the hill. BAD IDEA. I click my boot out of one of the skis, and as I put my weight on that boot, I immediately start to slide. I slide down a couple of metres, but the tops of some trees peaking up through the snow stop me. I instantly realize my mistake. I try to scramble back up so that I can get my ski back. As I scramble up, I start falling, but this time the trees don't stop me. I flail, trying to reach for anything that will slow my fall, but I keep falling faster and faster. I claw at the snow and scream; this can't be happening! I'm almost in free fall now, and I start to be tossed up in the air as I bounce off trees. One of my guy friends, a strapping young Dutch guy, later told me that he tried to get in the way of my fall but then backed out because I was falling so fast, I would have taken his head off. Finally, I face the futility and give up. I remember accepting the fact that this was the end.

I was completely free-falling at this point, only occasionally smashing on the ground just to be thrown back up into the air again. But I was utterly relaxed; I had accepted that I was going to die. The guys said I looked like a rag doll. I remember thinking that I had probably bounced off a bunch of rocks, and then I landed on my head and blacked out.

Then, all of a sudden, I came to an abrupt halt. I groggily lifted my head and opened my eyes to stare down into a rock ravine about 20 metres below. I'm on the very edge of the cliff, my legs hanging off. A small sapling caught me right between my legs, so perfectly between my legs that I didn't swing around it. It made no sense. The laws of physics weren't holding up. I looked back up the hill and saw that I'd fallen about 300 metres, the rocks that I thought I had bounced off were actually still the tops of trees, larger than the little sapling that had stopped me. How could I have fallen through a hundred trees but not this one? My friends slowly make their way to me. Crying, they're barely able to get out the words to ask me if I'm ok. I'm stunned, shocked, I feel my body with my hands, but there doesn't seem to be any broken bones.

A nice gentleman comes down with my skis. I put them on and ski down the rest of the hill.

To this day, I try to use this as a reminder to let go. I'm stubborn, so I've had to learn this lesson a few times, including after the Ebola outbreak. But giving up was literally what saved my life, or at least it's what prevented me from having any broken bones. I was so relaxed; there was no resistance that could be broken.

How to let go

I find a simple visualization can help allow us to let go. Sometimes I need to do this visualization over and over again.

1. Ground yourself either through the tree grounding
2. Imagine what you want, see it in the form of a postcard, and try to see as many details as possible.
3. Give it up to the universe. Perhaps this is through putting that picture inside a balloon and watching the balloon float up to the sky until you can't see it anymore. Perhaps it's through a

> beam of sunlight coming down and evaporating the image until it's all gone. It can be any image that resonates with you as long as it transports that image to the universe and out of your hands.

When I had the *knowing* that I needed to assist with the Ebola outbreak, I clutched too tightly to that knowing. I didn't give it room to unfold. I had a knowing of what I should do, and I created an idea of when and where and how that was going to happen. I was sure I was going to leave in September and go to Liberia. It was this closed view that created all the suffering.

Finally, after hitting rock bottom, I understood what the universe was trying to teach me—again. Here are some blogs I wrote at the time for highly sensitive empaths.

Change

Personally, there has been a lot of change for me over the last few months. In August, my husband very abruptly dashed to Liberia to assist with the Ebola response. Since then, I've been struggling with living with him so far away (and not worry about him) while also winding down my private practice and moving to an online business. It's made me want to write this post to share and sort through the lessons I've had over the last while.

As highly sensitive empaths, we love very intensely. I think that love also relates to moments. We love moments or situations, and when they change, it can feel like they are being ripped from our hearts, even if they were a little prickly to love in the first place. I think inherently highly sensitive empaths struggle with change. I know I have.

One of my thesis findings was that if you want to manifest reality, you need to have a balance. A balance between knowing what you want and having enough attachment to the outcome can propel your intention forward—but not wanting it so much that you don't release it and allow it to come to fruition. In other words, you need to have an idea of what you want and then let it go. If you have too much or too little attachment to the idea, then the likelihood of it happening is significantly diminished.

So what does this have to do with change? Well, I'm learning, in subtly different ways, that I need to have an idea of what direction I want to go into—for example, moving exclusively online so I can be with my husband. But I also need to be open and flexible to how my future will work (when and where I will be reunited with my husband). If I clutch too tightly or not tightly enough, then my dream has less chance of materializing. If I want change to happen more smoothly, I have to let go.

As an HSE, we often want something in the future; we forget the things we have right now until they are being torn from us. That has been my biggest lesson these last few months. Things will change, perhaps even suddenly. So instead of always planning, I need to sit and settle into the now. My focus for the next unknown while is to, a) have gratitude for what I have, and b) release the dream I have for the future into the universe with the hope that it will unfold—while being open to variations.

The universe usually has something a lot grander for us than we even dare to imagine for ourselves, but this can be disappointing because it doesn't come wrapped how we expected. Be open, be open to change, possibility, and be open to blessings even if they come in wolf's clothing.

Along with letting go comes acceptance. Acceptance of the situation right now, acceptance that we don't have control, and acceptance over whatever the outcome is. I wrote the following blog directly after I wrote about letting go.

Acceptance

Acceptance can be a bit of a controversial topic. I know I've had a ton of resistance to it, and even lately, I've had to heal another layer of resistance. We've all heard the importance of staying in the moment, being in the now. Acceptance is like that but even more profound. Acceptance is recognizing what is and witnessing and feeling what is. It is loving and having compassion for what is.

Many people might have resistance to acceptance because if we accept ourselves or the situation, then perhaps nothing will change. But acceptance is not the same as complacency.

My new year's resolution is to have more acceptance in my life. I am a perfectionist, as well as ambitious, smart and motivated, and so acceptance has been the antithesis of my life. Yet I have learned so thoroughly that if I want to fulfill my highest expectations, if I want to make an impact, transform my life and the life of others, then I need to start with acceptance.

I was recently at a workshop by Gordon Neufeld. He's a very well-known psychologist in the parenting field. He was talking about "tears of futility." Tears of futility are when you are frustrated and angry because you realize that you are not going to get what you want. He states how it's important for kids to experience tears of futility if they are to be able to move on from a situation. Tears of futility are about acceptance, about giving up your idea of what should happen, or what should be. It is not until we have our tears of hopelessness, not until we finally accept where we are and stop trying to change it, we can then see the infinite options of how to move away from where we are.

Soon after I wrote this, I finally got a job in Sierra Leone. My knowing that I had to join the Ebola response ultimately came to fruition. But it wasn't until I learned how to let go and accept that I wasn't in control that the job offers started coming in. I have found that cleansing my energy field has helped me become clearer in what I want to manifest and also supported me in coping with the uncomfortableness of not being in control and letting go of negative or uncomfortable emotions.

Cleansing yourself

I was emotionally exhausted with trying to make my future look how I wanted it to look. So along with practising letting go, I also had to practise cleansing myself. As I've mentioned before, we often take on other people's stuff to help them, or perhaps through internalizing their values. Or, if you're sensitive, you might even unknowingly pick up things from the environment. This can be like carrying a grand piano on your back as you're trying to hike up a mountain. It's not helpful, and it just makes life difficult! Whenever you feel overwhelmed or emotionally exhausted, take that as a signal that you need to cleanse yourself. The following are some techniques I often use on myself and with those I work with.

Visualization

Here is a clearing mediation that I use:

1. Ground yourself, either through the tree grounding, the cord grounding, or by taking some deep breaths.
2. Imagine a small purple flame in the centre of your chest. This flame burns up anything that you no longer want to carry: stress, negative emotions, thoughts.
3. See the flame getting bigger and bigger and start burning up more of your body: your whole torso, down your legs, your head, and then the space around you. Imagine you are resting in these beautiful purple flames.

If you prefer you can also imagine the following, but always start with grounding:

1. Imagine a bright sunbeam coming down from the sun/heaven/universe and coming in through the top of your head.
2. Feel this bright white healing light enter your head and imagine that it is vibrating so quickly it's just humming. This vibration shakes out all your cells and transmutes any negative energy that you don't want to hold anymore.

3. Have the light flow down your body, eventually filling your whole body with this beautiful bright white light. Feel the lightness and health of your body.

When I'm exhausted and feel like I want to give up, I do the following:

1. Imagine you are on a beautiful beach, lying down where the waves come up.
2. Just wholly relax, be a blob on the beach, let the beach support you and hold you up.
3. Imagine the waves crash over you, and as they slink back into the ocean, they pull out anything that isn't serving you anymore. Let them crash over you as long as you want, cleansing you every time they slide back into the ocean.

Exercise

Exercising is one of those incredible things that helps with everything: stress, health, anxiety, sleeping! If you feel like there is too much on your plate, you can always try a form of exercise that uses alternating sides of your body, such as swimming, walking or running. When you do this type of exercise, it's forcing the right and left sides of the brain to communicate, and it can help you process and digest things. It might help to give you clarity on what is going on for you.

I know when you are overwhelmed, you can often feel like you don't have time to exercise, but it's possible to squeeze it into your day no matter what. Force yourself to take the stairs, walk instead of taking the bus, take a walk at lunchtime. When we take the extra time to do these cleansing techniques, it frees up more time in our lives because we stop running in circles. We become more productive and more efficient.

Water

Don't forget to drink lots of water. Take a bath or shower, or go for a swim in the ocean if that's available to you. Water is physically and emotionally cleansing.

Alternative suggestions

Lastly, if you're so exhausted that all of this seems too much for you, then I suggest just putting some rose quartz in your pocket. Pink is the colour of compassion, and rose quartz can feel like a warm hug. Additionally, some people use sage or full moon rituals to cleanse themselves. As always, experiment, try different things out and use whatever works for you. Any type of ritual can be potent, even if you just make it up yourself.

My refusal and inability to let go created so much suffering for me! Everything had to be stripped from me before I was able to let go. I was only able to finally let go because I was utterly exhausted and hopeless and didn't have the strength to hold on anymore. I survived taking that path of trying to control everything. And I still take milder versions of this path, but we don't have to! If we can trust and let go, accept who we are, the situations we are in and that things don't have to work out exactly how we imagine they should, then we stop creating suffering for ourselves. Let go of your preconceived notions of what is right and what is wrong. Then life will be so much easier.

The Ebola response is hard to put into words. Never had I felt like I could die at any moment, never had I seen so much death all around me, never had I felt so rejected and hated by the world because of my association with the disease. But it was glorious! We lived in the moment, and we came together to defeat the disease. Ebola was declared finished on my birthday, and the party the country had was unparalleled to anything I have experienced. I received a medal of honour from the Canadian government for the work I did there.

It's easy to blame the universe or God for the suffering that we create in our life. But the universe wasn't trying to punish me for holding on; I was punishing myself. The universe was trying to tell me that everything's all right, that I'm not alone, but I refused to listen. Happiness and choosing love is not about being a better person, it's about finally learning to stop blocking the incredible person you already are. It's about letting your fears fall away and coming back to your true, magnificent self.

Chapter 5
Buying My Home - Trust

The literal wall of fire

We were driving full speed towards a massive wall of fire. It was so big that the flames were reaching up higher than our 4x4, and it was impossible to see past it. Dawn was just breaking, and I could only make out shadows quickly moving out of our way ahead of us. I heard a gunshot, perhaps to warn us to stop or to warn others as we hurtled full speed ahead. My security Manger yelled, "Faster! Faster, drive faster!" We were all bracing for impact, the driver, my security manager and I. All that filled my vision was the wall of flames that would soon envelop us.

This is what trust is like

It was 4 am, and my security manager had come to rescue me.

I had been back in Haiti, helping in the Hurricane Matthew response that had devastated parts of the country. On my way back from visiting some of the programs outside of the base, a big riot broke out, and all the streets were blocked with massive fires, semi-trucks and freshly dug ditches. I, along with some others, had found refuge in a hotel close enough to the rioting that we could hear the yells and gunshots just 200 metres away from us. I was huddled in a room with 20 other people breathing through wet towels. We were trying to soothe our burning eyes and lungs after we had been tear-gassed for the third time. I was suffering the most because I had run around the hotel as they were shooting tear gas at us, trying to herd everyone into safety. But in the scramble, I had managed to find my phone. When I could finally speak, I called my security manager to update him on the situation. He told me to stay put; he was meeting with the rebel leaders to see if he could get me out. He later called telling me to stay there for the night, and he would come to get me early the next morning.

I woke up at 4 am to a call from him, "Get up now, go fast we're in the front." I scrambled in the dark and ran to the road. My security guard was there with a car. I scuttled inside, and we started driving before I had shut the door and were racing to the main road. The rebels were already beginning to make a fire out of burning tires. We had to drive through it fast enough so that our car wouldn't catch fire.

We plunged right through the wall of fire, perilously missing a parked semi that the flames had concealed entirely. If we had been one foot more to the right, all of us would have been dead. I ducked down in the seat, trying to avoid any bullets if they decided to shoot. But they didn't.

And then it was calm, everything was quiet, I kept looking back to see if people were following us, but no one was. When I arrived at the office, they gave me the day off, but I worked anyway.

Trusting

I know that perhaps my life is more dramatic than most, but trusting the universe can feel as scary as driving through a wall of fire. We don't know what's on the other side. Careening full speed ahead seems like a crazy idea, and a death of sorts seems inevitable. But then you do it, and it's actually not so bad. Sure, you may have narrowly missed disaster, but you did miss it, and now nothing could convince you to go back to the place you left. There's a whole world of happiness out there. It's better and more beautiful than we could ever create or imagine for ourselves, but sometimes we need to drive through a wall of fire to reach it.

When knowing doesn't seem to make sense

Every single day I'm deeply grateful that I am cocooned here in my lovely apartment. I'm writing this during the Pandemic, and France has been in lockdown for two months, so I've certainly had to be in here a lot. There is no other place I would rather be, and I feel so lucky to have this sanctuary I can call home.

But getting here wasn't easy. Trust must go hand in hand with listening to your intuition and overcoming fears. I've found that the more I listen to my intuition, the more a pattern emerges of being very sure in what I must do and then being tested more and more as I try to do that thing. I have to drive through a figurative wall of fire. Buying this apartment tested me. Or rather, it forced me to let the things no longer working in my life to burn away. Following your heart is not the easiest path. Still, it does result in genuine joy regardless of the circumstances surrounding you. I hope that by sharing my struggles, you'll have more trust when you go through your fire because if you can overcome it, the rewards are priceless. Encountering a wall of fire doesn't mean stop.

Montpellier is one of those places that just really felt right. After staying here a couple of months, I knew I wanted to live here, even though I didn't have the knowing. My husband and I had been looking for a city to call home for the last five years. Montpellier was the first place that, for me, really felt like home. However, Francois didn't have the same feeling and so was reluctant to commit to buying anything. Two years passed, and my yearning grew, but Francois still wasn't sure. Little did I know it wasn't Montpellier he was questioning, it was me.

I believe there is always a solution where both people can be happy; you just have to be creative to discover it. So, as the next year went by, I started thinking of other ideas. Maybe we could work in such and such a place together and make a home there? Or perhaps we could continue with our current jobs for such and such a time and then do this other adventure? I tried so hard to come up with solutions that I overwhelmed myself with all the different options of what our future could look like. I was getting more and more lost in the maze of possibilities, trying to work around the yearning that I needed a home.

Then one summer day, Francois and I were visiting Montpellier. We were relaxing and reading in the sun on one of the many café terraces that dot the little streets. I was wholly engrossed in my book when suddenly I heard a "ding!" that came out of nowhere. It was so clear that it took me a moment to realize it was in my head. It was like the sound of a high-pitched small bell, and abruptly, I knew. I looked up and said, "It just hit me. I think we need to buy a place here and make it our home base." Francois looked at me skeptically. By this point, it had been three years since he had not decided what he wanted to do. Later, Francois would admit to me that it was because he wasn't sure if he wanted to stay married to me. But at the time, I just thought that he loved this city, but it still didn't entirely feel like home to him.

I don't believe in sacrifice or compromise. I think both of these sentiments come from a mentality of "not enough." So I always like to look for solutions where everyone wins. So, although I wanted Francois to want to live in Montpellier, I didn't want to coax him to do something he didn't want. However, I knew there was a solution. I asked him to think about it for another week to have time to start the process before we had to return to the Middle East. If he didn't want to buy an apartment with me, I would use the money I earned to buy a smaller one myself. We could use it as a base or rent it out if he didn't want to live there. I wanted to make sure I was making a request of him and not a demand.

At the end of the week, he decided that he wanted to buy an apartment with me. I was ecstatic. We began the process of looking at apartments, AKA, I started acting on my intuition. When all of a sudden, Francois freaked out and told me he couldn't buy an apartment with me. I was devastated. But I didn't question it. I had made a request, and so I told him it was no problem and that I would look for a smaller place I could afford on my own. It was not fair to punish him just because he wasn't doing what I wanted.

But I have to admit there was a part of me that was angry at Francois, although I tried not to be. I felt like he was playing with my heart, and why couldn't he just see that this was a good investment? I took some time to delve into my anger, and I realized that the anger was just a way for me to feel power. In reality, I was fearful of doing this on my own, and I was frightened that I was making a mistake. By now, I no longer felt the knowing, but I realized I couldn't put this on Francois. I had to trust the universe, that this was the right thing for me to do, that I really did hear that bell ring in my head. Once I had that awareness, my anger for him evaporated. Although I was still nervous, I was ready to buy an apartment on my own.

I spent the next seven months researching apartments, contacting real estate agents and figuring out exactly what I could afford. Francois and I had another trip planned to Montpellier. He had agreed to translate and help me navigate the French bureaucracy system of purchasing a property. I had only two weeks to find and make an offer on an apartment. At the last minute, Francois said he was only coming for the first week. So, I knew I was going to do this mostly on my own, but I was still not prepared for what happened next.

Over the last couple of years, Francois's and I's relationship had been struggling. I loved him with all my heart, but he said he felt numb. He became more and more distant, throwing himself into his work. He told me he wasn't sure if he wanted to be married to me. But then he'd tell me that we would never get divorced. I wanted a great love. It was horrible to feel like I wasn't part of his life, even though I had taken a job in the Middle East to be close to him.

Yet it was through this challenging time that I really learned how to love unconditionally. I knew Francois didn't know if he wanted to stay married to me, and although that hurt, through my self-love practices, I was able to give him space while at the same time keeping my heart soft and open to him. I was able just to enjoy the feeling of loving him, not needing anything else. I loved him unreservedly, regardless of what he did or didn't do for me. Regardless if he loved me fully or not. Learning that is something that I will be grateful for until I die.

And I also loved myself. After two years of carrying the relationship, I was no longer content with staying in limbo. Francois said he loved me, but his actions repeatedly stated something different. So, after two years, I needed a real commitment from him or for us to go our separate ways.

On the night before we were to fly to Montpellier, Francois told me he couldn't commit to me.

My heart shattered.

I cried so hard I could barely breathe, and yet even while I was crying, I remember trying not to because I didn't want to make him feel bad. I had felt the truth of his decision. I knew it was his truth, and I wanted to respect that. We had been together for eight years. We had travelled all over the world together, working in all sorts of disasters, and sailed across an ocean; it felt like there was nothing we couldn't overcome. But we had hit a crossroads that couldn't be bridged. Part of loving someone unconditionally is letting them go.

The kicker is that half the reason I wanted to live in France and learn French was that it was his heritage.

What the fuck was I doing buying an apartment in France?? Not to mention the fact that because of our jobs, we'd never gotten around to getting me French citizenship. So if I bought an apartment in France, could I even live in it?

I seriously considered giving up buying an apartment. Fuck intuition, fuck doing what's right. It wasn't logical to keep going with this mad plan. But we had flight tickets, so what else were we supposed to do? Spend our vacation in Iraq? We were both still in shock. I was like a zombie, blindingly following the course that I had already laid out for myself.

Here is an excerpt from my journal that I wrote during a layover on my way to Montpellier:

> What the hell are we going to do??? I mean, we've just basically decided we're getting divorced, and now we have to spend a week together in France, I'm supposed to buy a place?? Do I want to live in France still? Honestly, I really don't, I want to crawl under a rock somewhere and never get out, or sail out into the middle of the ocean and never return. How am I supposed to buy a place in a country where I speak the language like a donkey?
> How am I going to do this?
> How am I going to be alone?
> And now I'm crying in the middle of this café while a musician is singing "Stand by me" behind me. HA!
> Why do I have this feeling/knowing that I have to buy an apartment in France? I don't even know if I can get French citizenship/residency now. What the fuck is going on?
> I guess I'll just try to start with getting on the next flight and take it from there.

I was numb and operating on automatic pilot. I could no longer connect to the knowing that I needed to buy an apartment, but since this had happened before, I knew I had to just trust. I felt like a blind person fumbling around in the middle of a cloud, trying to find something solid to hold on to. Even though I'm a flexible person and can sometimes change my mind, I have never once found that it has shifted in all my many experiences of following my intuition. Once I have a knowing, I need to trust that it is still valid even when it seems like it is the craziest thing to do. Buying an apartment in France made no logical sense. My friends and family all thought I was mad to go ahead with it, and yet I had to trust that I had heard that "ding" for a reason. Perhaps hearing that bell in the first place was so that I could have the strength to go through all of this. I mean, who hears a "ding" anyway? What a strange sound to indicate that Montpellier is where I belong. Intuition does not equal logic.

I was barely functioning, and so I clung to Montpellier like a life preserver. I tried to visit the apartments I had chosen, except that the real estate agent would often forget that we had an appointment or would cancel at the last moment. It was demoralizing. Even though I knew my intuition would be challenged, this was over the top. How could I find a place in two weeks when I struggled to get out of bed, and people wouldn't even show up to the appointments?

It wasn't until the end of the first week that I found an angel. She had taken the form of an English-speaking real estate agent. She took me under her wing, and I was finally able to visit several apartments. Then Francois went back to Iraq.

> Francois has just left for Iraq after us spending a week together in France. I feel like I can actually hear my heart cracking into small pieces. I tried to hold my shit together all morning because I hate to make him feel bad or sad, but I kept breaking down. Now that he's left, I've been crying my eyes out. I'm so fucking petrified!!! I don't know what I'm afraid about, but I never realized how much I used him as my safe harbour!! He's just so fucking kind and wonderful, and I've lost him. I keep on hyperventilating. Why couldn't I be happy with

how things were, why did I have to push for us to get counselling? I would be happy with him ignoring me and not loving me than just walking away. He made me feel so safe, I never even realized how much I depended on his calm quiet. And at the same time, I know he made some bad mistakes, so I'm just so confused. What way is up? Where the fuck am I supposed to go from here? Was I using him to hide from life?

He's worried that he's making a mistake, but I know that he needs to do this and that his life is just going to get better. But what about me? This isn't my choice, my heart isn't telling me to leave him, so how do I know my life is going to get better? It feels like it's just sinking down a sewage drain. And yet I have to support him in this decision that is splitting my heart because I do KNOW it's something he has to do. Honestly, how am I going to get through this? How strong does the universe expect me to be???

Oh my god, I can't handle this pain.

Finally, I fell in love with an apartment. Even though it didn't have everything I wanted, I felt it was close enough. I put in an offer only to be told it had already been sold a few hours earlier. I spiralled deeper into despair. I was so angry with the universe; how could this happen? How could my life be falling apart like this? Why the fuck am I supposed to buy an apartment? If I'm supposed to do something, then shouldn't the universe make it easy? It felt like every possible thing that could go wrong was, and my heart was breaking in the meantime. Francois blamed the apartment buying for the end of our marriage, although I think we both know that wasn't why. All my friends and family were telling me to go back home to Vancouver. Why would I buy a place in France when Francois and I were divorcing? I was on a roller coaster, and no matter how hard I tried, I couldn't get off, yet all this time, I knew I had to trust.

I hate trusting.

Then I found it: MY apartment. It had everything I was looking for but had given up on, and it was in the exact location I wanted. As soon as I stepped in to look around, I knew. I can't describe the weight that literally lifted off my shoulders! Finding this apartment felt more than just that—I felt like perhaps the universe was looking out for me. I wasn't alone. I am on the right path! There is hope! There is a light in this bitter darkness that I am drowning in. It was and has been the one thing that has kept me afloat at this time in my life where everything seems upside down.

Here is my next journal entry:

This morning is completely different because last night it was confirmed that my offer for an apartment was accepted! I wish I could add a video here of the apartment so that you could see it. I'm still reeling from the fact that my offer actually came through. It means so much more than even just having a home. It means the universe is watching over me. It means that I'm not alone, it means that I'm not crazy and that I'm accurate in what I think my heart is saying. It means that I'm not alone. It means that little by little, everything is going to be ok and that it's going to work out. It means that I'm not alone. It means that I'm on the right path, it means that I am loved. It means that I'm not alone. I'm not alone. I'm not alone.

And what's more this apartment is so much better than the first one I lost, it's got a small balcony, it's bright, it has exposed wooden ceiling beams, it has a massive storage room, and it's actually in the same location as the first place, which is incredible.

I have tears, but this time not of grief or sorrow but of such profound gratitude. The universe is with me, I'M NOT ALONE! I am taken care of. I've found this absolutely incredible real estate agent that has totally taken me under her wing and was the one who did all the negotiating and will help with alllllll the paperwork right up until I take possession (to be honest it wouldn't surprise me if she was a literal angel). Even the gentleman selling it to me is kind and seems honest. How am I so blessed by the universe?

And thank God this worked out! It means that I really am supposed to buy an apartment here and make it my home base. I was starting to think I was on crazy pills, especially with Francois and I falling apart. But I wasn't. I can hear what I'm supposed to do. What I hear IS accurate.

Thank you thank you thank you universe. Thank you from the bottom of my heart!

I quit my job and took ownership three months later. After two years of working in Syria and my personal life in shambles, my heart was beaten to a pulp. As someone who works in mental health, I believe in practising what I preach. I no longer felt capable of being good at my job. Moving into my new apartment to heal was the only thing I could do. Francois generously lent me enough money to exist for a year, so I didn't have to worry about getting another job.

As I write this, I still don't know what's going to happen with my residency, but it's no longer a primal fear that overwhelms me. I'm already so much better at trusting. I keep on saying, "The universe got me into this. The universe can get me out." I do know that although I don't usually love material things, I love my apartment. It has been my refuge while I put together the broken pieces of my heart. It has been a womb that I've crawled into while my life went to shit. And I am so so so eternally grateful that I had this haven to retreat to as I recovered from my divorce.

I'm not sure why every time I know I need to do something, the universe seems to make doing it extremely difficult for a while. Then, at the last moment, everything falls into place. Why can't it just be easy right away? Why this wall of fire that we have to walk through?

After taking this past year to meditate and heal, ponder and write, I don't think we have to go through these difficult situations as a way to test us. I don't see the universe as something that doles out punishment or takes away everything we have to make sure we only love or believe in the universe. I think the universe is using these difficult situations to show us our own strength, our own power, our own ability to accomplish way more than we thought was imaginable. These demanding situations help us let go of things that aren't serving us any longer. If I had bought another apartment before I had found mine, then I wouldn't have found my place. Although I had learned how to love unconditionally, my marriage needed to end.

I think the universe was showing me just how big my heart is, and the container my heart lived in before was too small and needed to be broken open. In my journal entry, I questioned if I was using my husband to hide from the world. Now, a year later, I actually think I was. I needed to come out from behind him and stand on my own. As painful as these last couple of years have been, I don't regret anything. Change needed to happen, and sometimes that's painful. But we don't have to add suffering to our pain. Ending relationships is painful, quitting jobs is painful, losing loved ones or moving places, facing failure or being betrayed are all painful, and there's no way around it. But when we make that pain mean something negative about us, our worth, or what we deserve or not, that's when we create suffering. When we are confronted with other people's external fears, and we take them on as our own, that creates suffering for both parties. When we forget our pure magnificence, or that our soul is forged out of love, that is what creates suffering. Following our intuition and driving through the wall of fire, these are sometimes necessary acts that remind us of our true nature, our true strength. Most importantly, they teach us what love really is.

External fears are my father threatening to kick me out of the family, or my boyfriend not wanting me to go to Haiti. They are the news coverage of Ebola and even my ex-husband not wanting to join me in buying an apartment. External fears are other people's fears about themselves, the world, or you. They are expressions of their journey and what they need to heal while also reflecting your blocks or unhealthy relationship habits. External fears force you to develop, listen to and trust your own intuition and to gently and compassionately make healthy boundaries with those you love. Once they are identified and understood, external fears are gifts in understanding your path and surrounding yourself with nourishing people who support you in being your best self.

Part 2

Internal Fears

"If you are fearful, it is certain that you will endow the world with attributes that it does not possess, and crowd it with images that do not exist."

A Course in Miracles

Chapter 6
External Fears Versus Internal Fears

This section is all about internal fears. I'm fascinated by internal fears. Don't get me wrong, they suck, but they are also such windows into our soul! External fears are other people's thoughts or opinions that we take on, so they only require listening to intuition and healthy boundaries to resolve them. In contrast, internal fears are unavoidable and infinitely more interesting. External fears can deter us from our path, and they can distract us, while internal fears are our path. Internal fears are what we need to uncover and heal in this life; they are the reason we are here. They can be embedded in our outlook on life, and they tint how we see ourselves, others, and the world. They require you to delve into yourself, to discover and question conscious and unconscious beliefs. Only then can you fully understand that they are not real, that they can't hurt you, that they are just a nightmare in a dream we think is real life. The universe teaches us through contrasts, so if we are to understand love truly, then we must understand and heal our fears. Wisdom is the gift of internal fears, they are our purpose, and they are our path to knowing and being love, but only if we remember they are not real.

I am incredibly grateful that I was born with an anxiety disorder, a type of internal fear. Anxiety is a fear or worry about something, or in my case, everything, to the extent that it significantly negatively impacts your daily life. Although the concern is about things outside of myself, it is an example of internal fear because they are my fears, created, and resolved within me. I am the one who is fearful of all those things out there.

As a child, my mom took me to countless doctors to understand why I always had stomach aches, but at that time, doctors didn't know it was a classic symptom of anxiety in children. I used to be so anxious about being late for school that I would wake up at 3 am, get fully dressed, do my hair, clean my room, make my bed, set my alarm for 6 am and go to sleep on top of my bed fully clothed. I would lie like a corpse so that when I woke up at 6 am, I'd be mostly ready for school. But my anxiety made it so that I couldn't escape from internal fears, and so I was forced at a young age to look at my anxiety and decide if I would let it control my life. Internal fears can only be resolved by looking inwards. With anxiety, even if you try to change your outside environment, your anxiety will worsen because it's an internal thing.

I remember learning the definition of bravery: to do something, even though you're scared to do it. I decided that I wasn't going to let fear make my decisions; I wasn't going to let it stop me from doing things. As someone dedicated to choosing love over fear, I can't think of a better challenge to face and overcome at an early age.

Internal fears are what make up most of our existence. They are fears that we are consciously afraid of, such as public speaking, or rejection. They are also fears that are subconscious, such as us not being good enough, or unlovable. There's even research that shows that we can carry our ancestors' fears in our DNA; this is called generational trauma. All of these are examples of internal fears, and if we want to get past them, if we don't want to be controlled by them, then we must look at them directly and heal them. Unfortunately, our automatic and most common human reaction to fear is to run away from it, but trust me, that only makes it proliferate.

Fear grows fear

Anxiety is the most common mental illness in North America and more rampant than ever, with around 40 million Americans suffering from it. We're in a fear epidemic that's snowballing. What's more, we have anxiety about anxiety. All of society revolves around helping us avoid feeling or thinking too much: TV shows, buying more things, the beauty industry. We are told that all of these things will make us happy, yet they distract us and make us more anxious and depressed. We are running away from our feelings because we don't know how to handle them. We are taught that emotions are bad and to shove them down. Yet the more we live life not facing our fears, the more our fears get bigger. Research on phobias shows this. For example, you are terrified of mice and don't meet this fear, then your fear of mice could severely restrict your life. You might stop going outside because you're nervous that you'll see one. Then on top of that, it can also generalize or spread into a fear of other things that resemble mice, such as rats, and then that could spread to perhaps cats or anything that might remotely remind you of mice or any of your consecutive fears. The more we avoid our emotions, the bigger they get. This is especially true for fear and anxiety.

I find that in terms of our internal fears, we are often petrified of being scared. We have this first fear, but our fear of it grows and grows until it's much greater than that original fear ever was: it becomes terrifying to even think of facing it. It's like a cat in front of a light that casts a massive shadow. If we just have the courage to turn around and look at the source of what's causing the shadow, we'll find that it's not remotely as big or scary as we thought it was.

When you live in fear, you are locking up your heart in a prison of pain and distrust; every brick in the prison wall is of your own making. You have the power to undo or break down the prison you've made for yourself, find freedom from the agony you created, and wake yourself up from the nightmare you've convinced yourself is real. Love is the key to doing all of this, remembering that we are love and that love is the only thing that really has power. Love is the only thing that will disintegrate the walls: love is the key to your freedom.

If we want to choose love over fear, then we have to be clear about what are our underling intentions, what is truly motivating us. It's common for me to make a choice out of love and be totally petrified while making that choice. How ironic.

When my marriage fell apart, I was petrified of being alone. I didn't know who I was without my husband. But I wanted a great love, and I wasn't going to find that in my marriage. I loved my husband with all my heart, albeit he told me he couldn't emotionally commit to me. My love and respect for both him and myself overruled my fear of being alone and forced me to make one of my life's scariest decisions.

Conversely, it is easy to say, "I want to do XYZ because I love so and so." Often, we use this "love" to justify or explain actions that are potentially detrimental to ourselves and others. If I had used my love for my ex-husband to justify staying with him longer, I would have been betraying us both. It was petrifying to end our marriage, but if I used love to ignore how unhealthy it was, that's not me being motivated out of love, that's me being motivated out of fear of losing him.

I see this all the time in emotionally or even physically abusive relationships. What you are truly being motivated by is a tricky thing to uncover, I know it is. However, if we take care of our garden, if we take care of and listen and comfort our hearts first, we are already taking the loving path. Connecting and comforting our own hearts is a crucial step; only then can we truly heal any unconscious beliefs that are coming up for us.

Unconscious limiting beliefs

An unconscious limiting belief is an example of internal fear. An unconscious limiting belief is exactly what it sounds like: it's a mostly unconscious belief that you have about yourself that limits your happiness. When you are mentally and emotionally ready, these limiting beliefs will bubble up to the surface, often in the form of situations or people that especially annoy or upset you. People and situations are a mirror of our inner or subconscious workings. Whenever we encounter something upsetting, that is a sign that an unconscious belief is coming up because we are now ready to address it. We all have unconscious limiting beliefs, and even though I have been doing this work a long time now, I'm still finding beliefs that are bubbling up. That is the gift of life.

Thank goodness I (mostly) gave up trying to be perfect years ago, or else this journey can get quite disheartening. That's why I keep on mentioning how it's impossible to make mistakes because I'm hoping you, too, will try to give up the idea of being perfect. Perfection is a destination. Healing our unconscious beliefs is a reminder to focus on the process of our life. To heal these limiting beliefs, we need to focus on the present, not on some far away or unreachable outcome that we want for ourselves. An unconscious limiting belief drives our behaviour and decisions without us being aware of it. When we do something or have our actions driven by this belief and are unaware of our real motivations, then we strengthen these negative beliefs and continue to be stuck in negative patterns in our lives. We could be doing the most "loving" acts, but if it's out of an unconscious fear of something, then you are not acting out of love. That is why it is so important to uncover these beliefs. Without awareness, we just strengthen negative and limiting patterns.

I will give you a couple of personal examples.

I had an unconscious belief that I was selfish. When I look back,

I realize now that I had this belief about myself since childhood. The great thing about unconscious limiting beliefs is that when you are ready to heal them, they will come up. So, although I'm a massive fan of meditation and introspection, you don't even need to do these to uncover them because life will unfold more and more intensely until you are essentially forced to see them.

It was about 10 years ago, and I didn't even know about the concept of unconscious beliefs. I had heard about Freud's unconscious, and I loved Jung's collective unconscious, but I didn't think about how these would affect me. My washing machine had broken down, and instead of going to a laundromat, I had taken my clothes to my parent's house. I'm not sure what happened. Perhaps my dad was upset because they hadn't seen me much and felt like I was only using them for their washing machine. Whatever the reason, I got into a heated argument with him, which doesn't happen often, and my dad finished by calling me "selfish." This word hurt me so much, I gasped. Even though I couldn't remember why we were fighting or how it happened, I remember feeling so wounded that he thought I was selfish. I got so upset that I stormed out of their house.

I couldn't understand how my father could call me selfish. Me, selfish?! Me, who had just dedicated a year of my life volunteering in Haiti after the massive earthquake. Me, who dedicated all my time and effort to helping others. Me, who financially supported two children to go through school, donated to charity and protested for the rights of others. Later that week, I was still upset and knew that I was overreacting, so I brought it to my therapist (yes, therapists need therapy). That's when I learned about unconscious limiting beliefs.

It was like a door opened in my brain. I realized that although those things were terrific kind things, and although I had followed my heart and gone to Haiti to the detriment of my wellbeing, there was still an unconscious motivation underneath all these actions that I hadn't been aware of.

I was trying to prove to myself and the world that I wasn't selfish because deep, deep down, I thought I was.

I had dedicated my life to helping others. I was a complete overachiever. I was going out of my way not to be selfish, but I was still unconsciously motivated by my fear of being selfish, which kept me in the selfish loop. I was doing loving things, but not out of a place of love. Since I was being motivated by fear, I couldn't prove to myself that I wasn't selfish, regardless of how hard I tried.

When I went to Haiti, I listened to my intuition, but that's only part of the task. The other part is to work and act out of love. But I was operating out of the fear that I was selfish. Although I know I assisted a lot of people by doing my loving acts, I also know that it is what led to my total emotional destruction in Haiti. The beautiful thing is that the universe can use our actions no matter what our hidden motivation is. Now that I'm more aware, I believe that had I gone to Haiti out of true love, I would have avoided getting post-traumatic stress disorder. It's how I've avoided getting mental breakdowns in my missions after Haiti.

However, although I operated out of fear and crawled out of Haiti, I needed it. I needed to heal my unconscious limiting beliefs.

How to heal unconscious limiting beliefs

Well, the good news is that becoming aware is often the first and hardest step. It is very easy to go through life and blame others for the upset you experience, and of course, they certainly have 100% responsibility for their actions. Although we also have 100% responsibility for how we respond to those actions. I reacted to my dad by getting more upset with him and not wanting to talk to him, something that I know is out of character for me. Once I realized it was because I had the negative unconscious belief, it was my responsibility to heal that belief.

I decided to have a conversation with my dad. I told him that what he said hurt me and shared my deep fear of being a selfish person. Now my dad is wonderful, and I have a great relationship with him, so it was safe for me to do that. Unfortunately, you can't share your vulnerabilities with people that will use them against you. If the person who is triggering you is not safe, that means you need to make strong boundaries. You need to take care of the beautiful, priceless heart of yours that needs to be healthy and cared for if it is going to help the world.

While I was able to have a healthy conversation with my dad, stating that I didn't like how he spoke to me and sharing my vulnerabilities with him, I also worked on healing my unconscious negative belief that was fully conscious at this point. I have a technique that I use personally and for my clients whenever these beliefs make themselves known.

Step 1) Discover your unconscious limiting belief: Take a blank piece of paper and on the left draw yourself (I'm not an artist, so I just use stick figures). On the right, draw the person with which you have the conflict. Then beside the person on the right side of the page, write down all the things that person has said about you and all the things you think that person thinks of you. Just write a short phrase, such as how my dad said, "You are selfish." Try to write down at least three different short sentences.

Step 2) Read over all the phrases and pick the one that strikes the biggest chord. For me, I don't remember what else I wrote. I just remember the "You are selfish" phrase, and so that's the one I chose.

Step 3) Write that phrase in a little thought bubble above your character on the left of the page, changing it so that it now is a thought that you are having about yourself. For example, I would change the phrase to "I am selfish."

There are a couple more steps that I do with my clients, but you can use this as a starting point.

Some clients can see exactly how they have been projecting their own fears onto the other person, but it can be difficult to accept for others. In those cases, I have my client go home and spend the next week thinking about this and see if they can find these statements come up in the many areas in their life. Every time my clients have come back and been shocked. They found their self-limiting belief show up with the person, but also at work, with friends, in romantic relationships and sometimes during their hobbies. Once you see how much this is affecting your life, move onto the next steps.

Step 4) Create a mantra that is the opposite of your belief. I'm quite pragmatic, so I just do the opposite of what my belief is. Although, like any mantra, it's important to frame it in the positive. For example, "I am XYZ," as opposed to, "I'm not XYZ." Create a mantra of what you want to be. For instance, I could change "I am selfish" to "I am generous" or "I am giving" or "I am thoughtful." Try a couple out and see which one hits your heart deepest.

Once you have chosen your mantra:

Step 5) Spend the next week saying it over to yourself as often as humanly possible. I would put it as an alarm, or even as wallpaper on my phone. I'd write it on sticky notes and put them all over my house, and I would sit and meditate on it as often as I could remember. All in all, I would try to say it to myself between 30-50 times a day.

Step 6) Put your mantra into action. After a week of saying my mantra repeatedly, I would start to do actions with my mantra being the intention behind the actions. The actions don't have to be grandiose; in fact, many small actions can impact more than one big action. Like so much in life, it's not the action you do that is important, but the intention behind it. For example, I could give money to homeless people with the intention that "I am generous," or I could decide to buy myself a donut with that same intention, as that would be an act of me being generous to myself. Action is taking your mantra and making it a reality. I usually just need to do my mantra actions for another week, and then I no longer think of or am consumed by my negative belief.

If you find you are still struggling with healing this hurt, then you need to honestly ask yourself if you are ready to be rid of this pain. And the answer needs to be a heartfelt "yes!" and then "now what?" If you aren't at that point, then there are still some fears or motivations behind keeping this fear that you need to uncover. You can always ask for help from the divine, or if you aren't comfortable with that word you can use the term "light," and so say, "I release my limiting belief to the light," or perhaps, "Light, please come and heal my fear about _____." Say this over and over until it doesn't seem to be an issue in your life anymore.

It's interesting that once something is healed, it just kind of disappears. There's no ray of sunshine that comes down or angels singing; it just fades away. With some deep and powerful negative beliefs, I've had to heal different layers of them, and so it might take longer. But that's ok because life is now; it's not the end of a race. It's this step now that we are taking to heal our hearts and souls and show love to these beautiful parts of us.

Helping others

My first unconscious limiting belief was about selfishness. So, perhaps it's predictable that the one thing I have struggled with is the thought that it is selfish, self-centred, or egotistical to be focusing on myself when there are so many other people I want to focus on and help. I've also had many clients worried that they are egotistical or conceited for not helping others when they concentrate on themselves. Often, we use guilt to motivate us to be better people. But by beating ourselves up, we make it more difficult to have the strength to be there for others. When we heal ourselves, we can be healthier, more loving, and patient persons for our loved ones. I wasn't able to honestly believe this, however, until I was healing a different unconscious limiting belief. That was the negative belief that "I am not important."

I don't remember how I had uncovered my "I'm not important" belief. Still, I remember that I had been diligently saying the mantra "I am important" repeatedly, and I was now in step 6, where I was doing actions to make this mantra a reality. I had been doing actions all week when I was ordering a coffee. Usually, I am too timid to ask someone for something, especially favours, but I needed change for a parking meter, and I needed to practise putting my mantra in action. So, when I had finished ordering my coffee, I decided to ask the cashier if she could give me change for $5 (because "I was important").

I will never forget that moment. I think it went into slow motion.

The cashier looked at me and my outstretched $5. Then she looked down at the open cash register and then looked back at me while closing the cash register and said, "I'm sorry, it's too late. I can't open the drawer to make change for you."

Now, to be honest, before this exercise, my first reaction would have been to think, "You jerk!" and I would have been angry and upset at her blatant disregard for my needs. But instead, my honest-to-goodness initial thought was, "you're important too!" and I wasn't upset with her at all!

I was so surprised by my immediate reaction. It was so different to the reaction I was expecting from myself. I ended up grinning from ear to ear and genuinely wished her a good day and left. Instead of being hurt and annoyed, and it possibly affecting my day, that moment became one of those life-altering moments.

I finally understood that when we are compassionate to ourselves, it truly does make us more compassionate towards others. When we focus on ourselves and healing our internal fears, the whole world wins. When we take care of ourselves, we automatically take better care of others. Before this moment, I found it difficult to honestly believe that loving yourself can improve your love for others. But here was a tangible experience of just that. That day, I truly learned to the depths of my soul that me healing my shit genuinely makes me a better person to others. That experience helped my heart understand that when I genuinely embody how I would like to be to others, and to myself first, then it will naturally and effortlessly overflow to others. It's a win-win! You are not conceited when you take care of your heart. In fact, it is the most generous and loving thing you can do for the world. A Course in Miracles calls it being "Self-full."

We must take time to uncover, look at and heal our internal fears if we want to be a better person and if we want to make the world a better place. It is the most effective way to do both.

How do we know when an internal fear is taking control of our life?

When an internal fear is activated, you will know because you will have some sort of painful reaction. Often it is anxiety, or perhaps those of you who were taught that you couldn't be anxious might express it in the form of anger. Pain, whether physical or emotional, is a signal that we need to pay attention to something.

Some people might have cut themselves off from their emotions so much that they don't experience or feel emotional pain. Instead, an internal fear might express itself in the form of physical pain. Perhaps physical pain is the only safe way for you to express emotions. It is said that almost 80% of the cases doctors see are psychosomatic health problems; in other words, caused by emotional stress or issues other than a physical cause.

In my thesis, I analyzed the most cited studies in psychoneuroimmunology, which is where they study the influence of emotions and thoughts, and how they affect the immune system. Research has found a strong correlation between depression and a weakened immune system. The connection between emotions and the physical body is becoming quite well known. Take, for example, how my anxiety as a child often produced stomach aches.

I recently had a client who had suffered from a back spasm and had been confined to her bed. When we went into the pain and listened to why it was there, it showed us that she had a deep fear of being unworthy. We used the rest of the session to heal that fear. Within a day, she was walking again, and her pain had almost completely disappeared. Whether physical or emotional, pain can often be a red flag that you need to address and heal an internal fear.

You can also know if an internal fear is coming up if you are annoyed or angry with someone. If there is someone in our life who is pissing us off or creating a negative emotion, then that's a flag. That is not to say that this person isn't doing something inappropriate, they very well could be, and they are indeed responsible for their actions and behaviours. However, as I say to my clients, someone can poke you, and they really are poking you, but it's just annoying. Still, if someone pokes you in an open wound, where it's very sensitive, and perhaps that wound is infected, and you can even see the bone, then that same poke will hurt exponentially more than if there was no wound. We might not have known that injury was there if they hadn't poked us. Now that you are aware of the wound, you can start healing it while making appropriate boundaries with the poker. However, these boundaries need to be made out of love, not out of the reaction to being poked.

Another way to know if an internal fear is taking over or coming up for you is if you are self-sabotaging. This is a common experience for many people. Most of us would rather stay our same unhappy selves, than step past our circle of comfort into a happier way of being. When the same negative things happen over and over, that is self-sabotage, and that is the internal fear that you don't deserve anything better or that if you allow yourself to be happy, then you're just setting yourself up for more pain. Negative patterns that are happening over and over are a clear sign that an internal fear is driving your life.

Giving up outcomes

One internal fear that I'm currently wrestling with is the fear of losing my home through not getting a visa to stay in France. I know this is an internal fear because of the sheer illogical panic that it produces. The first step is acknowledgement, the understanding that this is where I am right now. But it doesn't stop there. The second step in this situation, and the hardest for me, is the giving up of outcomes. This last week I've been giving up the result of whether I'll get my visa. It is challenging, especially if I go into fear. Still, I'm so passionate about choosing love, operating out of love and living out of love that I'm entirely determined to come out of fear every time I notice that I slip into it. That means not being vindictive or angry or manipulative as a way to get my visa. It means being honest when I am these things, or I want to do these things and stopping that behaviour and then apologizing if I do something out of fear. It means not trying to control the outcome.

At the end of the day, it's not about what I think is best for me. Every time I slip into fear, I make sure that I stop and ask the universe to heal this fear of mine. I try as hard as I can to let go of the outcome and trust that the universe has a plan for me that is even better than I could even think of. I need to stop trying to control what that plan is. Sometimes I struggle with doing this so much that I actually have to stop every 30 minutes and consciously try to let go again.

I am also incredibly lucky to have someone in my life (my mom) who holds me to choosing love and reminds me of these standards. Others can feel protective of me, and so in their protectiveness, they encourage me to go into fear or blame because that's what society has taught us to do. Going into fear is how most of us live on this earth, and living out of love is a very tricky thing as it goes against social norms. You can't listen to most people's counsel, so you need to find that one person who also has the same value of love. Be picky about who you ask for advice.

I can say that after two weeks of intensive meditation, consciously trying to let go, and begging the universe to help me, I'm surprisingly quite ok. Even if I don't get this visa, I know that I will be fine, and I no longer feel the deep panic to control the outcome. I've done what I can, and now I need just to let life play out. It's a beautiful feeling, such freedom and peace!

*Now that I am reviewing this chapter, I can update you that I didn't get the visa, but because of the emotional work I did of releasing the outcome, I'm totally ok. I know that things will work out even if they didn't work out how I pictured them.

It's not about the outcome. It's about being as loving as possible, to ourselves, and throughout this whole process we call life. Don't hold on too tightly to how you think things should be. Relax your grip a little, and your life will unfold to be much more beautiful than you could have imagined or created yourself.

I can't think of a better way to live.

Chapter 7
Self-love

It wasn't until I was doing my master's in Psychology that I finally realized I had all the classic signs of generalized anxiety disorder. The thing about anxiety, especially if you're born with it, is that since you've had it all your life, you don't realize that there is any other way to live. So, it's quite easy not to know you have it, even though it might create a lot of suffering.

Since I didn't understand what was wrong with me at the time, I reacted the same way many people do; I shut down my emotions and hid in my brain. I became a philosopher at the age of 10. I much preferred to discuss ideas and concepts than anything to do with unpredictable emotions. No wonder I did my thesis on quantum physics. Quantum physics, to me, was a rational and logical way of explaining fantastical concepts. But my master's in psychology forced me to admit I had no idea about emotions. While I was delving into my passion for quantum physics, I was also getting certification in a psychological school of thought called Emotion Focused Therapy.

At this time, I also stumbled across being a Highly Sensitive Person, a concept developed by Elaine Aron. This then turned me towards studying the idea of empaths. These new understandings helped me to embrace the superpowers that were my emotions and paved the way for me to change my perspective. My extreme sensitivity, which had previously been a considerable burden, slowly transformed into what I like to call my superpower.

Thank goodness I finally started to delve into emotions and understand highly sensitive empaths. This training, along with my thesis, completely altered my focus from cognitive to emotional, which transformed my life and changed how I work with clients. In western culture, we aren't taught how to deal with our emotions; in fact, many of us are downright afraid of our feelings. We fear that our emotions are crazy or irrational or uncontrollable, and if we let them out, they'll wreak havoc on our life. We have the fear that we'll go off the rails or make a mistake or be looked down upon. These are all types of internal fear, and yet ironically, emotions are how we heal these inner fears.

Even in the field of psychology, there is an apprehension of looking directly at emotions. Freud often talked about "hysteria" as a mental illness, and now the most popular school of psychology in North America is called cognitive behavioural therapy (CBT). Of course, there is nothing wrong with focusing on thoughts (cognition) and behaviours; it's just that you're missing half the equation. Emotions are difficult to control, and they are tough to understand; they are indeed a wild card. It was only through facing my fear of emotions that I could start on the journey of healing my internal fears and blossoming as a psychotherapist.

The highly sensitive empath

For those of you who are highly sensitive, this concept might be eye-opening for you. For those of you who aren't, this concept will be crucial if you want to understand the highly sensitive loved ones in your life because it's a whole different universe of being. Additionally, my journey of coming to grips with being a highly sensitive empath

(HSE) is an excellent example of how you can overcome and heal your own perceived internal "defects" or fears.

Part of my abhorrence of emotions was because my feelings were a lot more sensitive than those of other people. Being a highly sensitive empath means that we are incredibly receptive to energy, the energy of those around us, and even the energy in our environment. This uncanny ability can lead us to believe that there is something wrong with us since no one else seems to be affected. There is also the constant message that we're too emotional. All of these messages develop into the internal fear that we are crazy and oversensitive. The HSEs that I counsel often struggle with anxiety and depression. There also seems to be more Millennials that are HSE than the earlier generations.

The Highly Sensitive Empath is an amalgamation of Elaine Aron's concept of Highly Sensitive People and the more new-age concept of Empaths. Highly sensitive people are biologically wired with a stronger, more active and fine-tuned parasympathetic nervous system. That means this trait can't be developed or changed. I have worked with a lot of highly sensitive people, and I found that there was a large subtype within highly sensitive people that were empaths. Empaths are sensitive to the moods and energies of people or the environment around them. That means they can often get overwhelmed by the news, and get affected by other people's anger, depression, excitement, etc. Unlike being a highly sensitive person, one can develop empathic traits with lots of dedication and guidance from your intuition. However, when you are born with these talents and don't know how to handle them, they can feel like a curse.

I have talked to therapists who don't understand this experience, and so it's common that those who are not highly sensitive not to comprehend what is going on for HSEs, and often just wish HSEs could "get over it" or "move on." But as an HSE, I can attest that this is extremely difficult to do.

I describe highly sensitive empaths as having enormous ears. We hear a lot about what is going on in the world. We hear the insecurities in others, the pain and struggle. We hear the terror in the news and the hopelessness in our communities. For some reason, it's so much easier to hear the negative emotions rather than the more positive ones like joy and happiness, although we hear that as well. Then, we hear so much that we end up with overwhelming amounts of information. It's as if we have a massive stack of paperwork. Others who don't notice much, just have a few pieces of paper, so it's easy to organize and file away. But for us with superhuman hearing, it takes a while to get through all the paperwork, and filing it can be more difficult because we have so many categories and subcategories of information. What often happens for me is that I'll feel an emotion, perhaps sadness, and it might take me a couple of days to sort out why I'm feeling sad, or where that sadness is coming from, and I'm a psychotherapist, this is my job!

I haven't found any way to make this process go faster, and I can't change this part of me. Instead, I have just accepted that I need more time to sort out what is going on for me. I make sure I prioritize time by myself, or time in nature so that I can regularly go through and organize this jumble that is inside. Please be patient with your HSE friends or loved ones, or if it's you that is HSE, then be extra compassionate with yourself because this is just how it is. We can't change our parasympathetic nervous system, and so we need to focus on adjusting our lives to adapt to how we are.

Our hyper-awareness can lead to another common aspect of HSEs, which is our small mouths. Small mouths represent speaking up for ourselves or making requests for what we need, although I find this trait has a lot of variabilities. Some HSEs are good at speaking up, while others can only do it for those more vulnerable. We can have difficulty speaking up for ourselves because we are worried that perhaps we'll hurt others, or that we are insane since no one else understands our perspective or notices what we notice. Often, we care so much about making other people happy that we can't even connect to what would make us happy. Our happiness is at the bottom of our priority list, which is perhaps why so many HSEs can suffer from anxiety and depression. (If you would like more information of HSE please visit my website at www.vanwyckconsulting.com)

Highly sensitive empaths and internal fears

It is thought that about 20% of the population is a highly sensitive person, and so of that, I would say 15% are highly sensitive empaths. That means that although I think this trait is rising with each generation, most people don't have this gift. Therefore, HSEs can often grow up feeling disdained and alienated. We learn to hate our gift and have this internal belief that something is deeply wrong with us. I think this is tragic.

I don't always believe in labels or categories. Although they can be very helpful, they can also be destructive. However, I feel the highly sensitive empath label is an important one if it allows us to accept what we are, instead of conforming to what we think we "should" be. We spend so much energy trying to change ourselves to be like everyone else. Only once we accept who we are can we start the journey of turning these gifts from curses into the superpowers they are meant to be. How incredible would the world be if all HSEs could genuinely learn how to assist those struggling? If they could step into their light so that they could raise the people around them? Highly sensitive empaths make the most incredible inventors, leaders, teachers and bosses; they can see the minute nuances surrounding them, and their intuition can be unparalleled. Unfortunately, without the knowledge of what a highly sensitive empath is or how they need to take care of themselves, they can often spiral into overwhelm, depression or anxiety.

So often, we humans have an internal fear that there is something deeply defective about us. That we should be more "X" or less "Y." We compare ourselves to others that we feel are better. But when you avoid understanding yourself, when you don't love yourself, you are fighting a hopeless battle. This doesn't mean not trying to be a better person, but it does mean knowing what you can change and what you can't. This stands for everyone, HSE or not. Learn who you are, accept yourself, and adapt your life around that. Self-love is the first step in becoming the person you wish to be.

Heart connection

So how do you love yourself? While much of this book is trying to answer this question, one thing I teach many of my clients, especially HSEs is how to connect with their heart figuratively. Connecting with your heart is essential for all people, regardless of whether you are an HSE. However, it is especially crucial for HSEs. Learning how to communicate with and take care of your heart is literally the most effective thing you can do to take care of your garden. Remember the garden analogy in Part 1? Where you have to take care of your plant because you're the only one who knows how to, and healthy relationships are those that meet at the fence? Well, HSEs are notorious for going into everyone else's garden except their own. Connecting with your heart is a way to bring yourself back to your garden and take wonderful nourishing care of your plant (heart) before you meet others at the fence.

Taking care of your heart is one of the holiest things you can do. Your heart is the engine of your life. It is the pulse of your existence; it is the connection between you and all creation. The heart connection visualization is simple but infinitely powerful and is vital for having healthy relationships, building self-esteem, and becoming a force for good in the world.

This heart connection technique is powerful on many levels. First, it separates you from your emotions. You aren't having the feelings, your heart is. This is invaluable in being able to be more in control of how you then react to your emotions. Secondly, seeing your heart as something separate makes it much easier to take care of and love, rather than trying to take care of and love yourself, which many people struggle with. Lastly, often your high self speaks through your heart, but without connecting to your heart, these messages can feel vague and challenging to trust. When you hear it from your heart, it's much more concrete, easier to hear, and easier to believe.

I do the heart connection through a visualization. The first time we connect with your heart, we focus on really seeing it. Then I'll lead you to sit beside your heart without saying anything and just being in the presence of it. The first time you connect with your heart, your heart might be distrustful or distant or even angry at you depending on how long you've ignored it (I know I sound crazy, but you'll understand once you try it). If that's the case, be gentle, work on showing your heart that it can now trust you.

Visualization: Heart connection

1. Start with grounding. (I start every visualization with this.)
2. Once you are grounded, turn your attention inwards and focus on your heart. Notice what your heart looks like. Is it a literal heart? Is it a cartoon heart? Is it something else entirely?
3. Take a moment to notice what it feels like. What are its emotions? Is it sluggish or agitated? Can you feel connected to it, or is it hard to feel? Just acknowledge the feelings and state what they are by simply saying, "It seems as if you are apprehensive of me right now," or perhaps "I'm so sorry you feel like you're losing it."
4. Notice any sounds? Is it saying anything to you? Is it making any type of noise?

5. Sit beside your heart for a moment and tell it that you're *sorry it took you so long to visit, you didn't know how to do it before, and you really care about what it's going through.*
6. Then ask your heart if it needs anything from you right now to be more comfortable? Remember that this is your imagination, so anything is possible. You could pull down a star for it or tuck it into bed if that's what it wants. You could go to Disneyland or give it a cookie. You can do anything for your heart, just as long as it doesn't involve hurting anyone else.
7. When you're finished or start getting distracted, tell your heart that you're going to leave now, and does it have anything it would like you to know before you go? Give it some time to answer, and if it doesn't, then say goodbye to it. Tell it you'll visit it again, and then gently and softly come back into the room. Give yourself some time to come back into your body.

For the first time, you might want to leave it like that. It could feel very strange to connect with your heart, and you'll probably feel like you're just making all of this up. That's fine, remember even if you are making this up, your brain can't tell the difference between imagination and reality, so it's still healing and powerful. Even if you can't see, feel, or hear anything, make sure you tell your heart that you will check in later and then make sure you follow what you say and check in with it later. This is the best way to build up trust. Often people's hearts don't trust them because we have been ignoring and shutting them down. This distrust makes the heart reluctant to share anything with you.

For others, their heart might be overjoyed with finally being able to make contact. There is no right answer or right way for your heart to behave and just trust whatever is coming to you. Remember, at the beginning of the book, when we talked about how your intuition can communicate to you? Use that information to connect most clearly with your heart and don't worry about if what you think it is saying is right or wrong, just go with whatever comes to your mind first.

My intuition is such that I'm able to connect with my clients and feel what their heart is saying and feeling. I do this only to help my client's trust in what they're getting. Usually, when I am starting to work with a client, I'll tell them what I'm getting, and then they can tell me if they think that's close or not. That helps build their confidence that what we are doing is real since I can feel what's there without them saying anything. The more and more we do it, the less I'll say and the more I'll have them tell me what's going on so that they trust their own intuition more and more. I will only say something if I feel they are skirting around an issue, but that doesn't happen too often. Trust in yourself, trust in this process, and, most of all, check in with your heart as regularly as possible so that you can create a strong relationship with it. The more you check in, the faster and easier it will be to do. Now, checking in with my heart is such a habit that I don't need to ground or even close my eyes to hear my heart. I can even check in while I'm talking to others, which is invaluable when navigating interpersonal relationships.

If you're completely unable to feel your heart that can mean one of two things: a) these techniques are not a good fit for you (see if you can tap into your intuition to explore if that is the case), or b) you have some deep blocks to self-love (that could be a result of trauma). In which case, I would suggest getting outside support to heal because it's extremely difficult to treat on your own.

Like most of my techniques, the heart connection is a simple one, but I can't stress how far the ripples of this action go throughout your whole being. This checking in, this empathizing with your heart can profoundly change you and your experience, although that is not why we do it. *We do the heart connection because this relationship between you and your heart is singularly the most important relationship you can have in your life.* If you don't have this relationship, then your whole life will be filled with chasing empty things, and looking for acceptance in places that will only give it to you for a moment. No matter how much praise or approval you get from others or outside things, they will never make you feel fulfilled. The relationship with your heart truly feeds your soul. Still, it is also the gateway to understanding your intuition, knowing what your path here on earth is, and indeed being able to experience real love, an essential precursor to being able to give it. Without this relationship with your heart, it is impossible to love unconditionally, and being able to love unconditionally is the greatest gift I think a person can experience.

However, listening to, empathizing with, and loving your heart is not the same as obeying its every passing emotion. There is a subtle but significant difference. My heart, for example, is dramatic. I mentioned how I grew up with very high anxiety, and that's because she's a little over the top about things (in a very endearing way). She stresses out that I said the wrong thing, or perhaps offended a person with a thoughtless comment. My heart worries that she spoke too much or that a person, event or possibility will hurt her. But this is ok, I listen to her, comfort her, and sometimes she makes me laugh with her antics, but all the time I help her understand what she's feeling. I feel and empathize with what she's feeling, send her love, and then I make my own decision.

My heart totally freaked out about going to Syria during their civil war, and I could understand where she was coming from. But I knew she was capable of it, and I knew how important it was that I would be a candle of hope and compassion in one of the most strict and violent parts of the world. So, I listened to her concerns, comforted her, and showed her I love her and still went forward. My heart is often scared of things she doesn't know or hasn't done before, and so I make sure I comfort her and hold her, and then we move forward into the unknown together. I treat her with respect, but she also doesn't control me.

Nutritious meals vs birthday cake

I have a metaphor that I tell my clients which relates to the infinite energy we can tap into as well as the importance of the relationship we have with our heart.

Imagine you are starving. You haven't eaten in weeks, you're weak and can barely function, and your friend has a birthday party. You go to the party but there isn't any food, just one big birthday cake. For some reason, in all the chaos of singing happy birthday, your friend forgets to give you a slice of this birthday cake, and before you can get a piece, it's all gone. How would you react?

I think it would be a massive deal! Here you are weak and starving, and here there was a birthday cake, and your friend didn't even bother to save you one piece. That could even be the end of your friendship because how could someone who's supposed to be your friend not care that you were starving?

Now imagine you are well-fed, and right before the birthday party, you had a big meal with all the nutrients you needed, and you show up to the party full. But the same thing happens, your friend forgets to give you birthday cake. What would your reaction be then?

You might be annoyed, but you might be grateful because you're trying to eat healthier and you were already full, so you're happy that you weren't pressured to eat birthday cake.

The same situation happened, the only thing that changed was your health and hunger levels before the birthday party.

Other people's love and acceptance is always birthday cake. It's lovely, it tastes great, but if that's all you eat in your life, then you are going to have some serious vitamin deficiencies that could severely affect your health. Sound familiar? It is so important that we learn how to feed ourselves; we are the only people we can control, so why not use it to our advantage? Once we can feed ourselves, crappy things might still happen, but they won't feel life-threatening. Plus, we will be so much healthier and stable when we feed ourselves nutritious meals. That's what being kind to your heart is. It is the most nutrient-dense meal you can give yourself, and once you are healthy, you can truly be there for your loved ones. It doesn't matter so much if they have cookies or candies, you can love them for who they are and not what they might give you. That type of love is the only thing worth living for.

I am so grateful for all the trials and tribulations that led me, or rather, forced me to learn how to take care of my heart. But it is a learning process. Sometimes my heart needs one thing, and then later, she needs something different. That is why I need to have a relationship with her. Sometimes she wants to play, or other times she needs me to cuddle her for hours. Sometimes, she just needs to be wrapped around me like an African baby so that she's close to me as I go throughout my week. Just like you can't make one meal and eat that for the rest of your life, so too must you regularly connect with your heart. The relationship you have with your heart has the power to heal any other relationships that might have traumatized you, including harmful relationships you might have had with your parents. The link you have with your heart is the single most important relationship you can have on this earth. It doesn't have to be serious, deep, or profound. It just has to exist.

The brain and the heart

When I take the time to listen to my heart and take care of her, it is a way of connecting my brain with my heart. When my brain and heart are connected, magic happens! If your brain and heart are not in agreement, then I'd put my bets on your heart winning. How often do you do things you know are bad for you, but you do anyway? Our emotions are extremely powerful, and unfortunately, in our society, we don't know how to handle them, so we shove them down and ignore them. This results in our life going off the rails. Emotions are potent and beautiful and wise, and they also need the direction and guidance of our brain to steer them, just like our brain needs the energy and passion of our heart. Your heart is the energy behind everything you do, and if you don't take the time to make sure your brain and heart are on the same page, then it is a recipe for an explosive disaster. If our body is a car, then our brain is the steering wheel, and our heart is undoubtedly the engine.

Visualization: Brain heart connection

A simple way to connect your brain and heart is to do the following meditation:

1. Ground yourself.
2. Turn all your attention inwards, see your heart and see your brain.
3. Imagine a cord running from your brain to your heart.
4. Imagine both your brain and heart pulsing at the same time. It might take a moment to get them to beat at the same time; that's ok.
5. Keep imagining this for as long as you need to.

Strangely enough, I find that my intuition comes through my brain, through my thoughts, but is then verified and strengthen by the knowing in my heart. That's how my intuition works. I'm not sure if everyone's works in the same way. My heart, however, has infinite wisdom. When I connect to my heart and ask her for advice, the answers I get seem straight from the universe. My brain was overdeveloped, so now, I focus more on the heart and emotions, but the essential point is that both need to be balanced.

Heart fuel

For our heart engine to work, then we need a source of energy to fuel it. That's where our connection to the universe comes in. We have access to an unlimited source of energy if we just know how to tap into it. This is also part of what grounding does; it allows us to tap into the infinite power of the earth underneath us. In contrast, prayer, meditation and connecting to our high self will enable us to tap into the universe's endless energy above us. Both are necessary for our heart to operate. So, if your heart is tired, then you need to spend time each day to open it to these infinite energy sources, and most of all, you need to learn to accept. The following visualization is what I use regularly and is what I will sometimes guide my clients through.

Visualization: Heart fill up

1. Ground yourself.
2. Connect yourself to your source: the universe, God, Light. Imagine that source is sending you beautiful pure love from above and coming down through the crown of your head and directly to your heart. See your heart filling up with love. Feel your heart filling up with being loved.
3. Once you feel like your heart is full, send love back up to the source, perhaps in the form of gratitude. Use whatever emotion works for you to activate the feeling of love and send that back to the universe so that you create a circle of receiving and giving love.
4. Once you feel like that cycle of receiving and giving is running smoothly, and your heart is feeling and giving love, then send out love to the earth underneath you which nourishes, feeds and supports you.

5. Then feel the earth giving love back to you, nourishing you and making your heart feel stronger. Imagine an infinity sign with your heart in the centre, giving and receiving love up to the universe and down from the earth.
6. Stay here as long as you need. Let your heart be strengthened and cleansed by being in the vortex of this beautiful infinity of love.

Sometimes, giving love just seems like too much effort, or sometimes you're exhausted and just need some support. In those cases, it is perfectly fine to just focus on the universe sending love down to you in a beam of beautiful white light that enters through the crown of your head and fills up your entire body. Play with both of these visualizations and see which one is most effective for you.

We are supported and have access to infinite energy, if only we just ask. Free will means that we have to choose to ask for and accept something if we want it.

I think the most stressful humanitarian mission I have done was the Ebola outbreak in Sierra Leone, from 2014 to 2016.

I had to work on receiving and accepting energy into my heart regularly, or else I would have collapsed in the first month. When I arrived, the situation there was horrendous. Everyone was dying. There was no time to keep up with cremating all the dead. Families were left wondering where their loved ones were, or if they had survived. Medical aid organizations would arrive at villages to take the sick and give them care in the Ebola treatment centres. Still, people would die so quickly, and there were so many people sick that in all the chaos, it was difficult to keep track of where all the patients had come from. It resulted in villagers thinking that ambulances were cursed with black magic and refusing to call for help if someone was sick. Furthermore, they would throw stones at us whenever we drove past.

Part of my job was to open up the communication between the

Ebola treatment centres and the communities so they would know what had happened to their loved ones. I also connected with community and religious leaders and witch doctors to create mutual relationships of respect so that they would trust us. Most of the cases were spread because of the burial practices where the whole community would wash the body of the dead. With Ebola, once the patient dies, that's when the viral load is the highest, and so whole communities would get infected with this disease that had a 60-70% fatality rate. Furthermore, they believed that if they didn't clean the dead and bury them correctly, then the deceased would haunt them and future generations. That is why it was so important to work with the religious leaders and witch doctors in coming up with alternative funeral ceremonies and treatment of the sick. But in doing so, there was constant stress that we ourselves would contract Ebola since it was impossible not to interact with people, and often children would come running up to hug you.

Furthermore, the Ebola symptoms are the same as almost every common disease you can get there (the flu, malaria, dengue), including food poisoning. I only got food poisoning five times in the two years I was there, but each time I had to be quarantined. People in hazmat suits would take a blood sample, and I had to face the reality that I might die. The eroding from this fear of being on the brink of death and witnessing thousands of others on the brink of death, or others who were the sole survivor of large families, was immensely depleting of my heart.

I was in charge of creating programs to give psychosocial support to communities, Ebola workers and Ebola survivors who were often ostracized from their families for fear of Ebola. Then, on top of my day job, I also provided counselling for humanitarians that were suffering from PTSD or severe burnout because of their work since the beginning of the outbreak. My brain knew that we couldn't help everyone, but my heart was breaking at seeing all the pain and death. I remember having to connect my brain and heart regularly, comforting my heart and also helping her understand that I have limits too.

The only way I could continue to do my work was because daily, I used a variety of techniques to fill up and comfort my heart. These techniques allowed me to stay longer than most of my colleagues, even though I'm a highly sensitive empath. I think they are the reason that I eventually received a medal of honour from the Canadian government for the work I did there. Accepting energy and love from the universe allowed me to then give that to others.

Accepting can be difficult. At least it was for me because it made me feel vulnerable and worried that I'd become dependent, and what would happen if suddenly whatever I was accepting would one day leave? But the universe is infinite, it has always existed, and it will always exist. It has boundless love for all of us. If we can accept the love from source, think of the gift you can be to the world! Think of the love you could be capable of.

When you are capable of that kind of love, then rejection or abandonment doesn't affect you very much because you already know infinite love.

Chapter 8
Internal Fears in our Daily Life

Internal fears affect all aspects of our lives. What is inside us always gets projected to our outside world. Not too long ago, Turkey had threatened to take over, through any means necessary, a part of Syria, the place I had called home for two years. I was utterly devastated. I was frantically texting my friends and staff to see how they were. It just seemed so unfair; they had already been through so much! The Islamic State and the ensuing conflict to retake the land from ISIS had decimated their city and lives. They had lost everything and had just started to rebuild, and now they would lose everything again. I couldn't believe the injustice! But I was powerless, just like we all were, to do anything. When the news broke out, I was in Oslo visiting some friends. To soothe my heart, I decided to go into the Nobel Peace Center. As I wandered around reading about the remarkable lives of so many inspiring people, I came across a quote from Bertha Von Suttner, the first Nobel Peace Prize Laureate. She said, "Seek not good from without: seek it within yourselves, or you will never find it."

This quote shot like an arrow right into the centre of my heart.

Now I'll admit, there's a cynical part of me that felt like: "There's no way you going within yourself is going to help your friends and staff," but really, what other choice did I have? There was nothing else I could do. So, I went within, I searched for the peace and compassion that was hiding within me, I delved into the forgiveness and understanding that was buried. And it worked.

By "worked" I mean that I was able to find, hold and feel peace and love, and I could finally offer them to my friends in Syria. Then there turned out not to be any bombing or violence. I believe Turkey took over, although that's still unclear. At any rate, my friends there who were scared and upset are no longer feeling that way. This big catastrophe that I thought was unavoidable and unstoppable just kind of fizzled out. Now, I'm not suggesting that my meditations were responsible for preventing violent conflict. Still, it did allow me to completely change my perspective on how I saw the situation and therefore shifted my reactions to the situation and to the people I was supporting through it. If we are violent and aggressive inside, then we will see the world as violent and aggressive. If we are compassionate and loving inside, then that is how we will paint the world. If we want the world to be different than it is, then we need to change our internal perceptions.

In fact, over a dozen peer-reviewed articles since the '60s have shown the significant peaceful impact that a group of meditators can have on reducing crime in the city they are meditating in. Currently, we don't quite understand how connected to each other we are. However, you can feel this ultimate connection, this oneness, through meditation. Once you have that direct experience, it makes sense that healing ourselves or finding peace within ourselves can directly affect others.

Internal fears and work

Many of us spend most of our time at work, and so it only makes sense that our internal fears are going to spill into our work experience. My work is quite frankly my passion; it takes up and gives meaning to most of my life. However, other people have jobs that they aren't passionate about but do them to provide for their family or to sustain the hobbies that they love. I don't think there is any right or wrong answer as to what your job means to you, as long as you have followed your own inner knowing.

Regardless of what your job means, our inner fears will always come out in our work. This may be in the form of relationships with your coworkers, how you perceive your boss, or what kind of manager you are. If we let our internal fears run rampant, then we will suffer in all areas of our life, including our job. If you find that you dislike something about your work, then take some time to ask why? Try not to focus on the outside, such as your boss is a jerk, concentrate inside. What are you afraid your boss thinks of you? What are you worried your coworkers think of you? What are you afraid of in terms of your job? That you're not good enough? That people will find out that you don't know what you're doing? That you'll let other people down? That you can't handle the workload? That you feel like you aren't reaching your potential?

Perhaps your internal fears are what paralyze you to stay in a job you don't like or takes away the joy from a job you really do like. My passion for being a humanitarian was tainted by my fear that I would let other people down. That I wasn't good enough, or that I was unworthy of their respect. As a humanitarian, it is so important that I am in a healthy headspace myself before I am deployed on a mission. I have found that so often, people with big hearts feel that they need to help everyone. Often, highly sensitive people can feel like there is something wrong with them, and so they focus on helping others to make them feel like they are a good person. On my mission to Haiti, this is what I did. I ran myself ragged trying to help others because I was afraid that was the only way I could prove I was of worth. But please hear me: *you don't need to help anyone to be valuable.* We are all valuable just from being born; that's what human rights are all centred around.

Incredible things happened in Haiti, and I know I did help a lot of people. I had children named after me, and I got to name babies. I know I was able to help a lot of lives and prevent suicides at that time, but still, I ended up getting post-traumatic stress disorder because I pushed myself to the brink. I felt so guilty that even though these 5,000+ people were grateful to me, there were still millions and millions I had not helped. What's more is that even though I was trying so hard to empower them and not let them put me on a pedestal, I was putting myself up on a false pedestal. I thought (subconsciously) that they needed me to survive and felt that if I left them, I would be abandoning them to sink again into abject misery. Which, quite frankly, was not the case, and was actually egotistical for me to think.

The biggest lesson I learned in my humanitarian career was after the Haiti earthquake. I realized, to my bones, that people survived before I arrived, and they would continue to survive after I leave. My job is not to save anyone, but rather to be a candle of love in times of dark despair. To remind people of their inner strength and wisdom when they doubt or even forget it exists. I can try to show, as best as I can, that the world cares about them, and they are valuable no matter how others have treated them. That's it, that is all my job is. Of course, I do assessments and create programs to try to address the needs communities are wanting to be met. Still, shining a light and reminding them of their own loveliness inside them is at the core of every program I create. The most effective way for me to do this is to be a living example myself.

I am often surrounded by other humanitarians who are struggling with post-traumatic stress disorder or compassion fatigue or just highly stressed. The decisions we make when in this headspace and the outlook we have can often be detrimental to the populations we are serving. It's not just what we are doing; it's also HOW we are doing it. When I look back at my time in Haiti, I was a mess. I thought that everyone depended on me and I had to save them all. I had no self-love, and my reserve for kindness had been emptied. When I went to

Haiti, I was operating under my unconscious limiting belief that I was unworthy, unlovable and selfish. I was using my work there to prove to myself that this wasn't the case. If I want to be a shining example, I have to face and heal my internal demons.

When I went to Syria to assist women and children living under the Islamic State rule, I had a much clearer outlook. I focused on being a light in a time of darkness, not in a western missionary type of way. In fact, I often defended Islam and differentiated it from the form that the Islamic State practised. Still, I highlighted love and compassion and taking care of our hearts and each other's hearts when we could. We were able to create a community to prevent women and girls from killing themselves because they thought their life was hopeless. We showed how important a role each of them has in their society and in their families. I advocated against honour killings and trained de facto police forces and community leaders on the importance of women as part of a healthy community. We offered information and support, but only after we had created a mutually respectful relationship with the community. Only then did we create conversations about how we could address issues that were coming up in the community. How much healthier of a relationship is that?!

Our program was very successful and widely accepted in the community. My staff went on to become compassionate sources of care. When I first arrived, I was told my work was too dangerous, and people literally laughed at me for even caring about women. And even though I've been gone for over a year, many of them are still working in this area. Some people were not interested in our services, and that was ok, we didn't force them on anyone. However, because we had such a respectful and relationship-based approach, we were one of the only organizations that were asked to provide training on how to prevent gender-based violence to some of the armed groups, as well as to some of the local governmental structures.

If you don't respect yourself, then you can't respect others. If you always feel you need to prove yourself, you'll only focus on possible ways people are disrespecting you. If you are hard on yourself and use violent self-talk, you will see the world as hard and brutal. There will always be insecurities and internal fears that come up, that's part of our path. Still, if we create a habit of facing them and healing them, then it doesn't entirely control you to the same extent when the next one comes up. Through the process of transmuting your internal fears layer by layer, you become less controlled by them. Each time you heal an inner fear, you strengthen your sense of self, and you step more into love.

I know that people will survive without me and that I'm not essential to anyone in this world. However, I also know that I can still inspire and love and shine love to people that are in abject misery. Then, those people might go on to assist others. I'm not indispensable, but I can still have a positive impact. That impact can be exponential, but only if I take care of myself, and that means taking time to really look inside myself and heal those parts of myself that are ready to be healed. Most of all, that means choosing love over fear in even the seemingly small decisions of life.

Internal fears and relationships

Internal fears affect us mostly through relationships. It is said that everyone is just a mirror of ourselves. So, relationships are the primary way we discover what our internal fears are. It was through therapy that I was shown that I had an internal fear of being unlovable. I had been struggling because I felt incredibly lonely like no one really knew or understood me and because I had difficulty connecting to others.

During a session, I had brought up that another friend of mine had started to hang out with other people and less and less with me. She was no longer feeling depressed, and so didn't need me anymore. My therapist pointed out how this was a pattern in my life. I would befriend depressed people or those who had just moved to the city. I would help them feel better, and then they'd find other friends they liked better. Through therapy, I realized that it was because I was positioning myself as the saviour. I was helping them and having them depend on me. This relationship was so unbalanced that once they got back on their feet, they didn't know how to relate to me anymore, and I didn't know how to relate to them. I was so afraid of rejection that I only befriended people that weren't capable of really seeing me. I was just as responsible for filling my life and picking out these people to befriend as they were in leaving me once they felt more confident. Friendship is about equality, about giving and receiving. Giving is a beautiful feeling, and I didn't let people ever give to me. So, when my friends didn't need to receive anymore, we could no longer relate to each other.

From then on, I really focused on trying to be open to equal relationships. At first, it was a bit like keeping score. Do they care about how I'm doing? Am I bringing up what's going on in my life into the conversation? Are they there for me when I'm sad AND when I'm happy? When something good happens to them, am I truly happy for them, or do I get jealous? Sometimes I still have to force myself to talk about what is going on in my life so that the friendship doesn't fall into an uneven balance. It's challenging to bring up my problems and successes with others, I don't want to bring them down, and I don't want to make them jealous. But this book is about owning and being true to who you are, stepping into your light, and choosing to be your glorious self instead of staying hidden by fear. Seeing and understanding our inner fears is essential. That is the first step, and then we have to make particular choices and changes to not fall into them and to choose love instead.

My fear that I was unlovable gave me an almost compulsive desire to prove my worth to others by devoting my life to helping them, thus proving I was lovable. I felt that unless I was serving others, I had no value. But because I was operating out of this place of fear, I just kept on perpetuating the same cycle of friends leaving me and of me feeling rejected. When patterns happen in your life, there's one thing that they have in common: you. That means you need to look at what it is about you. What fear are you operating out of that is perpetuating this pattern?

Three-chair technique

One of the most potent ways to really look at some of your inner fears is by doing this three-chair exercise with your inner critic. This is an extremely powerful technique, although you feel a bit like a crazy person when you do it. I've recently done it and forgot how deeply healing and transformative it is.

1. Have three empty chairs. One chair is where your high self sits, or your wise self, the essence of you that is all-knowing and loving. In the second chair sits yourself, and in the third chair sits your inner critic.
2. Sit in one of the chairs and take a moment to be that part, talking for that part. It doesn't matter how harsh you are, just let the emotions flow.
3. After that part has said all it needs to say, move to another chair for the part that wants to respond. Have that part say everything it needs to, including perhaps how the other part annoys or hurts it with what it just said.
4. Keep moving between the chairs as the different parts want to speak. There is no agenda here, just to voice and understand all the parts as much as possible. Perhaps if it feels right at the end, the self-critic can be given a new job. Since it's often the tough, forceful part of us, maybe instead of attacking us, it can become our defender. However, the most crucial thing is that all parts

get a chance to speak and be understood and hopefully decide how they can all work together.

Blaming others

A common way to run away from internal fears is through blame. We blame others for our suffering or others for our pain. If it's someone else's fault, then we don't have to deal with it, right? It's out of our hands. But that's precisely the problem. When we put our fears in someone else's hands, we are preventing ourselves from being able to heal. We are giving them our fear and our power. When we give away our fear and therefore avoid our fear, we then make it bigger. By giving them our control, we are making it impossible for us to do anything to change our life. I'm not saying that people aren't responsible for what actions they have done. Still, I am saying that we are responsible for how we respond to their actions.

I previously talked about how we can't take 200% of the responsibility for other people's reactions and emotions. That's self-blame, and I still stand by that. Blame in any direction is not helpful. However, now I am talking about when we are blaming others and giving away 200% of the responsibility. We still need to take 100% responsibility for our own reactions and emotions. When we say, "It's their fault I'm like this," or "It's their fault this happened," then what we are saying is that we have no control over our current state, that we are a passive victim to their whims and fancies. This is simply not true. They might have lied to you, or betrayed you, or been violent towards you, which is certainly on them. But are you going to let their actions define your worth? Define your identity? Define what it means about you? You are glorious! You are made from stars! No one's actions or inactions can diminish that.

Understanding our responsibilities and other's responsibilities is different from blame. Blame is saying everything is either our fault or their fault. Responsibility is saying that they did something, and that was hurtful, and now what am I going to do? Blame makes us a victim. Blame makes us weak and helpless. Blame is saying they are responsible for their actions and my reactions.

I, too, have been seduced into being a victim, into blaming someone else for my pain. I would confide in friends, and they would agree with me, "I can't believe he did that! You deserved so much more!" But frankly, this is bullshit. No, I can't control how others treat me, but I can always control how I respond. It's imperative that I take ownership of that. I have been deeply hurt by other people's actions, and those people are responsible for what they did, and it was not my fault that they did those actions. HOWEVER, the ball is now in my court in what I'm going to do. Am I going to forgive them and go back to the same relationship, letting myself be hurt over and over? Or am I going to forgive them and place a compassionate boundary where they no longer have the privilege of getting close access to my heart? Or am I instead going to choose to surround myself with others who treat my heart with respect? There are a thousand choices you can make, and the decision itself doesn't matter, as long as you consciously choose and take responsibility for that choice.

Anger is not the same as blame. If people hurt us, then we might get angry with them, this is different than blame. Anger can be part of a healing process, and there is nothing wrong with that. If we get stuck in anger, however, and we give away our power by blaming them and not taking responsibility for moving past the situation, then that's on us. If we get stuck in anger and blame, then what we are telling ourselves is that the thing we are afraid of is true and so powerful that we can't even question it. Anger can give us the energy to make an essential and needed change; blame keeps us stuck in circles.

Internal fears from childhood

I often work with clients who have a lot of blame toward their parents. There is a lot of blame for our current suffering because of how we were raised. If this is you, then take a moment to check how this thinking makes you feel right now?

I bet pretty horribly. When we have anger or blame others for something, we are often suffering more from it then they are.

Now I get it. There are some genuinely terrible parents out there, some of whom had no right to have children. Even if your parents weren't horrible, there is not one of us that wasn't hurt by our parents' mistakes. I want you to understand I'm not minimizing that pain; I see that pain. Many people suffer from the conscious or subconscious belief that they are unlovable or unimportant, or unworthy, and often that can stem from childhood.

Internal fears are fears that we have about ourselves, others, or the world around us. Many of them can be formed in the first five years of life. Attachment theory states that our experience in this formative time creates internal beliefs about whether we are good or bad, and whether others and the world are good or bad. If, for example, you are a baby under six months old, and you often cry because you are hungry, but no one comes to feed you, then you might create a belief that the world is terrible. At one time in Europe, it was advised that you let babies "cry out." But the current parenting theory is that parents should always attend to the crying baby, especially if they are under six months. Attending to the crying, whether it's because they're scared, hungry or need a diaper change, shows that young brain they are taken care of in the world. Of course, if this did happen to you as a baby, you may not "consciously" remember it or be aware of the subconscious fear or distrust that this would create in your adult life. Although with some types of therapy or deep introspection, this might come out.

Another example is a child that has a lot of different caregivers before the age of five. The child might then learn that they can't depend on one person and that they will be abandoned and might view themselves as bad because once they start caring for someone, then they leave. On the other hand, if a child has different caregivers but also one consistent caregiver, then that belief can be mitigated. According to attachment theory, these beliefs created before the age of five can stay with us as we grow up. They significantly influence our ability to form, or not, secure attachments with romantic others. This isn't to shame parents as everyone is doing the best they can with what they have. This is just meant to be an example of how we can create some subconscious internal fears without even knowing it.

I'm not one of those therapists that likes to delve into the childhood of my clients. However, I will if I think delving into my client's childhood will help them in the present moment. Understanding where our hurt comes from is understanding "why" we have pain in the present moment. Understanding why someone has a particular fear can *sometimes* support my client in having compassion for themselves. If I think the why will help my client, then we will delve into the past. Understanding attachment theory is like understanding the "why" and can help us have compassion and not meant to create blame. Often, we can think there is something wrong with us for having these deep fears. In fact, most of us will struggle with the fear that there is something wrong with us. However, sometimes the "why" can elicit blame. This is the ego's way of derailing you from the healing process that you've started.

As I've mentioned, anger can be healing. It's ok to feel anger towards your parents or others for the mistakes they've made. But now what? If you think about it, you'll realize that the past doesn't actually exist. It only exists in your memories, in your thinking, in the moment right now. Are you going to let people who hurt you in the past continue to ruin your present? Anger is an emotion with a lot of energy, and you can harness that energy to have healing conversations, or motivate yourself to get assistance to heal your internal fears. But if you use anger to blame, then you're immobilizing yourself. You're wasting the energy that anger gives you to just go around and around on the hamster wheel of bitterness. Regardless of who hurt you, is being stuck on this hamster wheel for your highest good? Is it giving you any joy or peace?

Attachments can be healed, just like all internal beliefs. You need to first see them and acknowledge them. This doesn't mean you have to figure out if you were left crying as a baby. The "why" isn't essential when healing fears. What's important is your awareness and labelling of the current fear, such as, "I'm scared that when someone sees the real me, they'll leave me." Once you realize you have this fear, and can have compassion for yourself for having this fear, that's when it often just evaporates. Understanding the fear means labelling precisely what you are afraid of and how this fear is negatively impacting all aspects of your life.

This is why I prefer to focus on the present and what's going on right now. Understanding the why is not necessary and sometimes not even useful. Let go of your focus on "why" something happened. Face the fact that it is. If delving into the past can increase your levels of compassion, then it's useful. If, however, it increases your level of blame, then it is detrimental. Regardless of why we have our internal fears or where they came from, the most important thing is that we need to acknowledge that we do have them. It's taking responsibility for the fact that YOU are the one holding this fear, and only YOU can heal it. Once you know this, you'll be able to loosen your grip on your fear, and once you loosen your grip on it, it will often heal and evaporate.

Relationships and healing fears

Relationships with others are like holding up a mirror to yourself. They show you the fears that you are harbouring, and they reveal the hurts or wounds that need to be healed. We need to understand this correctly, so we don't blame others for our injuries or wounds. We need to realize that our wounds were always there, and this other person is now helping us to see them. In fact, I would argue that relationships are the most effective way of seeing and, therefore, being able to heal the wounds all of us are carrying. However, we can also use relationships to reinforce our wounds. We must take the time to look at ourselves first and get support in looking at what is coming up for us.

As someone who felt too much when I was a teenager, I struggled with intimate relationships. So I tried as best I could to be an island, to not need anyone. This was tragic because we need human connection, and I was robbing myself of the opportunity to deepen my self-understanding and what I need to heal. It also didn't work. I was successful in alienating everyone, and I fell into a deep depression.

I've also tried to heal all my own shit by myself so that I didn't have to work things out with other people. Sometimes, this can work, but other times I need to communicate to the person about what is upsetting me. Even if there is no solution, just the communication often makes it evaporate. Similarly, I tried to heal all my stuff so that I could "attract" healthy partners. Still, there is no way we can heal everything. This process is a journey. I don't want people to think they have to have everything sorted before they can get into a relationship. Relationships can actually help you sort through all your stuff, but only if you are aware and don't fall into the trap of blaming your relationships for the pain you have.

No matter how creatively I've tried to avoid intimate relationships, both romantic and friendship, it never seems to work. We need others. We need others to show us what we need to heal, and we need others to heal. There just doesn't seem to be any way around it. So, don't avoid relationships as a way to avoid pain, or in an effort to wait until you've fixed yourself. Just make sure you take care of your heart, take responsibility for your actions or reactions, and don't take responsibility for their actions or reactions.

I still need the assistance of others even though I'm a great therapist and energy worker, and I dedicate lots of time working through and healing my own stuff. We are just too close to our own lives, and we are blinded to things that we don't even know we are blinded to. All of us need someone we can trust to help us keep everything in perspective, to help us remember to face our fears and choose love.

If you want to face your inner fears, then you need to surround yourself with people who will help you do this. It's not a path we can do on our own; we need the support and the learning that other people provide for us. Yes, others can hurt us, but if we know how to take care of ourselves, if we know how to comfort and love our heart, then when others make mistakes, it's ok. It hurts, but it's not catastrophic. If we stay out of blame and take responsibility for the decisions we make, relationships can be incredibly healing. They can be a true expression of love. But we can't give what we don't have, so we need to make sure we love ourselves first if we want to have truly loving relationships.

The biggest mirrors of all are those we are in close relationships with. If we don't heal or acknowledge our internal fears, then we can co-create some toxic relationships.

Chapter 9
Abusive or Toxic Relationships

Although there are hundreds of unconscious fears that can show themselves, there are a few that seem universal, regardless of culture, gender or even age. One such fear is the fear of lack, the fear that there is not enough. Perhaps it is a fear that there aren't enough good partners in the world and so we need to settle for the one we have. Or maybe it's the fear that there's not enough money and so we need to stay in a job we hate, or perhaps it's a fear that there is not enough happiness and so we need to sacrifice or compromise our happiness so that we can ensure there's enough left over for the ones we love.

Sacrifice and compromise

I first came across the concept that compromise is an expression of fear over 20 years ago. I remember I had so much anger at the idea. But the more I mulled it over, the more and more it made sense, and the more I've tried to incorporate it into my relationships and work. I always try to find "win-win" solutions.

Sacrifice or compromise is a fear-based mentality that there are only finite resources or love in the world and so if you give up some of yours, then others will have more. But that is the ego's way of seeing. When connected to love, when connected to the universe, we experience an abundance of everything because we are everything. When we remember we are created from love, we are love, the idea of lack seems insane.

Of course, I understand that there is famine, disaster, war and unemployment. I have seen all these things firsthand. I know they exist, but I know they also exist as an expression of what my personal beliefs are. If I believe the world is dangerous and violent, that is how I will see it. If I have parts of myself that are violent and dangerous, that will frame my beliefs. Explosions and gunshots have surrounded me, and I have succumbed to the hopelessness that death and pain and suffering are inevitable. Yet, in those same circumstances, I have also had moments of peace, joy, compassion, and gratitude. I have seen kindness and love, even in some of the darkest places in the world. I know, I know that darkness can only affect me as much as I let it affect me and even then, it will only be for a finite amount of time. We are Love. Love is what we are made of. Love is our natural and pure state. Love is at the core of all of us. Everything else is just an illusion. All fear, all evil, all darkness, is just a cloud that is temporarily covering the sun that is us. Yes, I experience the shadow, but that does not make the sun any less bright, it does not make the sun any less brilliant. Just because we forget that we are abundant, it doesn't mean that lack is real.

Love is infinite; there is no limit to love. Just because you love one person, it doesn't mean that you then have less love for other people. You never have to give up love for yourself so that you can give more love to others. The exact opposite is true. The more you love yourself, the more love will bubble up for others. Love creates more love, and so the more you love yourself, the more you can love others, the more love you'll have and the more love you'll receive. We've spoken about the adage of putting the oxygen mask on yourself before putting it on others, and it's no different with love. If we "love" someone else so much that we are sacrificing our well-being for him or her, then that is not love. That is fear.

Sacrifice means that there is not enough. But that is precisely a fear-based way of looking at the world. When I see people sacrifice or compromise, it is out of fear because that's what they have to do in order to save another person or people. They are often martyring themselves for the good of someone else. That's what I mean by sacrifice. It's a belief that you have to give up something of yours, or your well-being so that someone else can have something they want or need. Compromise similarly is the idea that we must give up a little bit of what we want, and they must give up a little bit of what they want so that we can meet in the middle. In negotiation, this is considered a lose-lose situation, because neither side is happy.

I often see empathic people or highly sensitive people in relationships with people who constantly sacrifice their own happiness to accommodate. I have worked with hundreds of highly sensitive empaths (HSEs) and am one myself, and one common belief for HSEs is that we are unlovable. When you believe that you're unlovable and can handle suffering more than others, you will often sacrifice yourself for others. That's not healthy love.

Sacrificing yourself for others can be done in the smallest ways. Like constantly focusing on what the other person wants or needs so that you don't even know what you want or need. But sacrifice can also be made in significant ways, for instance, by being the sole caretaker, never asking for help until you become burnt out, or by giving up jobs or dreams to accommodate others. That is not real love! That is not living out of love; it is living out of fear. Fear that unless you sacrifice yourself, the person will be destroyed. The parent-child relationship is the only exception. It's imperative to see the infinite love in yourself AND the magnificent love in others. By sacrificing for their good, we disrespect their truth. I'm not judging or blaming because I have been in this place, but I want to be a big road sign: Caution! Continuing down this road will only lead to pain and suffering, and that will continue to worsen until you decide to change your ways.

Instead of sacrificing and compromising, we need to change our perspective, and we need to look at ourselves sincerely and honestly. Only then once we have done this can we make a choice based on first taking care of our heart and then deciding how we can best express the love that wants to overflow from our heart after it feels truly self-loved. We need to see ourselves and our loved ones as whole and then make a decision based on that perspective.

Here is a journal entry from when Francois and I were doing long distance. My ex-husband and I had agreed that we wouldn't be separated for more than three months and a maximum of six. Francois had said he would only go for a couple of months, but it had been four months already, and I had told him that if I couldn't get a job to join him, then I wanted him to come back home after six months.

> All right, I'm still at it! I talked with the wise and lovely Dianne (literally thank GOD for her!), and it became very apparent that for me to "put my foot down" with Francois was very incongruent of me. I've always talked about how love is complete, is everything, and my love for Francois is just one part of love (as completely important as it is). And it's true and for me to make him stop working would be the same thing, plus that's not me! I'm full, and I'm independent but not in that I don't need him, but in that, I don't need him does that make sense? I am stronger and happier when I'm around him, but I can't strangle him to keep him near me. So I talked to him and told him all of this, and he said he was so relieved and that he really appreciated what I said and is going to think about it. After our phone call, I burst into tears and have been crying for the last hour or so, but I need to release him. I'm so scared that by doing so, he will float away (or I will push him away in hurt), but I do feel so much more congruent. I don't believe

in sacrifice, mine or his, and if he stopped working there because he felt he needed to take care of me, then that is not really love, and of course, he would feel resentment and bitterness. It's tough because Dianne is really the only one I can talk to about all of this, I'm realizing how steeped in fear most people are! Everyone thought it was about time that I said something to Francois, although maybe they were just trying to support me. Regardless, I have to release the outcome (just like I have to release every bloody thing jeez!), and honestly, deep down I feel better. It means that I will be all right, and I don't have to choose between my life's work or Francois, that I can have them both. Both are out of love, both are just part of love as is love and belief in myself. It's funny if I think about it, I've been feeling so dependent on Francois, and if I'm dependent on him, then why should people look to me for wisdom? I do feel so much more whole now. I had to believe in myself, hey? Thank god I'm more in control now of my future and I can make my own decisions instead of just waiting on Francois. Although perhaps he will choose to leave and join me in Feb… But I need to let him choose and not push him to choose to stay (which I could totally see myself doing) I need to trust his decision will be the best for him and ultimately us.

I love you.

Trust.

Believe you are stronger and more loving than you think.

You can do this!

A few years later, my ex-husband and I were faced with a similar predicament. He was on a mission in Iraq and didn't want to quit to join me in France. I never want to force anyone to do anything, and so I looked inside and asked my heart what she really wanted and needed. She wanted to be with my husband and reminded me of a moment of intuition I had had with my all-seeing eye. So even though I had no desire whatsoever to work in the Middle East, I chose, out of care for my heart, that I would go to the Middle East. I got a job and moved there to join my husband. However, what differentiates this from sacrifice or compromise is 1) I took the time to go down into my heart, listen and first take care of her, and 2) I took complete ownership of my decision to move. If I hadn't taken ownership of my decision, being very clear that it was only me responsible for this choice, then I could have used that move as something to hold over Francois, as something that his needs owe me. Or I could have perhaps held deep and silent resentment towards him for "making" me move. It wasn't easy, and I sometimes wanted to use it over my husband, "I moved here for you, so you owe me XYZ," but I didn't. And every time I felt that way, I made sure to go inside and take care of my heart, which felt lonely and unloved.

Sacrifice and compromise are a way of subversively blaming others for us not getting what we really want. It's giving away our power. Instead, we have to be very honest and take responsibility for the choices we make and continue to execute. We need to ensure that we are making those choices to take care of our hearts first before we take care of another's heart, while also respecting others who make choices that are taking care of their heart. Self-love is a type of magic love that is the only thing that will truly nourish and comfort our hearts; other types of love just don't have the same vitamins. The more we give ourselves this type of love, and the more we encourage others to provide themselves with this type of love, the healthier the world will be.

It even goes deeper than this. Another layer is that when you get in touch with your heart and its magnificence, and you truly experience that, then you will understand that it rarely needs those outside details such as prestige, power, respect, or even acknowledgement, to prove that it's majestic. Your heart already knows these things deep down, and so when you truly connect to its magnificence, when you can tap into it and are submersed in it, sacrifice or compromise seems genuinely insane. My heart has everything; she is everything. There is nothing that could diminish her amazingness, not disease, not torture, not even death. How can you sacrifice anything when you are profoundly complete? How is giving something sacrificing when you are overflowing with abundance? It's impossible. Sacrifice and compromise imply that once you give something, you don't have it anymore, but when you are in touch with your gloriousness, you'll realize that you are infinitely abundant. It's only when we are stuck in our ego, our sense of pride, or our self that is ruled by fear and lack, that we can even conceive that sacrifice or compromise is a thing.

The same process is needed when trying to make decisions. When I went into Syria, many people, including myself, were worried about my safety. I was going to advocate for women's rights and take care of women who had been raped and beaten and often shunned by society or had their life threatened by their family. I worked in places that had been controlled by the Islamic State for up to three years. As a white foreign female supporting women, I could be on the top of the kill list. And yet, when I got in touch with my heart, I knew that although this might happen, there was nothing that ISIS could do to damage my essence. They could damage my body, but not my heart. Only I can damage my heart by not taking care of it or basing my self-worth on what other people think or do to me. So, when I listened to the fear of my heart and comforted her and then asked her what she truly wanted, the answer was clear: to be a face of compassion for those surrounded by hate. So that's what I did for almost two years until my heart started to get tired and bruised and needed to retreat, which is when I quit and moved back to France.

Some people think I'm a hero for doing what I do, but I honestly am not. I'm simply listening to my heart, which is perhaps a little more dramatic than other hearts. A bus driver who genuinely smiled at me when I was struggling with suicidal thoughts had profoundly changed my life. That smile helped me get back on my feet, and 25 years later,

I still remember that smile. You don't have to go into war zones or epidemics to change the world. You just need to connect with your heart, take care of it, and let the love flow out naturally. You aren't required to compromise or give up anything of value; you just need to tap into the ocean of abundance that is all around you.

Unhealthy relationships

Along with the fear that there isn't enough, the fear that we are unlovable or that we will be abandoned are some common universal internal fears. It is said that the greatest human desire is to be truly seen and loved, and yet the greatest human fear is to be seen and rejected. These specific fears can be so deep and have so many layers that it takes some time, sometimes a lifetime, to heal the different ways they show up in our lives. They are often the reason why we stay in toxic or unhealthy relationships.

Unhealthy relationships are a reflection of unconscious limiting beliefs that need to be healed. What shows up in our lives is a reflection of what is occurring in our subconscious. Whatever is going on in our unconscious, we hold it to be true without realizing it consciously. For example, if we subconsciously think we are unlovable, then we will attract situations where we will feel unlovable. This can either be through people treating us poorly or through our interpretations of people's actions.

Unhealthy relationships can come in a variety of forms. They could be familial, friendship, or romantic. They are unhealthy when the balance is off, and one person is consistently putting in more effort to make the relationship work. There will be understandable situations where people are struggling and so can't put as much effort into other areas of their life. But if this is something consistent, if this is a recurring phenomenon, then this relationship is unbalanced.

Using the garden metaphor; it means most of the time is spent in one person's garden. A healthy relationship is when two people meet at the fence, they are both doing their own work and then supporting, but not controlling the other person's life.

An unhealthy relationship is also when two people come together whose gardens are both a mess. They may be using each other as distractions from tending their garden, or they may agree to switch gardens and take care of the other person if the other person takes care of them. This is unhealthy because no one can take care of our garden for us. If we don't have self-love, then we can't grow the fruit of love. We can be kind to others, but if it's because we need them to love us so that we have worth, then that's not sincere kindness. Additionally, if we don't love ourselves, then we'll never believe that someone else really loves us. We'll continuously require assurances from them, but these are only short-term fixes.

Unhealthy relationships result from us not taking care of our garden, of us not tending to the wound of being unlovable, unimportant, undesirable, or disgusting. These painful relationships happen so that we can make these unconscious beliefs conscious and then heal them. This is how we can use unhealthy relationships to grow. They force us to pay attention to our own garden that is withering and dying. This doesn't mean that we need to stay in unhealthy relationships, it means when we are in unhealthy relationships, we need to take a good hard look at what beliefs are showing up.

Often, what keeps us stuck in unhealthy relationships is the fear that we are unlovable. Perhaps there's a part of us that doesn't believe that we deserve anything better. Or that we won't be able to find anyone else. Or if we kick this person out of our garden, there will be no one taking care of it. When we are in a place of seeking others to complete us, heal us, or fulfill us, then we are trying to get our self-love from outside the self, which never works. The same goes if you are with someone who doesn't love themselves. You can love them with all your heart and spend all your time proving this to them, but it won't make them love themselves. They have to make that decision and do that work themselves.

When we have an unconscious limiting belief that is propelling us to get involved in relationships that are detrimental to us, then we will continue to attract circumstances with new people and situations that continue to point out to us what wounds need healing. I don't believe that we always have to learn things through pain and suffering, but frequently pain is the only thing that gets our attention and motivates us to face our fears and change our beliefs.

The process of loving yourself first before you can love others needs to be used in personal relationships. I have been in relationships where my partner has hurt and betrayed me deeply, and I had to ask my heart what she needed. She always chose forgiveness, although forgiveness with boundaries. If the same hurt keeps happening repeatedly, she chooses to draw more definite limits, and in some cases, that means ending the relationship. When I first started my journey, I felt that sacrifice was the ultimate show of love, and if I did that, then surely they would love me. But this is a red flag. That was me being a martyr or having a saviour complex. That was me acting out of the unconscious fear that I was unlovable, and I had to prove my worth. It was me behaving out of fear, not love.

Acting out of love is knowing and feeling your magnificence and wanting to have that overflow to others. When I martyred myself for others, which I did in both my work and my relationships, I was operating under the belief that there isn't enough joy for both of us. So, I would rather they have it than me. So now, when I notice I'm thinking that way I go deep, I comfort and love my heart because she is frightened that something bad will happen to someone she loves, or she's scared that unless she sacrifices herself, she won't be loved. I have to address those needs first before taking any actions. I have to water and feed my beautiful heart before I can meet anyone at the fence.

Let's take this out of the garden metaphor and into real life. Let's use the example of cheating. Cheating is a red flag that you are in an unhealthy relationship. It is an example of betrayal and often involves deceit. There can be many reasons why a person cheats, and again, I want to be clear that this book is not intended to create blame or guilt. All people in the relationship need to take time to look at why this has happened.

I have had two partners that have cheated on me, but I reacted differently to each circumstance. The first one I broke up with as soon as I found out even though he denied it. I "loved" him with such an intensity that I felt my life and happiness depended on him. Our relationship had been such a roller coaster that my physical health was deteriorating. I had pushed away all my friends because he didn't like it when I spent time with others. I had already been doing most of the work to keep the relationship together, and so when I heard that he was cheating on me, it was the final straw. On one level, I felt like it was a kick from heaven to give me a clear reason why we shouldn't be together anymore. Of course, even though it was a clear deal-breaker for me, it doesn't mean it was easy for me to get over him. I wrestled with myself and whether I had made the right decision. Maybe I should give him another chance? But I knew deep in my heart that it was a toxic relationship.

Getting over him is what opened my eyes to the fact that so many of us stay in unhealthy relationships because we perceive the potential. We see how beautiful their garden could be if only we go in there and clean it up a bit. But that never works. Many of us stay in unhealthy or toxic relationships because we think we can "love them healthy," that if we love them hard enough and strong enough, they'll get better. Just listen to the love songs out there; this is a common message. But I want to strongly and thoroughly tell you that this is an illusion. This is false. *We cannot love people healthy.* It is impossible to love someone enough so that they'll love themselves. It's impossible to go into someone's garden and make it beautiful, to feed it and water it so that it thrives. The only way someone can thrive is through self-love. I have tried over and over to love people healthy, and it always ends up in disaster.

I truly believe in assisting others, but only if they are willing to do their work. All relationships require both people to do 100% of their work in the relationship. Too often, we get stuck in relationships where one person is doing 100%, and the other is doing 20%. If this is a temporary thing because of some crisis, then that is understandable, but if this is a pattern, then it is our responsibility to speak up. If things don't change, then we need to take action out of self-love first, and then once you have that out of love in general.

I had another partner who was lovely. He had the most beautiful heart, and he also cheated on me. It took me completely by surprise. I'm intuitive, and so I'm good at picking up on very subtle things, but I had no idea this was happening until he told me. I was devastated but took some time to comfort my heart. After she felt loved by me, I then asked her what she wanted to do. She wanted to forgive him and work on trying to heal the relationship. So that's what I decided to do. I focused my attention on the relationship. I took ownership of that focus and didn't hold it over him, and I made our relationship a priority. I was genuinely choosing love out of fear, and looking back, I still don't think I wasn't operating out of any unconscious fears.

Except relationships involve more than one person. I can take responsibility for my outlook and behaviour, but I can't take responsibility or control the other person's behaviour. He ended up continuing to cheat on me. Again, I had no idea or suspicions until he told me—I had to be responsible for what I wanted and what he was capable of. I had tried to love him healthy, but I couldn't, even though I have a massive heart and can love a lot! I forgave him again, but I ended the relationship. It wasn't easy to end that relationship, but it was a lot easier than it was the first time it happened to me because I did it out of self-love. My heart shattered, but it turns out that it needed to shatter so that my heart could grow even bigger.

I don't think I made the wrong choice in forgiving him and staying in the relationship. Even though he cheated on me again, I still had a strong sense of self-love when I decided to stay, and I'm proud of that. But just because I have self-love, that doesn't mean I can control the actions of others. I had been doing most of the emotional work to keep the relationship together because I saw the incredible potential in him. Still, no matter how hard I tried to love him, at the end of the day, he didn't love himself, and that was out of my control.

There is no blanket decision that is always right, and even if we act in all the most perfect ways (which don't exist), others might not behave with the same standard. Still, when we act out of love, regardless of the outcome, we will be ok. We would have the strength and self-love to weather any storm that would have shipwrecked us if we didn't have that inner strength.

In general, I'm not a fan of cutting people off. I believe in forgiveness and compassion. But there are some people in our lives who we can forgive and have compassion for, but let them live their life in a different proximity to us. If a friend hurts you once, then express how it affected you and request how you would like them to treat you instead. Take the time to look at what your wound is and try to heal that as well. If you've done work to heal your wound and that friend continues to do the same actions that are hurtful even after you've communicated their effect, then perhaps that person is just not compatible with you. There are enough people in the world that we don't need to be compatible with everyone.

I've had friendships where I spent most of our relationship trying to love them so that they could love themselves, but they couldn't. I was spending all my energy trying to show them how magnificent they were, that I had difficulty enjoying my own magnificence. I even felt guilty about being magnificent. I feared shining my light because

I didn't want to make them feel uncomfortable. That, unfortunately, is not a healthy relationship.

We could all be in relationships where we help each other be the best we can be, shine the brightest, and be the biggest force of love in the world, where we share each other's pain but also each other's successes and joys. It is our responsibility to surround ourselves with friends who are encouraging and loving and supportive. It's not about blaming others for supporting you or not. It's about all of us taking actions to ensure that we surround ourselves with people who bring us joy.

A Course in Miracles states that it is the function of all relationships "to make happy." Are your relationships making you happy? If not, then there is something you need to look at.

Abusive relationships

I have been working with, pondering, and discussing the issue of emotional abuse over the last few years. Because I'm such an advocate for love over fear, many people, justifiably so, are worried that we use "love" to justify abusive behaviour. There is a distinct difference between abusive relationships and unhealthy relationships, and therefore we need to approach them in different ways.

Unhealthy relationships are damaging and harmful, although not to the extent of abusive relationships. Both are damaging to our sense of self, our self-love, and our wellbeing. But emotional abuse is when there is a consistent pattern of abusive words and bullying actions that destroys self-esteem and even the sense of self of the abused person. I can't say if the abuser does it consciously, but it is done systematically. Bit by bit, the abuser will cut off their partner from support systems or forms of independence, such as finances until the abused partner feels, or is completely dependent on their abusive partner.

At no point do I want to judge or blame any person that gets into relationships like this. I hope that people in these types of relationships might read this chapter and realize that they are in an abusive relationship and seek outside help. Often, people in abusive relationships tell themselves that "it's not that bad," or they try to justify the abuser's actions. But remember, you are made of stars! You deserve to be treated with respect and kindness. If you feel like you might be in an abusive relationship, please get help, you don't need to go through this alone.

When it comes to emotionally abusive relationships often, the abusive partner has slowly chipped away at the sense of self of the other partner. The relationship doesn't start as abusive, but it gets more and more toxic. The underlying goal of the abuser is to discredit, isolate and silence their partner. Research has shown that emotional abuse can be just as harmful as physical abuse, which is extremely difficult for survivors to leave.

Emotional abuse can be subtle, so here are some signs of emotionally abusive relationships:

- Think about your interaction with the abuser (it could be a partner, a friend or a family member). If you feel anxious, hurt, confused, worried, depressed, misunderstood, or worthless most of the time when you interact with them, that is a red flag that you might be in an emotionally abusive relationship.
- The abuser has unrealistic expectations of you, either in the things you do around the house, how you dress, the tasks you perform, how you spend your time, or if you share the same views as them.
- They don't respect your thoughts/views/emotions. They may say you are crazy or too sensitive. They don't accept your feelings or think you shouldn't feel how you do. They might accuse you of being needy or too demanding when you express what you need.

- The abuser can have very different mood changes, pick fights for no reason, say opposite things or behave erratically or unpredictably so that you feel like you are walking on eggshells. They are chaotic and destabilizing.
- They often blackmail you emotionally. This can be done by manipulating you or trying to use guilt. Holding your mistakes over you or using your vulnerabilities or compassion to control you. They could punish you through the silent treatment or withhold affection when you don't do what they want.
- They try to control and isolate you. The abuser tries to prevent you from spending time with your friends or family. Or they might hide or take your car keys, or not give you access to the bank account. They could try to keep track of all your movements, perhaps through texting all the time or even using a GPS tracker.

If your partner is exhibiting even some of these behaviours, then reach out to a domestic violence service near you. If that seems too drastic, then at least reach out to a therapist or search the internet for more information.

In these cases, how do you love yourself if you don't even have a self? If you are dependent on your partner? The slow chipping away makes it so you don't even realize how bad things have gotten. It's like the metaphor of the frog, where if you put him in a pot of boiling water, he will jump out, but if you put him in a pot with cool water and then heat it to boiling, he will stay until he dies.

We always hear that "relationships take work," so we have an expectation that we should be compromising or "working" on our relationships. But although all relationships take work, at least 80% of the time, they should be contributing to your happiness, and they should always be supporting you in being a better person.

Being in an abusive relationship is dangerous. If you are in an abusive relationship, it is highly unlikely that the abuser will change. We often feel like we can fix them, or feel like if only we were better, or it is our fault in some way. These are all untrue. If you want to find real love, then you need to first take care of your heart, decide what you are ok with, and what boundaries you need to put up. STOP BLAMING YOURSELF! Take 100% of the responsibility for your actions and 0% responsibility for their actions. Remember: you are not alone. There is a reason why abusive people don't want you to have a support network; it's because they give you strength. Lastly, make an exit plan and be aware that you might be in some real danger. The overwhelming majority of women who are murdered are murdered by their current or previous partners. It is really important to get help, professional or otherwise so that you can stay safe. It is possible to leave, no matter how much the abuser wants you to think it's impossible.

Stockholm syndrome

Stockholm syndrome is not just for those who have been kidnapped or held hostage. If you are in an abusive relationship, you might also suffer from Stockholm syndrome. In psychology, emotionally bonding with our abuser is seen as a way to survive.

For Stockholm syndrome to develop, four conditions are present:

1. A perceived threat to your physical or emotional survival. This can be to your life directly or also the lives of your friends and family. It could be through direct, clear statements or subtle threats or actions that make it clear that if you displeased your partner, you or someone you love would be in danger. Even witnessing violence directed at someone else or something else can be interpreted as a threat. This is also one of the many reasons why it is so detrimental for children to witness violence, even if they are never harmed physically.

2. A glimmer of hope through small acts of kindness. If the abuser is seen to give a small act of kindness, even if it's through not being violent when the survivor expects them to be, the survivor then feels a moment of gratitude or hope. This can also include seeing the "soft side" of the abuser. These small acts of kindness give the survivor hope that the abuser isn't all bad and sympathizes with the abuser. The abuser uses this to justify their actions, and the survivor has a false sense of hope that the abuser might change.
3. Focused on the abuser's perspective. When an abuser is easily or suddenly angered, those around them can feel like they need to "walk on eggshells" to avoid upsetting them. This then forces the survivors to see everything through the abuser's perspective so that they can better predict and avoid being abused. The survivor can become so ingrained in the abuser's perspective that they can even get angry or upset with loved ones who are trying to assist them.
4. Perceived inability to escape. This could be through having no access to finances or being worried that you or your loved ones will be harmed. The abuser may also use emotional blackmail, for instance, through guilt or by threatening to harm themselves if the survivor leaves.

Stockholm syndrome is characterized by the survivor trying to avoid upsetting the abuser at all costs. That means avoiding topics of conversation, doing chores exactly how the abuser wants and avoiding friends and family who might upset the abuser. It's not that the survivor doesn't love their friends and family; it's just that not upsetting the abuser becomes the most important goal. If you are a loved one of someone who you think is in an abusive relationship, then it's important to keep regular forms of communication open with the survivor. Try not to criticize or bring up the relationship as that will only create conflict and distance between you and your loved one. If you would like more information on how to get out of or support a loved one in this type of abusive relationship, please look into this website: https://counsellingresource.com/therapy/self-help/stockholm.

Remember, there are resources and help available for you. Please reach out to your friends, family, or a local domestic violence association. You're not alone. There are many forms of support to help people in these situations.

In any relationship, we can use the fact that we "love" someone to continue to let him or her treat us poorly. This can be especially dangerous if we are in an emotionally toxic or abusive relationship or friendship. That is why it is very important to start with self-love when implementing a lifestyle of choosing love over fear. It is not possible to truly love someone else unless you love yourself first.

Real love

So how do we have a healthy relationship? Sometimes it can seem daunting, and it is certainly something that we need to work on continually. This book is geared towards creating real love, and although it's simple, love yourself and let that love overflow to everything around you. It's tough even to know what real self-love is. Furthermore, we avoid loving ourselves because we often feel so strongly that if only we were truly loved and admired by others, we would finally be happy.

This focus on things outside of ourselves is addicting. If we have lots of money, then others will admire us. If we have lots of power, then others will respect us. If we are beautiful, then others will love us. But we need to learn again and again that true love and true happiness and fulfillment can only come from within. Until you learn this, you will be like a dog chasing its tail, and you'll never be able to find happiness and love.

Self-love

Loving yourself first is about learning to really love your heart, having that love overflow to others, and learning to accept the love that others give us. It is impossible to give what we don't have. To really love someone, you have to love yourself. I know you've heard this, but I hope you really hear this in your heart. *You cannot love another unless you have love for yourself.*

Self-love is the foundation of all love. It is the foundation for everything. Just like I was finally able to believe that other people were important only after I first healed my negative belief and genuinely believed that I was important. So too can we not truly love others until we love ourselves.

We will never truly believe that someone loves us unless we love ourselves. So often, we wish and pray for someone to love us like the love you see in the movies, but when we get that, we don't trust that it's true. We shrug off their love, aren't attracted to them, or don't really believe that they know us, and if they did, they wouldn't love us anymore. If someone compliments you on something you are insecure about, then you won't believe it, or you'll shrug it off.

Self-love requires that we look into ourselves and discover the dark bits. Notice the emphasis on the word discover? We don't need to change those dark bits, just acknowledge them and bring them into the light where they can be a part of us. I used to think that love solved everything, especially when it came to the dark bits inside me. But as I've delved into the universe that is my soul, I've found horrible parts that don't want love. In fact, they adamantly rejected it. But then I realized that I was trying to "love" these disgusting parts of me so that they would change. I was offering love to the side of me that wanted to be vindictive, with the condition that it would be "healed" and go away. That wasn't unconditional love; it wasn't even acceptance. However, once I learned how to truly love unconditionally, I could see these parts and appreciate them precisely for what they are, and then they would evaporate or transform in front of my eyes.

For example, there was a bitchy and bitter part of me that wanted to lash out and hurt another person. I first tried to send love to that part, but she told me to "fuck off." So I sat with it, and I understood why it wanted to be bitchy and vindictive. It needed to protect me, and it craved to stand up for me. Once that part felt that I understood it and accepted it, bitchiness and all, it calmed down. I then explained what I needed: that I aspired to choose love and have my integrity regardless of what other people did. Because I first spent time understanding my bitchy part, it was able to listen to my point of view. Then we worked together to transform it into a new role; it was now my alarm system when I needed to care for my heart.

Self-love exercises

Here are a few really powerful techniques that can help on this journey. These techniques require practice and consistency. Just like you can't spend one day in a garden and expect it to be great for the rest of your life, so too do you need to do these techniques regularly so that your self-love is maintained.

- Look at your eyes in the mirror for 5 minutes a day, try to see into the depths of them, and try to see the beauty of your deep inner self.
- Breast massage! This is mainly for the women, although if you're a man, let me know if this works for you too. The breast area is the area of self-love as it's right by your heart. There are many nerve endings in the breast and nipples, and when you massage them, you inspire more self-love and help release the emotions being held there. Use massage oil, or you can massage over your clothes. Put both hands on the outside of your breasts and

stroke down the sides and then up through the centre. Do this over and over for a few minutes, just feeling all the emotions there and letting them flow out. Then cup your breasts and shake them a little making an intention for yourself of what you would like to feel. Perhaps you want to be a goddess or have self-confidence, anything that resonates with you and is supportive and loving. Try to do this every day.

- Look up amazing or fun facts about the body on the internet. For example, did you know that bellybuttons grow specialized hairs to catch lint? Or that the average person produces enough saliva in their lifetime to fill-up two swimming pools? Our bodies are magical. Take some time to learn about the fantastic things they do for us. Appreciate all the work it does to support you even when you mistreat your body.
- Meditate. There are many different ways to meditate, and not all methods are suitable for everyone. Some people find mindfulness meditation helpful, and some great apps can help you do this. Others prefer prayer, running or yoga as a form of meditation. Find something that enables you to process your thoughts, relaxes you, and helps you get in touch with the very centre of you. Psychologists and spiritual teachers agree that at our very core, there is happiness and love. It just gets covered up by our negative thoughts and beliefs. Meditation is a glorious method to gently push the clouds away to get in touch with our inner light, joy and peace.

Loving ourselves is the first step in having healthy relationships. Since most of us are so focused on things outside of ourselves, and it is so ingrained that we have to be in other people's gardens, let's go over the difference between being in other people's gardens and meeting them at the fence.

Meeting others at the fence

When you go into someone else's garden, you take on the responsibility of meeting their needs, regardless of whether other people should meet those needs or not. Or perhaps you take responsibility for how they feel. For example, you will take responsibility for making them happy, even if their reason for being unhappy is that they aren't following something their heart says or because they are not following their doctor's orders and taking medication. When they are happy, we take credit, and when they are sad, it's our fault. When you meet someone at the fence, however, you don't do things that others should or can do for themselves, you only do what they need you specifically to do for them.

There is a story of a child who found a cocoon. For hours the child watched as a small hole was created in the cocoon, and a tiny butterfly struggled to get out. The butterfly struggled and struggled, and then it stopped fighting for a while. The child was worried, got a pair of scissors and gently cut the hole bigger so that the butterfly could get out. The butterfly soon emerged, but its body was swollen, and its wings were small and crumpled. It tried to fly, but its wings were too broken, and its body too big. It then spent the rest of its life crawling around, never able to fly.

The cocoon's small hole ensures that the liquid in the body is squeezed out into the wings. By cutting the hole bigger, the child prevented the butterfly from going through something difficult but essential for its wellbeing. Struggle is not a bad thing; sometimes it's essential for our development. Going through strife or seeing other people grapple is a vital part of life, there is nothing wrong with it.

When you meet someone at the fence, you recognize that your behaviours affect others, but it's their beliefs that create their emotions. We can do any number of actions, and there will be as many reactions as there are people. We can't take ownership or responsibility for people's emotions, even though we have to take responsibility for our behaviours. Therefore, we can't take on responsibility for others' emotional states, whether that be positive or negative emotions.

When we interfere in other people's lives, we expect others to live up to our expectations, to do things the way we do them because we know what's best. If they don't do things our way, then we get upset. But when we meet people at the fence, we don't make demands of them. If they do something against our advice, we don't get upset. We give others the freedom to make their own mistakes, and we don't feel guilt or blame when they do. When they succeed, we feel genuine joy, and we aren't jealous of their success. We celebrate their happiness.

When we have co-dependent relationships, we see others as an extension of ourselves. We see their behaviour as a reflection of us. Their behaviour can make us embarrassed or proud. But when we do that, we are not seeing them for themselves, as their own person. We have lost boundaries in the relationship. When we meet them at the fence, however, we realize that they have thoughts and habits that are unique to them and don't need to be controlled by us. They have their path and individual lessons that they need to learn that are different from our path and lessons. When we meet them at the fence, we can see other people for who they really are without needing to control them.

When we are in other people's gardens, we can often feel tired, burdened, trapped or resentful because so much of our energy and focus is about the welfare of other people. When we meet others at the fence, we feel relaxed and free, and we feel peaceful and content because our hearts are full and filled with energy.

Relationships can be complicated, but they are also so healing and essential to our wellbeing. We can't achieve happiness without connections with others, and most of all, we need a relationship with our heart.

Part 3

Learned Fear

All these things shall love do unto you that you may know the secrets of your heart, and in that knowledge become a fragment of Life's heart.

Khalil Gibran

Chapter 10
Fearful Experiences and Primary and Secondary Emotions

So far, we've talked about taking on or being influenced by other people's fears. However, when we think about fear or talk about things we are scared of, it's usually because of the fear we will now be addressing: learned fear.

Learned fear

Learned fears are anxieties we have because of an adverse event or circumstance that we have experienced. Or even a perceived event that we've heard about happening to someone close to us. Learned fear through someone else's misfortunes is a type of vicarious learning. Vicarious learning can be beneficial; I always say I wish I could learn everything vicariously. Still, sometimes it can get overwhelming, especially with the news so focused on only negative things that are happening in the world. We see this in how people can become quite afraid of something they heard on the news or even in movies. For example, crime is always reported in the news and sensationalized in how it's published. Many people think that crime is increasing globally, especially in our home countries, but research has shown that over the years crime is consistently on a downward trend. Furthermore, homicide, war, poverty and malnutrition are all going down, and yet that's never what we hear.

Additionally, the human default is to focus on what might be a threat to us. If we pay more attention to the sabre-toothed tiger than the gently budding flower, we will have a higher likelihood of surviving. But this focus on the negative, the fearful, can get out of control and fill up our perspective so that it's all we see. When all we focus on is what could potentially harm us, our lives are filled with fear, and our mood is progressively more and more miserable. A research study was done on the amount of fear in different populations, and it was found that Americans were more fearful than Syrians during the Syrian civil war. That's pretty crazy, and I attribute the news as being a big part of creating this epidemic of learned fear.

The news can generate so much fear, that as a highly sensitive person, I have stopped watching it.

If you find you are quite fearful or anxious, I recommend not watching the news. If you want to know what's going on, then find less stressful ways of keeping up with current events, such as comedy late-night shows that make you laugh while you're getting updated on what is negatively going on in the world. I also recommend Positive News, a UK newsgroup that reports on all the incredible things that are happening in the world today, which are quite astonishing and inspiring. News is not current events; it is negative events.

Furthermore, fear is contagious. If we directly experienced a fearful event, it can make us afraid of that event happening again. Our anxiety can even spread to objects or events that resemble that traumatic experience. For example, if someone has a panic attack in a shopping mall, that person could become fearful of shopping malls, or perhaps going into buildings, or even going outside. This is called generalized fear, and when we don't face our original fear, then generalized fear can become more and more contagious and can increase fear towards more and more people, places and things. That is why it is vital to face our fears because that is the only way to see that we can, in fact, handle them, and they aren't as dreadful or horrible as we think or even remember them to be. Fear is like a shadow, it can look like a giant and menacing monster on the wall, but when we look at the source, we see it's just a mouse eating cheese.

I had a breakthrough at the wise age of eight years old. I had been suffering from stomach aches for the last three years, and although now doctors would know they were a classic sign of child anxiety, we went from doctor to doctor to discover what was wrong. I had undiagnosed generalized anxiety disorder. During this time, my parents had, unfortunately, tasked my older brother to take care of me while they both worked. Every time I knew he was going to babysit me; I would get terrible stomach aches. Finally, I remember sitting and thinking about what to do regarding my brother. I didn't know that my stomach aches were connected to my fear of being left by my parents, but I did see that I had to decide whether I would let fear control me.

I was terrified of my brother beating me up, but I hated being told what to do. Even though he was five years older and way stronger, my stubborn and independent nature refused to let him "win." This often resulted in a battle of wills that became physical, and I would almost always lose. One afternoon, I remember thinking: I could be submissive and listen to what he tells me to do, or I could face the consequences, do what I want, and try to run away before he could hurt me. I decided to choose the latter and quickly learned how to make my poor brother so angry that he couldn't move, which would increase my chances of getting away. Those early experiences probably paved the way for me to go into psychology, but also represented my first conscious step of facing my fears and not letting fear dictate to me.

From then on, even though I was anxious in all areas of my life, I would never let my feeling of anxiety stop me, and soon after, my stomach aches stopped.

Not knowing

Often, the scariest things are the things we can't see because we can't physically face them. During the Ebola response in Sierra Leone, which happened 10 years after the civil war there ended, people would tell me over and over that they preferred the war because at least then they knew who their enemy was. It's similar to the Pandemic; we don't know who has it, how long it's going to last, or when a cure or vaccine will be developed. We were told to stay at home and socially distance for months, and even when that ended, we weren't sure when borders would open up again, whether we would still have jobs, if we would be able to find new employment, or if there would be a second wave.

Not knowing is often the most fearful thing of all, and in these circumstances, how do we face our fear?

When we go through painful experiences, we try to avoid going through them again. To do this, we feel that if only we could control our environment and ideally everything in it, we can protect ourselves from everything we are afraid of. Except we can't control our setting. Perhaps we get our heartbroken, and then we might be reluctant to let ourselves be vulnerable with the next person. Maybe we become suspicious of the next person we date, and we try to change their behaviour. We try and try to control others, control our jobs, our physical environment, and our children, but it's an impossible mission. Just like we need to face our fears, we also need to face the fact that we can't control anything outside of ourselves. Even when we try just to control ourselves, we aren't taught how to deal with our own emotions. Not knowing what's happening or what's going to happen is the ultimate feeling of being out of control.

As a society, or perhaps as humans, we need to become more comfortable with being out of control and the uncomfortable feelings this creates. We need to sit in our unknowingness, and we need to let go of trying to have control and just be. We need to ground ourselves and allow the fear of not knowing flow through us and eventually flow out of us, and sometimes we need to do this multiple times a day. I wish there was a way we could avoid feeling these uncomfortable emotions.

There was a long period of my life where I did as much as possible to avoid my emotions and perfectly control everything around me. But unfortunately, no matter how hard I try, no matter how hard I see those around me try, it's impossible. Being uncomfortable, out of control, not knowing, and experiencing pain is an inevitable part of life. In all my desperate searching, in all the work I've done in disasters, with the abject poor, and the extremely wealthy, I have not found a way to avoid uncomfortable emotions or painful situations. But I have found that if we sit in them and let them flow through us, they are WAY less disturbing than we predict, and they rarely last as long as we dread they might.

If we are to process our fear around external situations, events, people and things, it's essential to know the fundamentals of how emotions work.

Primary and secondary emotions

Emotions are energy in motion; they are flowing, changing states of being. We can have any number of emotional reactions to situations, and we often base these reactions on our beliefs—conscious and especially subconscious. However, the opposite is also true. Our emotions can have an unconscious effect on our beliefs. That's one reason why it's important to understand feelings because they can offer deep insight and huge energy to provide the change we want to see in our lives.

Emotions are like a layer cake. We have different layers of emotions, but to get to the core layer, we need to acknowledge and process the layers that are over the top of it. There are two main categories of emotions: primary and secondary. Primary emotions are core emotions. Primary emotions are the genuine reactions we have to things, such as seeing a snake and being scared, or someone stealing our food and being angry. These are root emotions that are natural reactions to circumstances. Primary emotions are often one of four emotions: sadness, fear, anger or happiness. I love primary emotions because they usually have a message for us. Perhaps it's that we need to take that leap of faith and change jobs, or that we are ready to go to the next level in a relationship.

Primary emotions are a close connection to our intuition. They guide us in what is and isn't working in our lives. They help us see what we need to heal, and which relationships will support us in our healing process. Primary emotions are the energy of life. They are the engine that motivates us to return to love. Primary emotions are the signs on our path that tell us which way to go. Even the primary feeling of fear is such a gift because it tells us that there is something dangerous ahead, and we need to change directions quickly.

I remember when I was in Syria, I was in a car waiting to go through a checkpoint. All of a sudden, there was automatic gunfire coming from about 10 metres away, and I automatically crouched down in my seat to hide, without looking to see who or why there were gunshots. My driver started laughing at me because it turned out it was just the soldiers operating the checkpoint and simply shooting in the air to disperse the large crowd. But I'm glad I had my reaction. At that moment, fear was the perfect reaction to have!

Secondary emotions, however, are much more diverse and complex. They are the emotions that cover the primary emotion and are emotional reactions to our primary emotions. They are emotions that are used to reduce or make our primary emotions more bearable.

The feeling of fear is particularly challenging for people to stay in or process because it makes people feel vulnerable or weak or powerless, which is a very uncomfortable feeling. Therefore, anger is a prevalent secondary emotion in response to primary fear because anger feels much more powerful; one feels more in control and in charge when they have anger. For example, a mother who has lost her child only to find them later will often respond in anger to finding the child. She will scold the child for running away, and this anger is a secondary emotion. Deep down, she's not angry with the child, deep down, she was frightened that something had happened to the child.

It is documented that in disasters, domestic violence and gender-based violence increases. This is because people are stressed, and to deal with that stress, they become angry with those who have less power. This anger is an attempt to make perpetrators feel more in control when there is chaos. However, beating your wife because you are stressed is not a healthy or helpful way to deal with fear. Not only will it increase your stress and anxiety, but it will also increase your guilt and slowly destroy your support systems.

Conversely, I regularly see clients who are genuinely sad but then hate themselves for being depressed. The primary emotion is sadness, but the secondary emotion could be disgust or self-loathing. Secondary emotions are our way of reducing uncomfortable feelings within ourselves, but they can often cause more problems than they are trying to solve because they distract us from primary emotions.

The more we consume ourselves with the secondary emotions, the more convoluted we get, and the more we avoid and leave the primary emotions unresolved. For example, I will often tell my clients that for the next week (sometimes longer), they are not allowed to answer the question, "why?" This is because I find people often use confusion, or trying to understand "why" as a way to evade what is. Someone might be heartbroken because a relationship ended, but instead of just facing that heartbreak and processing it, they try to circumvent it by being consumed with what went wrong, and how and why it ended. When they get answers, they don't listen to those answers and continue wrestling with why the relationship ended rather than accepting it's over and processing the hurt, pain, and sadness.

I find it useful to distinguish between primary and secondary emotions because it helps us know where we need to focus. Secondary emotions need to be acknowledged and accepted before a person can drop down into primary emotions, but they don't need to be overly focused on them. Secondary emotions give us insight into our unconscious beliefs and any wounds that we might have that need to be healed. They are the expression of what needs to be accepted and integrated within us. Primary emotions, on the other hand, need to be felt, processed and listened to. We don't need to obey what they say, but they often have profound wisdom that we need to hear. The subconscious mind is sometimes referred to as the feeling mind, and so paying attention to, processing and understanding our emotions is the gateway to healing our subconscious beliefs.

Physical care

Just as emotions are essential to listen to, it's important to note that some emotions come from our physical state, and our physical body affects the state of our thoughts and emotions.

If you are going through a difficult time, don't underestimate the power of the physical body. Notice if you're more depressed in winter, or irritable when you're hungry. Sometimes our emotions are just telling us that we need more sleep or sunlight. In my first session with clients, I always try to ask about their exercise, eating and sleeping habits. We don't need to make everything profound. If someone isn't sleeping or eating well, their emotions will be all over the place. It doesn't matter what other healing modalities you use. It's crucial to ensure you are getting the sleep and nutrients that you need. Sleep is vital: the body can last longer without food than without sleep. It's also possible to get too much sleep. All of us need different amounts of sleep, so find what works best for your body,

Often when we are stressed or depressed, we can either stop eating or overeat, especially processed or carb-heavy food. Undereating and overeating are both common symptoms of distress, but they can make our problems more difficult. Get the help of a nutritionist if you are struggling and try to eat five servings of fruits and vegetables a day. New research is emerging, which shows a correlation between gut health and anxiety. So, if you find you have anxiety, then try increasing your consumption of probiotics.

In terms of exercise, I can't speak highly enough for it; it's one of those five birds with one stone type deals. Exercise helps with physical health, helps improve sleep, reduces stress, increases self-confidence, and is just as effective in treating some types of depression as anti-depressants! Additionally, when you do exercise that alternates each side of your body, such as walking, running, swimming or biking, that aids the communication between the right and left hemispheres of your brain, which helps in processing events and emotions.

If you have taken care of your physical needs and you're still struggling with uncomfortable emotions, or you have experienced a difficult event that you know you need work through, there are some simple techniques you can do to process your emotions. Processing your emotions can help you get down to the primary emotions and clear away all the unnecessary heavy emotions you might be carrying around.

Processing emotions

The human body/mind/spirit is very resilient, and so sometimes it can heal on its own without any specific techniques or outside assistance. For example, in the humanitarian field, it is well known that it can be detrimental to use the method of "debriefing" people after a traumatic event. Research shows that forcing someone to talk about a traumatic event over and over when they don't want to causes harm. For others, talking about a traumatic event can be healing. The central difference between harm and healing is the willingness of the person. Don't feel like you have to force yourself to talk. Try to listen to your inner wisdom when choosing techniques to heal and always exercise compassion when going through this process.

The following is a straightforward technique that I often use to process my uncomfortable emotions.

1. Take some time to sit still and in a comfortable position.
2. Ground yourself.
3. Label the emotions that you are feeling right now. Start with the biggest emotion. For example, "I feel angry."
4. Let the emotion flood you. Let it fill up your whole body. Really delve into feeling the emotion. Feel the emotion crashing over you like a tidal wave. If you start to feel scared that the emotion will overwhelm you, remember your grounding.
5. Then imagine your heart is breathing in that emotion and then breathing it out to release it. Have your heart breathe the emotion in and out until the emotion fades, and perhaps a new one comes up (in which case you start from step 1 again). Do this breathing through your heart until you feel a sense of peace or perhaps numbness, which is your heart's way of saying it's processed enough for now.

At first, I tried doing this technique by just having the heart breathe the emotion out, but I found I wasn't able to release it unless my heart breathed it in first. I'm not quite sure why this is the case, perhaps it has to do with acceptance. Breathing an emotion in is like accepting it, and only once we've acknowledged it are we able to breathe it out and release it.

If getting flooded by your emotions seems too intimidating, you can always try good old-fashioned journaling. Journaling is fabulous if you want to process emotions and notice patterns coming up in your life, but you don't want to talk to anyone about them. Journaling is like being a therapist to yourself. It's a beautiful way to sort out and untangle the jumble of emotions in our head and heart. We are often worried or anxious about something and think about it over and over in our minds, which makes it seem exponentially larger than it is. Once we finally express what's inside us, we realize that the problem isn't nearly as big as we thought.

Furthermore, for us to make progress, we need to acknowledge and express the emotions we have, and we need to do this before we can do anything else. Many times, people want to jump to the solving part, but as I tell my clients, you can't fly from Vancouver to London unless you know where Vancouver airport is, go there, and check-in. Journaling can help you sort out what is truly bothering you and what your primary emotions are. Just knowing these two things can sometimes make the problem evaporate. Dream journaling is also an excellent way to see patterns from your subconscious that keep coming up.

Self-compassion

As with all fear, if you want to overcome it and choose love, you need to start with self-compassion. There are many things you can do for yourself that can assist in your healing journey. But to process any emotions, especially uncomfortable ones, self-compassion is essential. Often, we create suffering by judging ourselves for how we reacted to an event. For example, you can be upset with yourself for not doing more when someone robbed you. Self-compassion is massive. You already have to overcome the ramifications this fearful experience has elicited in you, don't add self-judgment or self-flagellation.

I have often seen what is called "survivor's guilt," where people witnessed something terrible happen to someone else and feel guilty that it didn't happen to them. I encountered this a lot in disasters I have worked in and have experienced this myself after I came back from Haiti. This way of thinking is not only unhelpful but detrimental. I can't tell you why our life unfolds the way it does, but guilt is one of those secondary emotions that only deflects us from looking at the heart of the issue. Guilt is rampant in our culture and has no positive benefits. So have compassion for yourself! Know that there are a hundred ways to react to any single situation and don't compare yourself to others. An easy method to increase self-compassion is to please take the word "should" completely out of your vocabulary. Instead of saying "should" you can say "I choose to" or "I choose not to." These are much more empowering statements.

The heart connection technique is one of my all-time favourites and helps create self-compassion. When you can visualize your heart and hear what it's saying and feeling, you separate yourself from the emotions you are experiencing. This allows you to understand and have compassion for your heart as it is having all these emotions. Self-compassion involves being able to label the different emotions that you are having and accepting the fact that you have these emotions. It's not judging yourself or the situation, or why or if you should have these emotions. All emotions want to be seen. Once you see them, and only once you see them, can they then transform or evaporate or give you wisdom as to what you need to do or pay attention to in your life.

In the coming chapters, I will detail how I have experienced external fears, how they have affected me, and how I've processed both primary and secondary reactions to these fears.

Chapter 11
Haiti – PTSD

A couple of times, I mentioned how I ended up scarred from my deployment to Haiti after the earthquake in 2010. I think I struggled so much because I had some unconscious beliefs that were motivating me and because I saw some truly horrible things.

The earthquake was unlike anything many of us had seen. The destruction and ruin, and the sheer number of people that died. The UN estimate that around 300,000 Haitians were killed from this incident. It was complete pandemonium as we humanitarians scrambled to assist. Many non-government organizations (NGOs) will state that the earthquake response was a disaster. There were so many organizations that it was almost impossible to coordinate. There were ad hock "camps" everywhere where people made live-in structures from sticks and tarps. Many people were afraid to stay indoors, even if there were spaces for them to live. Basic necessities were hard to get because governmental corruption was rampantly preventing the ability to bring in much-needed supplies. The security was perilous, with up to 52 kidnappings happening per day as people desperately tried to make money to take care of their families. No systems such as electricity, sewage, or even street signs were in place, and many of the roads remained blocked with rubble more than a year after the earthquake had struck. It was complicated trying to complete seemingly simple tasks.

This is a blog entry that I wrote in December 2010.

Phew! A lot has happened in the last week! After the election results came out, there was total chaos in the streets. I was woken up in the middle of the night by the sound of protesters shouting and marching. We heard gunshots and helicopters, and there was smoke everywhere from all the barricades that were set up on every street.

On Wednesday, there were zero cars out, anyone driving in a car got rocks thrown at them, and there was no point in driving because of all the blockades. We were even told not to go on the balcony of our guesthouse for fear of people shooting at us, as there is a lot of anti-white sentiment (which I can understand).

Thursday was a little better, so we went for a walk staying near to our guesthouse. It wasn't long until we encountered a crowd of people protesting when all-of-the-sudden this massive crowd of people came running towards us. We were paralyzed and stopped in our tracks, not knowing what to do. Then we heard gunshots, and the three of us panicked. We all ducked into a side street, which amused a group of nearby Haitian men who laughed at us. I laughed awkwardly and made signs of my heart beating way out of my chest, which made us all laugh, and they made motions of the gunfire just being the police shooting into the air. Sheeesh! It served to be a bit of a bonding moment between the Haitian men and us, and we talked to them a bit about the election in a mixed mash of languages. But soon after, we retreated to our guesthouse.

Not to be defeated, however, the next day we went out again (despite the city STILL being shut down) we walked around our area again and met some more Haitians in an IDP camp nearby. We told them that we did workshops on techniques to deal with stress and trauma and met with the director of the camp who was extremely organized and set up a tent and benches to do our presentation. The presentation went all right, but it's hard for people to understand how doing relaxing techniques can help them improve their lives when they haven't eaten for a day. I can understand where they're coming from... we learned that we have to frame it in a way that is tangible to them. Common symptoms of trauma are not being able to sleep, lack of motivation, and increased anger, all of which inhibit their day-to-day survival. However, we are trying to work on a plan that can address their many physical and mental needs. That is the complexity of Haiti.

By Friday, the roads had opened up again (although not the airport or the Canadian consulate) and so we went back to the big camp we had been working in before all the lockdowns. It was chaos there, with the pastor being in worse condition. We agreed to pay for him to go to the hospital. I then led a healing group, which was incredible. People were really open and although we still got lots of requests for food and medicine (and houses, and a medical clinic, and a school, and an orphanage) people really felt the difference from before we started the group compared to after, and they are excited to work with me throughout the year... so it was encouraging.

The tricky thing about this place is that it has so many problems with so many layers and so many roadblocks trying to solve the issues, but it just requires one to be more creative, right! The good news is people thought there were going to be lots of manifestations all this week, and there haven't been any thus far. Perhaps the UN trucks that regularly patrol the streets with their soldiers out and their rifles poised are intimidating the public not to protest. But somehow, I think all hell is going to break loose as soon as they declare the election recount results, which is December 20th. People say that the reason "Sweet Micky" is so popular is that he is "not a politician," which is seen as the most redeeming quality of all of the 19 candidates. But I digress.

So far, I am very happy, scared at times, and often nervous and overwhelmed, but generally content. The people are incredible! And so friendly (despite disliking us whites in heated moments) and they are so strong! I have such an admiration for these people, and I feel honoured to be in this country! Not to mention the wonderful weather.

On one of my first days, I worked with a new translator. I had him drive me to the camp on a rented motorcycle, or "moto" as they are called there. Here is my blog entry from that day, which will give you an idea of how a seemingly simple day can get off track and complicated quickly.

My newest catchphrase is "it's Haiti" this is my explanation for anything and everything that goes wrong. Many of you have heard me say it when Skype intermittently shuts down, or as a response to your inquiry about what that strange and deafeningly loud sound is in the background. It's often the answer I give when people ask how much I've accomplished in a day. But nothing has been as much of an "it's Haiti" day than today.

Today was the first day trying out my new translator. First, my translator's nickname, as I found out on the way back, is "Sex" yep, Sex, that is just one inkling of what a character he is. Additionally, me being trusting (no not gullible, trusting), I believed him when he said he was good at driving a moto. In his defence, he is quite good, although only by Haitian standards. Also, in his defence, he rented a crap motorbike, so we were bound to have some issues.

The day started with a five-minute endeavour to get the thing started. I should have seen the foreshadowing in that, but like I said, I'm trusting. We did get it started, and yes, it did stall a few times, but usually, it would begin back up again within ten to twenty tries. However, getting it going wasn't the only problem. Balancing also seemed to be a bit of a challenge, as was navigating the hundreds of potholes (if you can call them that, some made ponds in the middle of the road). Add to that Haitian traffic, which is a kind of uncontrolled chaos, and already you have a heart-stopper.

We weaved in and out of oncoming traffic, narrowly missing trucks that were barrelling towards us. Seriously, I've never clenched my thighs so hard for fear of my knees getting clipped by either trucks coming towards us, or vehicles that we were passing. Daniel AKA Sex found me endlessly entertaining, declaring that I "really was a girl" (something I have entirely no problem being). He would vacillate between laughing at me, swearing at the moto, and waving and yelling at people we passed that he knew (which is EVERYONE in the city of Port-au-Prince).

I don't mind his popularity; in fact, it's quite nice because it opens up a lot of doors for me and has facilitated a pretty genuine peek into local Haitian culture thus far. But the fact of the matter is that when he waves and shouts at people, he simultaneously looks back at whomever he's yelling at and is therefore not looking at the road ahead of us. Add to that the fact that he inadvertently swerves in the direction of his wave and the inevitability of this then causing us to hit a pothole head-on, giving my bum a couple of seconds of a free throw, and I started to very much mind his waving.

Then we ran out of gas.

Thankfully, his popularity secured us some gas that was sold out of a dirty old cooking oil container from an equally dirty street vendor. Although it still cost us four times the amount than what is sold at the gas station, hey, "it's Haiti." We then proceeded to precariously make our way to the camp to find that the people I was meeting were running an hour late. So, I went around visiting camp dwellers until they were ready.

After my meeting, I thought it would be nice to visit another nearby camp. Yesterday I had been quite excited that a random person had called me. He was from the nearby camp and had gotten my number from a local psychologist (yes, I'm getting famous too). He wanted me to come and meet him so that we could do work with his camp as well. However, because my first meeting was delayed by an hour, our stroll ended up being situated right under the midday sun. But we were told the camp was right beside the camp we were in right now.

Two MOUNTAINS later, we finally made it. We only had time to have a quick five-minute introduction between the director and me, before we had to rush back so that I could be in time for my group lesson, although looking back, I laugh at my naivety.

The Haitians, bless their souls, are for the most part, very helpful people. So, on our way back as we were following a tiny path, and I realized we had gotten lost, some very kind people willingly walked us towards the "correct" direction. Thank goodness when I travel, my sense of direction is at its best, so it only took me an hour to realize that we were not going in the correct direction. Enter the second batch of "helpful" Haitians. This time it only took me 30 minutes to spot that again we were quite a bit off our target destination. Being "clever" as Daniel calls me, I decided not to follow any more Haitians and finally, with me leading the way, made it back to our original camp only three hours late. The hike was actually quite nice, and Daniel (who is also a famous rapper) played a bunch of songs on his phone and gave me a mini introduction to Haitian hip hop so that our steps were often light and accentuated with raising-the-roof motions. We miraculously arrived at Canaan 2 with enough time to get to my group lesson back in town, but not enough time for me to lead a group in the camp. That was until someone pointed out that the tire was flat on the moto.

It only took a couple of minutes for the repair guy to get the tire off. This led to the discovery that the hole was not a new one and had been previously repaired by simply tying, with string, the segment of the tire into a bunch, so that the hole resembled a deflated balloon. It did take them an hour to try and melt some rubber over the hole to seal it and then gave up and resorted to returning the tire to its previous condition, albeit with more air. This then gave us a limited amount of time for us to go home before I assumed the flat tire would return—that added pressure (pun intended) to the fact that the moto wouldn't start. At first, I laughed at the sight of Daniel on the bike and two guys pushing it running as fast as they could. But after another two hours, the joke got a little old even for me. Then Daniel disappeared for about an hour, my phone died, his ran out of minutes, and I had long given up hope of making my group and instead was trying to stay optimistic about getting home before dark. Finally, after what felt like hours, Daniel and co. got the bike started again. The tire was still functioning, but we were both all too aware of the perils of stopping lest the bike would never start again. Off we went on our journey home, which was again filled with the chaotic-too-horrific-for-a-video game way home. Seriously, there was a point in which a truck blew out this giant billow of thick black smoke so that there were more than a few seconds where we couldn't see anything, and other cars, therefore, could not see us coming. But we managed to get through.

And then we hit a dog.

Daniel, of course, kept on driving, ignoring my cry of dismay, and I was able to look back to see the dog safely stumble to the side of the road.

I made it home, and Daniel has just called me to let me know that he made it home too and that he misses me. Really what more can I say than hey, "it's Haiti."

The beautiful thing about Haiti was that it seemed like anything was possible. However, that was a double-edged sword and part of the reason why I got PTSD. These entries paint a picture of what it was like, but it wasn't until the end of my time that I got glimpses into the darker sides that are a part of every society, but especially when there is no sense of law. It was the senseless death and hopelessness that shattered my heart.

One time I was called to a camp because there was an emergency. The camp residents were stoning an eight-year-old boy because he had raped a six-month-old baby. A colleague and I had to intervene to save the boy from being killed. In my mind, if a boy that small knows how to have sex with something, he probably had been sexually abused himself. It broke my heart that someone so young was in pain and causing pain to a baby because of his own dark experiences, and that poor baby girl who didn't know what was going on and was just crying with the blood of her broken hymen on her tiny white dress.

We mediated between the little girl's family and the boy and his family, and the organization I worked with was able to get the boy to safety. We ended up having to evacuate him to another part of the country so that he wouldn't be murdered. Then, over the coming months, we worked with the baby girl's family to assist in healing. I'm glad I was able to give compassion and kindness to that little boy who was so hated by everyone else and was silent and stone-faced. Although I don't know if the little boy understood how what he did was wrong, and how was he going to get healing? I also worked with the baby girl's family. Although the girl won't have a conscious memory of what happened, she'll have a bodily memory. Being raped could be quite debilitating to her in the future without her consciously knowing why. I'm not sure if her family will tell her what happened once she's old enough to understand. Sometimes, as a humanitarian and a psychotherapist, you get especially affected by certain cases. This was one of those cases. I still think of that little boy and the baby girl. I hope they're ok.

Then, a couple of months later, a colleague of mine was killed. It was an utterly senseless death that happened because he got in a drunken fight with some people. They allegedly got so mad at him that they ran over him repeatedly with their motorcycle. I'm not sure if the police did an investigation to find the people who did it. Before this incident, another humanitarian had been killed because he fell off the roof of a place I had stayed at for two weeks. And then I had also found out that another humanitarian had died because they had gotten malaria and dengue fever at the same time. I've since known many people who have died this way.

Having these deaths happen one after the other in a short period beat me up emotionally. But my breaking point occurred after about 10 months of being there. I had just emerged from being bedridden because of a debilitating bout of Typhoid that affected not only my physical strength, but also my mental strength. I felt fragile and barely able to get out of bed, even after two weeks of being sick.

I was taking a moto with my translator to the main camp where I worked. There was another moto driving one metre in front of us, and a semi-truck was passing both of us. I can still see the driver on his moto starting to sway fiercely back and forth, trying desperately to maintain his balance as the semi-truck drove closer to us both. Pushing us to the edge of the road and nearly into some of the people and stalls lining it (of course in Haiti, there aren't lanes that people drive in), the moto started swerving more violently. And then, in slow motion, I watched as he swerved so forcefully that he fell over right under the semi-truck.

We veered abruptly and avoided hitting him, but I still saw the wheels of the semi-truck run over him, and I heard the crunching of his bones. I waved frantically at the truck driver to stop, but he stopped right on top of the man, so I frantically motioned at the driver to reverse so the truck would be off him. I remember seeing the man have a seizure and thinking that I didn't even know of a hospital that we could take him to. He died soon after, and all of us on the sidelines felt utterly sick and hopeless.

I was sobbing as we finally left to continue on our way to the camp. When I arrived, the people did not care about what we had just seen. But I guess how could they when they had already too much to deal with themselves? But they tried joking to me about how one of the camp leaders was now in the hospital because he had been beaten "within an inch of his life" and wasn't it funny? And wasn't he stupid? And I just went numb with how cheap life seemed here, how easy it was for people to die. How much did people have to shut off their hearts to deal with the daily tragedies?

But my final breaking point was right after making jokes. One of my staff pulled me aside to ask me if I could take her child with me when I went back to Canada. I knew that sending your children away is a common practice for those with little money, to the point that they will pretend their kids are orphans in the hopes they will get adopted. Parents believe that their children will have a better life with wealthier people. But it has led to a whole industry of child sex slaves, where these children certainly do not have a better life. I knew that this woman trusted me so much that she was willing to give me her child, and I should see this request as an honour. This lovely little boy who had been with her every day as she came to work and who I'd seen grow wonderfully over the year. And she was willing to give him up? I got it. I got where she was coming from. But I was already so shattered that I interpreted it as a sign of hopelessness, and for some reason, it just destroyed my heart that she wanted to give her boy to me.

And I broke.

Thankfully, I only had a month to go before my contract finished. By this time, my team was confident, compassionate and powerful leaders in their own right. I stepped away from leading groups myself and focused on just supervising and getting things as organized as possible so that things could continue after I left.

Perhaps if I hadn't been driven by my unconscious beliefs that I was selfish, or that I was a bad person or the mistaken belief that they needed me to survive, then I would have been able to handle it all better. I went in wanting to help, and I got completely and utterly overwhelmed with the misery, hopelessness and suffering that I encountered. I had an agenda, and instead of witnessing and meeting people where they were, I wanted to change them, to make them happier because that would prove to my insatiable internal fears that I was a good person. I was so focused on what I couldn't or didn't achieve that I drove myself to a mental breakdown. No matter how hard I tried, I wasn't going to take away the suffering of the Haitians. They would still have to live in poverty and violence. Although my heart was in the right place, and I do believe I was able to empower hundreds if not thousands of people, I didn't see that in the end, they didn't really need me. This mistake cost me my own well-being and sanity, which wasn't necessary.

I don't know for sure, but I believe that if I had healed my unconscious fears and had operated out of love and respect for humanity, then I could have been more effective, and I wouldn't have crawled out of Haiti. I could have supported and empowered more people without the mental and physical destruction of myself.

From that day forward, I became a shell of a human. I could no longer connect to emotion of any kind. My heart felt numb. I drank alcohol to a destructive and detrimental degree. I lost myself and who I was and what I was doing. I had given my word to stay for a year, and so I did, right down to the day, but I should have left. My word is less important than personal integrity, and I lost my integrity. I lost my ability to love and to care on that day.

It took me two years to heal from Haiti.

A phenomenal therapist and now a dear friend of mine, Alyson Jones, talked to me while I was in Haiti. She could see before I could, how run down and coming to pieces I was. She offered to make me an associate in her practice in West Vancouver and convinced me to return to Canada. So, after travelling around Central America for a couple of months, I returned to Vancouver. With her help, I started my own private practice, which became very successful. For the next two years, I dedicated myself to my private practice and focused on my mental and emotional healing. I started gradually letting go of the overwhelming guilt I had for leaving Haiti. I began to meditate more regularly and did yoga.

I hired a therapist to help me deal with my secondary trauma and the flashbacks of dead bodies that kept on intruding in my brain. I regularly had sessions with an energy worker, Heidi Reid, who does Bodytalk. Slowly but surely, I started to heal. The flashbacks came less and less often. I did a technique called Lifespan Integration to fully heal my traumatic memories. Then I learned the technique to assist my clients who had post-traumatic stress disorder.

But most of all, I learned that I could care, but I can't drown in my own caring. I finally learned not just in my head, but in my heart as well, that people have their own inner strength and wisdom that I need to respect. I don't need to be anyone's saviour. I don't know and will never know the ins and outs of another person's life, of their struggles and joys, of their successes and failures. Most of all, my job as a psychotherapist and humanitarian is to help people get in touch with these wise, strong, beautiful parts of themselves. To respect those who are suffering, to know that they survived before they knew me, and they will survive after I leave, and I need to trust in this. I can't fix anyone. I can share some techniques that many people have found useful. I can be a guide, but they have to take the actual journey.

Post-traumatic stress disorder and secondary trauma

There are different levels of fearful experiences, and our reaction to them is not necessarily based on the intensity or negativity of the experience. An experience to one person can create a strong negative reaction, whereas the same experience might not affect another person. Our responses to fearful occurrences are influenced and moulded by our previous experiences, personalities, way of thinking, the support systems we have in place, our age, sex, and level of resilience. There is no right or wrong reaction. We have to honour the emotions that come up for us and not judge ourselves for having different feelings than what other people appear to have.

So, if you have suffered a trauma, if you have felt overwhelmed by the pain and sorrow around you, please try to focus and get in touch with your inner strength, your inner knowing. I hope the exercises thus far, such as the heart connection, are able to help you on that journey. Please know that you are not alone. You can and will succeed if you keep on trying. There are many people you can ask for assistance on this crazy journey of life.

Post-traumatic stress disorder (PTSD)

Sometimes our bodies, minds and hearts can't deal with particular events. This can be for many reasons, some of which we don't quite understand. It could be because of unconscious beliefs or childhood experiences or the simple nature of the events. When you suffer from a trauma or even witness one firsthand, you could develop PTSD. Symptoms include having such a high level of fear that it is affecting your life in a substantial and limiting way, such as, preventing you from socializing, affecting your physical health, interfering with your sleep, or making it difficult to do your job because it's difficult to concentrate. If you've had these symptoms for six months or longer, then you might have PTSD. If you think you might be suffering from PTSD, which can affect those who have gone through anything from car accidents or sexual assault to something that was perceived traumatic by you but might not have been for others, then make sure you seek professional help. You can visit your doctor, a psychologist or a psychiatrist to see if you are suffering from PTSD.

Secondary trauma is when you've seen, or even just heard about someone's traumatic experience, and it really upsets you, and you can't get over it. Usually, it's someone with whom you have an emotional connection. There are too many symptoms to list here, but secondary trauma will often negatively affect your worldview or how you see things. Frequently to cope, you shut down emotionally. Secondary trauma is a confusion of boundaries and can happen to those who are very empathic or who regularly hear about the suffering of others. Instead of joining in someone's pain, you are merging with it. When I was in Haiti, I had poor boundaries, and I merged with the pain of the people I was working with. That's what led to me getting traumatized.

Even though nothing traumatic happened to me personally, I also developed PTSD because of some of the things I had directly seen. I have since endured more extreme events than the ones I witnessed after the earthquake, but without getting PTSD. Perhaps it was because that was my first real humanitarian mission, and I probably had so many unconscious beliefs that drove my outlook and behaviour, so that mission created some post-traumatic symptoms for me. It's hard to really know or predict what will traumatize us. Many events can create responses of anxiety, stress or trauma, and these events will be different for each person.

Healing post-traumatic stress disorder and secondary trauma.

If you are diagnosed with PTSD, then research has shown the symptoms will not go away with time. Often, time heals wounds, but in this case, it doesn't. PTSD is notoriously difficult to treat, as can be seen by the high suicide rate of war veterans. If you or someone you know might have it, please make sure you or your loved one gets professional assistance. Some medications can help, and there is new emerging research on psychedelic drugs being helpful as well, but there are also forms of psychotherapy that can help. Research has shown that Eye Movement Desensitization and Reprocessing (EMDR) has been quite successful in treating PTSD symptoms, and a technique called Lifespan Integration. Both these techniques are useful for treating PTSD, secondary trauma or other troubling memories or events.

EMDR

EMDR facilitates the processing of traumatic memories or other adverse experiences. It is not only used for those who have PTSD, although it has been shown to be successful in treating PTSD. It works by clients briefly thinking of the stressful event while also focusing on an external stimulus such as the therapist tapping their knee or visual stimulation if that's preferable. This external stimulus that happens as you recall the stressful memory facilitates communication between the right and left hemispheres of the brain. The therapist helps the client process the stuck traumatic memory by improving rational and logical thinking and connecting the traumatic memory to other, more pleasant memories. This creates new learning for the client as well as new insights, which can be powerful. It also helps the client build new skills for more adaptive functioning. I have not been trained in EMDR, and so my understanding of its benefits and intricacies are limited. However, I know of many people who have been successfully treated with this technique.

Lifespan integration

When I returned from Haiti, I used Lifespan Integration, energy work, and a lot of my own self-work to heal my PTSD. Although this combination was very effective for me, all of us will gravitate towards different healing modalities. I have since learned how to do Lifespan Integration and have been continuously amazed at how well it works.

Lifespan Integration is based on the premise that we have a core self. Whenever something stressful or traumatic happens to us that we don't know how to process, we slice off a piece of our core self and leave it with that event in a box and shove it down. If there are many of these events, our core self gets smaller and weaker and less able to handle future traumatic events. An event in the present can trigger or remind us of previous events. This trigger generates a more substantial reaction because we are reacting to both the current and past events.

The technique involves writing out simple, one-sentence memories from your life so that the therapist can train your brain and make new, stronger neural pathways into the present. We are teaching your brain that you are no longer in that traumatic event but have survived it and are here now. As it makes these neural pathways, it also collects those parts of your core self left in the past so that your present core self becomes more integrated and robust.

Trauma is like a knot in your brain, and emotions and memories get stuck in that knot, replaying your trauma repeatedly. With the Lifespan Integration technique that knot becomes untied, the right and left hemispheres connect and process the event, and emotions can freely flow. The result is that you remember the event, but you forget why you were upset over it. Before I begin Lifespan Integration with my clients, I have them rate how disturbing the event is. If I don't, then once we've finished the process, the memory is such a non-issue that they forget why we were focusing on it.

One of the traumatic events that was giving me flashbacks was of the moto driver being run over by the semi-truck. The practitioner had me write out one sentence memories of that event step by step and one sentence memories after that event until the present. Then the therapist would read these memories in quick succession to me as I'd visualize them. We did this until we got to the present moment, and then we would start the whole process over again. It is incredibly tedious, but by the end, I was able to see the event yet not be emotionally triggered by it.

It is vital that if you do this treatment, you ensure that a registered therapist trained in Lifespan Integration is conducting it as anything involving trauma can have the possibility of re-traumatizing clients. For more information on Lifespan Integration, please go to lifespanintegration.com.

PTSD is an example of a learned fear. It's an authentic reaction to a very real event. Your body is warning you to avoid situations like that in the future; however, your body goes a bit overboard. Again, you must get outside assistance in dealing with this. Your brain is stuck, and it needs outside help to get unstuck. Once you understand that you have these fears, which you've learned directly or indirectly, it's a lot easier to process and heal them. As always, acknowledging and labelling what's going on needs to be the first step before you "solve" any issue.

Chapter 12
Attacked in Sierra Leone

Most learned fears don't traumatize us and are just labelled as frightening. These events can still paralyze you and negatively impact your life without giving you PTSD. Processing fearful events and then healing from them can seem daunting. You will process in your own way, and for some people, pretending like it's not a big deal or that it never happened can work for them. For me, doing that just made my life infinitely worse, so I hope you can be true to yourself and also learn from my mistakes.

In my 38 years, I have hitchhiked all over the world, almost died in a ski accident, been robbed and forced to sleep in a park in Manila, been attacked by a herd of elephants and almost trapped in a bush fire. But I had never experienced someone physically harming me until I was in Sierra Leone. Even in Haiti, where kidnappings were common, I felt mostly safe. I led a stress management group for all the prominent gang leaders in Port-au-Prince, so all the most dangerous people knew me and often went out of their way to make sure I was protected. But in Sierra Leone, I encountered firsthand one of the scariest events of my life.

As part of the Ebola response, I was in Sierra Leone, one of three

West African countries with a large deadly outbreak. The Ebola epidemic was challenging and stressful for a variety of reasons. First and foremost is the fear that you may get Ebola, which I think many people will be able to relate to with the Pandemic. Another stress was the hatred, or at least the dislike and fear that I felt aimed at me from people and governments worldwide, especially from those in my own country. Although I knew how Ebola was transmitted, there was lots of fear and misinformation around the world. Although I knew it was impossible to be infectious unless I showed symptoms, others were terrified of me. Those of us who worked that epidemic felt like global lepers. For me, who knew the facts and was careful never to put others in danger, I felt profoundly rejected and even hated by the world.

It was not much better in Sierra Leone. Local people believed that foreigners brought the disease, and they were convinced the USA created it as a type of biowarfare. This idea was insidious, resulting in fear and hatred for anyone who was white. When I worked for the Red Cross, our cars would get pelted with stones as we drove. Health care workers would get attacked and sometimes killed. There was so much death that a new job sector emerged: burial workers. But because burial workers couldn't follow traditional burial practices as that is what spread Ebola, they were seen as traitors and driven from their villages and kicked out of their families.

Part of my job was to create a psychosocial support program to assist communities, survivors of Ebola and specifically burial workers. Burial workers not only dealt with the death and fear of contracting Ebola but like Ebola survivors, they also had to deal with the rejection and hatred by their friends and loved ones. I also worked with witch doctors, community leaders, pastors, and imams to facilitate accurate, up-to-date communication on how Ebola is spread. We would collaborate on how they could keep their communities safe. I mediated between exiled community members and their communities to get them reintegrated. Lastly, I facilitated dialogue and trust between communities and non-governmental organizations to increase Ebola case reporting. I eventually was awarded a medal of honour from the Canadian Government for the work I did during this time.

But even with the fear of getting Ebola, death all around us, and the hatred both in Sierra Leone and around the world, what rattled me the most was what happened on New Year's Eve, 2015.

The Ebola outbreak had finished with no new cases since October, and Ebola was declared officially over in November. For New Year, I was at a beach hostel with my husband, Francois, and my brother Max, who was visiting for a few weeks. There was a big beach party that night, but thankfully Francois and I had decided we weren't going to drink. We all danced on the beach with everyone having a good time. The three of us were the only white people and so stuck out quite a bit. Some people were either remarkably kind and welcoming to us white people, while others became increasingly hostile. Francois and I often came to this beach hostel on the weekends, and so I knew some people. But there were thousands of people there from all over the country. Ebola had only been finished for a little over a month, so, having big gatherings was still a novel and exciting thing.

I, having the smallest bladder in the world, had to go pee. It was past midnight and the atmosphere was getting harsher as people started getting drunker, so Francois and my brother thankfully accompanied me to the bushes on the beach's edge. As we walked back to the beach and talked about calling it a night, a group of guys approached us and asked Francois for money. They seemed pretty out of it like they were on some sort of drugs, or perhaps they were just really drunk. Being the only girl, I wanted to get myself out of the way so that I would be less of a liability and hurried ahead of the group of guys, trying to get to our bungalow.

I don't know how the leader was able to ninja towards me, but he did. The next thing I knew, he grabbed me around the neck with both hands and started gently strangling me and dragging me away towards his friends. My brother and Francois froze, and the last thing I could see as he dragged me away was the remainder of the guys moving towards Francois and Max and slowly starting to surround them. I knew I was on my own.

The guy was strangling me, but not to the point that I couldn't breathe; it seemed more like he was trying to drag me away by my throat. He was forcing me further into the darkness.

Time literally slowed down.

I remember thinking that I wanted to hurt him, but not too much that I would kill him or leave permanent damage, but just enough so that he would let me go and not come after me. I decided that I would punch him in the nose, but not too hard to make the bone go into his brain. I now realize that I didn't have to worry about doing that because I'm not that strong. But at the time, I really thought I could, and you never know how strong adrenaline makes you. I managed to twist myself a bit so that I could make a sweeping punch right to his nose. I caught him off guard; he stumbled back slightly and ever so subtly released his grip on my neck. I pounced on the opportunity and twisted out of his grasp, elbowing him in the stomach to propel me away.

I ran as fast as I could in the sand.

I screamed, "Help! Help!" as loud as I was able, but no one did anything. No one dancing even looked at me. I felt so utterly helpless. I was worried that the guy was running after me and that Francois and Max were getting beat up. Still, I didn't want to waste a second in pausing to look behind me. Thankfully, my brother and Francois heard my screaming. They thought that I was in new trouble and so got away from the group of guys to run towards my scream; they were completely unharmed. I think I was in a time warp where it felt like I was being dragged forever, but in reality, I escaped before the group of guys had even reached Francois and Max.

We went back to our rooms, shaken. I was numb and bleeding from four fingernail scratches across my neck, but I was ok.

Now I want to be clear that I am fortunate that I keep my wits about me in emergencies. In terms of either the fight, flight or freeze response, I can fight. In our security training, they teach us that this is an innate trait and that it's very difficult to change your innate responses. Instead, you have to plan for them. Many people in my situation would have frozen or tried to run away but not been able to, and there is no blame on you if that is your reaction. I feel so lucky that I could fight my way out of a situation that would most likely have ended up in me getting raped numerous times and possibly killed. Be compassionate on yourself if you have acted differently in a similar case and know that sexual assault is never your fault.

Processing fearful events

If your intuition tells you that it's time to process an experience and you don't have PTSD symptoms, then it is possible to use the techniques in this book. However, I always recommend that you get support. Humans need each other. You don't have to go through this alone.

First and foremost, remind yourself that you are safe. We talked about Lifespan Integration in the PTSD section, and a big part of that technique is showing your brain that you are now safe. We can take that concept into these situations and repeatedly remind ourselves that it is over. Such and such has happened, but now you are here and safe. Perhaps saying this aloud to yourself will be even more helpful as that helps things feel more real. Unfortunately, in my situation, I elected to pretend nothing had happened and tried not to think about what I narrowly escaped.

Additionally, some research suggests giving your body a thorough shake after a stressful incident to release all the stress hormones that have flooded your system. Sometimes people will have seizers that do this instinctually. But I like just to give my arms, legs and then body a shake after I've experienced a stressful event. If you watch animal documentaries, you'll find that after they escape a predator, they will often give themselves a shake. It's a comforting way of signalling to your mind that you're in the clear, and the stressful event has passed. I love simple techniques that don't require too much effort.

Stressful situations are where grounding is critical too. Try to ground yourself as often as possible. That will help your body to process the event on its own without you even knowing it. You can ground using the visualizations of the tree roots growing out of your feet or the cord attached to your spine and connecting you to the centre of the earth. I constantly ground myself, and I think that was my saving grace after this event, for which I am thankful.

Lastly, there is something called the "butterfly technique" where you cross your arms over your chest so that it's almost as if you're hugging yourself. Rest your right hand on your left shoulder and your left hand on your right shoulder. The crossing of the arms on opposite sides helps the right and left hemispheres to connect and process emotions and thoughts, including trauma. Gently alternate between tapping each hand a couple of times and say a comforting or healing statement. Some examples of healing statements could be, "Even though I'm scared, I know that I am safe," or "Even though I'm lonely, I know that I am loved." It's good to have the first part of the statement acknowledge what you are feeling right now, and then the second part to be where you want to get to or a phrase of love or healing. Make sure you don't use harsh or hurtful statements because then that gets tapped into you. The butterfly technique is also a great thing to teach kids.

After that assault, I was in shock. I wasn't able to process what had happened, and certainly not what could have happened. This attack occurred a year after I had already lived and worked in the Ebola outbreak, and I think it was too much for my brain and heart to compute. That is ok. Our body can only handle as much as it can handle. Above all, it's imperative that we are compassionate to ourselves when trying to process events like these.

Healing painful events

Processing and healing are slightly different. All events need to be processed. Processing an incident is just letting your body know that the event is over, and you are now ok. It's accepting and understanding what happened. Healing painful events is deeper. It involves healing the fears or the pain or the hurt that the incident might have caused. Not all events need to be healed, and just because you have processed an incident, it doesn't mean you have healed it.

If you want to heal, you need to forgive. I know that word can be difficult, daunting or even triggering for a lot of you, so I think it's helpful to break down the steps to forgiveness and then the steps of forgiveness as I see them.

1. Self-compassion- Like many of the techniques I have mentioned, this one is fundamental for so many different situations. You must have compassion for yourself in how you acted or didn't act. You did the best you could with what you had. We all make mistakes because we are all human. There is nothing wrong with making a mistake. We just need to get back up and try again. Not trying is the most harmful thing we can do to ourselves and others. The whole purpose of this life we have right now is to experience it. Brené Brown talks about getting in the arena, being vulnerable, and trying our best. If you've done that, then that is the most important thing. Making mistakes is inevitable; it's what we do in response to those mistakes that define us. A wonderful human being sent me a magnet that says, "I never make the same mistake twice…I make it four or five times just to be sure." I look at this every time I start to feel shame in the mistakes that I've made. If you are struggling with self-compassion, you can try the butterfly technique above. Also, keep reading as this whole book is geared towards helping all of us find the love within ourselves.

2. Compassion for others- If possible, see if you can get to a place of compassionate understanding for all actors involved. I know this is easier said than done. Still, your compassion for others (after you have first had compassion for yourself) will significantly improve your own life and well-being. As a humanitarian, it is so vital that we are neutral and willing to assist all sides of a conflict. When I was in Syria, working in places devastated by ISIS, I was still able to have compassion for ISIS soldiers. It didn't mean that I agreed (at all) with what they were doing or had done. But it did reduce the anger and hatred living inside of me. If my goal is to show others love, then I have to be loving to all people. Sometimes I'm more successful at this than other times. I struggled with having compassion for the men who did honour killings on their family members. But it wasn't until I was finally able to have compassion for them that I felt our program became more successful and effective. It's not what we do; it's HOW we do it. How can I assist others if I don't understand where they are coming from? Having compassion for others means understanding their pain and their struggle. You don't need to agree with it, but you must understand it. I believe that everyone is a reflection of yourself, so compassion for others is a natural extension of compassion for yourself. Just like self-love naturally extends into genuinely loving others. Once you are able to have compassion for others, you can start the process of forgiveness.
3. Forgive- I know this is a loaded word for many people, and this can be a crazy concept, but forgiveness is THE key to self-healing. It is at the cornerstone of everything. It is the most powerfully loving thing we can do for ourselves. It is the only thing that will free us from the pain and suffering that fearful events can create. It is the only thing that can free us from our ego. Now to be clear, forgiveness does not mean forgetting.

It also does not mean giving up boundaries. I have forgiven many people, which doesn't mean I'm still going to let all of them live close to my heart. Some yes, but some I have let go. However, once I forgive them, it means there is no longer any resentment connecting us. Forgiveness is different from trust. I can forgive someone, but that doesn't mean I trust them. If they have done something very hurtful and trust has been broken, they still need to rebuild it. However, I'm not holding their mistake over their heads or using it as a bargaining chip. A Course in Miracles says that we are all one with only the perception of separateness. Therefore, when I hurt another, I am hurting myself, and when I am kind to another, I am kind to myself. Forgiveness is the only act that can bring us out of our perception of separateness and back into unity. The three steps of forgiveness are:

a. Exposing- be honest about the hurt the person's actions had on you, understand what you need to forgive, stop and notice different emotions and thoughts that come up and welcome them.
b. Accepting- not judging yourself for what it looks like or feels like, letting it be whatever it is.
c. Handing it over- release the hurt and pain and anger to the universe/holy spirit/high self, don't hold on to it. Let it go, and then it's gone. Forgiveness is a thought of peace when you are in a state of inner turmoil.

Ho'oponopono

Ho'oponopono is a potent tool for forgiveness. It was developed in Hawaii and is the practice of reconciliation and forgiveness. The word Ho'oponopono means "to correct" or "to make right." It was made famous by the work of Dr. Ihaleakala Hew Len, who is said to have been able to heal everyone in a state-run mental hospital over four years by using this process. The hospital treated those who have psychosis and other psychiatric disorders. In his book called "Zero Limits," which he co-wrote, Dr. Len says that he healed each patient without ever seeing them by looking at their file and doing ho'oponopono to mend the part of him that the patient represented. The foundation of this practice is that everything outside us is a reflection of what is inside us. Therefore, when we heal inside ourselves, we also contribute to the healing of others outside of us.

I used Ho'oponopono just recently in healing the last remnants of that assault in Sierra Leone. As I've been delving into and trying to reconcile the racist parts of me, it led me to understand that the anger and hatred that the man had towards me reflected what I have to heal deep down inside of me. Through practicing this technique, I was able to acknowledge my wrongdoing, my own malicious beliefs regardless of how buried they are, and then ask this man for forgiveness. I did this technique over and over until I felt a clearing and lightness in my mind. It was a beautiful moment.

Ho'oponopono is very simple to do.

1. Think of something that is upsetting you. (Perhaps it's how your boss treats you.)
2. See if you can focus on the part of you that is reflected in the situation. (Maybe it's how you act in similar ways to your boss.)
3. Then say the following phrases over and over again to that part of you that resembles hurt (your boss). Do this until you feel the charge has evaporated.
   I am so sorry
   Please forgive me
   Thank you
   I love you.

Many people struggle with saying this to someone they are angry at, and the important thing to keep in mind is that 1) we are all connected, so your anger towards someone else is also anger towards yourself, even if it doesn't feel like it, and 2) our outer world is a reflection of our inner world, so if someone has done something hurtful to us, that means we have that same capacity to hurt, even if we haven't acted on it.

If you can't connect to any of these concepts, that's ok. Try doing the exercise and see if it works, regardless if you fully understand the ideas here. If it doesn't, then perhaps it's not the right time yet, or maybe you would benefit from outside assistance. Like all the techniques I describe in this book, you don't need to worry about if you believe in them wholeheartedly, they will work just as long as you are open to the idea of them working. Just focus on being a teeny bit open, and that is enough.

Unconscious to conscious

Being attacked created a genuine and powerful primary emotion of fear. Still, the shock numbed this emotion, and I shoved it down to my unconscious until my body was ready to explore it a few years later. When I finally started to think about the event, I could still feel remnants of shock and then a hint of anger, which increased as time went on. Both anger and numbness were secondary emotions. But because I was still suppressing them, I couldn't process them, let alone heal my buried primary feeling of fear.

As time went by, my secondary emotions morphed and changed. The shock wore off, and the anger became more insidious. I was frustrated at Francois and Max for doing nothing (in my eyes) to help me. But I also didn't talk to them about it because I didn't want to offend their masculinity, which, as a feminist, is a ridiculous thing to be worried about.

My suppressed fear of that evening slowly and unbeknownst to me generalized and spread to become a fear of some men, and then expanded to a fear of all men. Then my resentment morphed into hostility towards all men too. It was so unlike me. I've never been one to hold on to grudges. Still, because I was so unaware to look at what my heart was feeling, my emotions spiralled into more negativity. Although these fears and feelings and beliefs were not overt at first, they slowly got stronger without me realizing that I even had them. Then, once my anger was so intense that I couldn't help but feel it all the time, I got triggered into hostility more and more easily. It still took me a year to understand what was at the root of my anger. It wasn't until I had another incident in the Middle East that I could heal my then overt hostility and resentment that had generalized to all men.

Racism and sexism

Both racism and sexism are types of normalized fears that are often unconscious. As a white woman and spiritual leader, as a psychologist and a humanitarian, it is my obligation to bring up topics of racism and sexism, even though it makes me uncomfortable. I'm embarrassed because I have both racist and sexist tendencies. Both racism and sexism are learned fears that are unconsciously programmed into us. They are not systems that I created, but they are systems that I uphold. We are not born with them; instead, society and family systems slowly and quietly condition us. Instead of understanding how the system we live in continuously gives more advantages and opportunities to one group at the expense of another, we unconsciously accept the teaching of the system that keeps down one group so that another group can profit. We start to believe that we are smarter or work harder and so deserve where we are in life and that those marginalized then also deserve where they are in life.

If we want to choose love over fear, then we need to delve into how we are complicit in this system. None of us created the system of racism or sexism. Still, we do play into it, strengthen it and protect it in ways we are often unaware of. I can't dismantle white privilege or sexism, but I can use my privilege to assist others with less. That does not mean I have to be ashamed or guilty for the colour of my skin or my sex. No one can control how or with what they were born. But it does mean that we need to take a good hard look at ourselves to see how we are perpetuating and leveraging these systems for our profit and how we can do our part to advocate for and be an ally to those who are repressed and discriminated against. I cannot separate my journey of fighting for women's equality from fighting for the equality of Black, Indigenous and People of Colour (BIPOC), or the rights of any marginalized group.

Feminism

Many people think feminism means women have to stop wearing bras or shaving their legs. Yet, my understanding is that it only means women are equal to men. I have been working in women's rights and as a feminist for some time now, so it seems bizarre that we still need to debate what appears to me, an obvious fact. However, my recent delving into my white privilege has helped me understand the perspective of women and men who are still part of the sexist system our societies promote; and how I still hold some of these unconscious beliefs.

I feel more comfortable writing about feminism because I identify as a woman, so I'm justified to use my voice to share the impact that sexism has on us. Although I am still apprehensive about shouting that I'm a feminist because I feel like "real" feminists will criticize me and point out all the ways I subscribe to sexism. I need to take ownership of my fear, that's my responsibility, and I think our fear of being judged is precisely what makes it challenging to have honest conversations with each other about what we know and don't know.

Judgement creates a sharp divide, with all of us being scared not to be racist or sexist, and so we stay silent. This is a problem.

I have not studied the history of feminism deeply, but to me, feminism is not anything radical; it is merely the belief that women have the same value as men. This is the core, and yet it affects many different aspects. Women's work should be valued the same as men's work and compensated likewise. Women-heavy sectors should be as prestigious as male-heavy sectors. Teachers for elementary and high school, for example, used to be mainly men, and the profession was highly respected. The more women entered that field, the lower the pay went, and the less valued and respected the field became. In any sector, the contribution of both men and women is essential and needs to be treated as such. Sadly, women are often seen as an add on if there's space, but not vital.

Women having the same value as men also means that women are not objects. They can be beautiful and sexy and freely express that part of themselves but always knowing that their worth is more than how they look. They have more than just a body; they have emotions and thoughts and should always be treated as such. Of course, the same is also for men. However, we don't mention it as much because it is not the norm to objectify men. There is sometimes a trend that since women are so objectified, we should then do the same to men, but where is the healing in that? Additionally, women who objectify themselves can have the freedom to do that, AND they can still be seen as human beings with innate worth.

Throughout the ages, societies have been fearful of women's sexuality and have tried to control it. Women having the same value as men means that they get to dictate how they use their bodies. Women's sexuality is so beautiful and profound and intimate, and when we suppress it, all of society loses. Sex is not just about procreation. It is about emotionally bonding, trust, and vulnerability. It's an energetic explosion that some cultures even use as a path to enlightenment. We lose so much when we try to control those parts of ourselves.

There are many people with conscious or unconscious beliefs that women are too emotional, not reliable, not good at managing, or making tough decisions. Even though there is a plethora of research that shows that female world leaders are fantastic for the countries they rule. Research has demonstrated female leaders tend to have a more peaceful foreign policy and more robust democracy at home. The more women there are in parliament, the more there is a reduction in human rights violations by that country. Female world leaders are more likely to take decisive action than their male counterparts.

In the private sector, those with more gender-balanced management teams significantly out preform those with male dominate management teams.

Women and men aren't the same, but neither are men and men, or women and women or trans and hermaphrodite. Just because we have different outside appearances or gender identification doesn't mean we aren't all worthy of love and as valuable, just because we are alive. Human rights aren't just for one group; they are for all humans.

Just like it is unrealistic and unethical to expect minorities to be responsible for a more equitable and just world, so too is it impossible to put the responsibility of changing sexism on women. Why are people with the least amount of power responsible for changing the system? All of us need to work together to ensure that all races, genders, and sexual orientations are valued and respected. In so doing, we dramatically increase our happiness and the safety of our world. Let's try to stop judging each other's qualities and worth based on how others look. In fact, let's try to stop judging people's worth in general. When we reject or harm others, we are rejecting and injuring ourselves. Instead, let us look at those gross parts of ourselves, try to understand them, have compassion, forgive and then heal. It's scary to look at the ways we are sexist and racist. I get it. But it's imperative that we do.

White privilege

As a white woman, I have profited from the systems of white privilege. I have not had to struggle with racism or worry for my life when I interact with the police. The incident in Sierra Leone was the only time I felt I was attacked based on my gender and skin colour, something that black people, indigenous people and people of colour (BIPOC) have to struggle with every day. Even during Ebola, where I experienced a lot of hate and aggression because of my skin colour, I still had white privilege. I was still respected and given audience to powerful people because of my skin colour, and their perception that I could provide those I liked with access to the resources they needed. That is how I was able to mediate between communities and people. (Although to be clear, I was always very transparent with what I could or couldn't do and assisted whomever I could without any judgement of whether they worked with me or not.) Working in various countries has given me a small glimpse of the struggle that BIPOC people regularly face, and even that small glimpse was terrifying.

As I write this, protests are happening worldwide over the murder of George Floyd who was allegedly killed by a police officer kneeling on his throat while three other police officers stood by and watched. This horrendous event has finally forced me to face my own racist beliefs, which I have been too cowardly to face until now.

I am so ashamed to admit that I have known that I needed to educate myself on white privilege for some time. We talk about it at school, and I try to address racial concerns in my work, making sure that I always say the right things and promote equality. But I have always shied away from taking a good, long hard look at myself and how I consciously or unconsciously uphold the system of white privilege from which I profit from so much. I used the fact that I'm a humanitarian, an environmentalist, and a feminist, to argue that I've got too much on my plate already and can't take on another cause. But that thinking right there is an example of my white privilege. I got to choose whether or not dismantling the system was a priority, and I decided that it was not.

Before writing this book, I had a third existential crisis, the crux being that I need to delve into myself and find all the dark, disgusting pieces of me. I need to bring those pieces into the light and integrate them into my being. Recent events have shown me that it is time that I look at these racist parts of me. I acknowledge them and bring them into the light so that I can finally heal them. I hate that I have these parts of me, and I know I will make countless mistakes in even this chapter of writing. But love over fear means that I need to try. I need to embody my belief that we are all one, that we are all deserving and equal. Finally, I need to take responsibility for the actions, thoughts and beliefs I have that contradict this.

I am just beginning this journey, and so I am reading the book titled: "Me and White Supremacy" by Layla F. Saad. It's an important first step, and I highly recommend it for any of you who are willing to face this part of themselves.

Both feminism and racism are types of learned fear because they aren't biases we are born with. Instead, they are biases and fears that we learn to have. We are taught that black, indigenous and people of colour are dangerous or are involved in more criminal activity, or that women are weaker, too emotional and less reliable.

When you experience something that doesn't fit into a belief or worldview, you experience cognitive dissonance. To resolve that dissonance, your mind will "forget" that experience or explain its occurrence in a way that helps you to maintain your belief. For example, if we believe women are over-emotional, we tend to remember times when we witness women being over-emotional and forget the times when they aren't. This way, our beliefs get strengthened, and it prevents our brain from having to create new beliefs every time we are confronted with conflicting information. That's how stereotypes can be detrimental because they develop a lens of how we see the world that is then very difficult for us to change. Furthermore, because emotions are scary and unpredictable, we relegate them as nonsense and only give value to rational, logical thought.

We aren't to blame for being taught these fears. It's the society we were born into. However, we are responsible for looking at our learned fears, at the biases and beliefs we have, and at the injustices of the systems in which we live. After we have the courage to face these inner terrors, we need to decide what we will do with our situation. If we benefit from the system, how will we use that to assist those who are discriminated against? If we don't benefit from it, then what are we going to do? How do we want to act?

As with all learned fears, we need first to realize that we have them before we can unlearn them. I was just talking with someone who was telling me that there is no sexism in Lebanon. How can he heal something he doesn't know is wounded? Often healing or releasing learned fears involves first understanding that you don't know what you don't know. We need to take time to look honestly at ourselves and to notice and uncover that vast part of us that doesn't even realize how truly racist and sexist all of us are.

Learned fears require us to process what we've gone through and then delve into ourselves to heal the experience. My learned fear of men through my experience in Sierra Leone needed to be uncovered and looked at in more depth to heal the roots of it. I think that life is geared towards showing you what you don't know through the experiences we come across. But if we focus only on blaming others for the lessons we encounter, then we can easily miss out on this learning opportunity. That man was responsible for assaulting me, and I'm going to take my power back by using that experience to heal those parts of me that have fear and resentment towards others based on what they look like.

Chapter 13
Moving to the Middle East - Integration

The incident in Sierra Leone remained unhealed in my subconscious. A couple of years later, it started to come into my consciousness in the form of anger. Still, I wasn't forced to look at the beliefs and emotions I had stuffed down until I was deployed to the Middle East. I lived in Iraq and Syria for a couple of years, developing and implementing programs for women who were suffering from gender-based violence (GBV). GBV includes inter-partner violence, rape, sexual assault and fundamental human rights. In the Middle East, we worked on preventing honour killings and child marriage as well. Working in this field makes you incredibly aware of the injustices and pain that women in particular endure. Seeing these injustices brought up my own emotions about men that had been fermenting subconsciously more and more since Sierra Leone. The attack that I went through was paltry compared to what I have seen and heard other women and girls survive. However, I want to use my small example so that you can have an understanding of how processing and healing events can look. Please remember that processing and healing is a very individual journey and that everyone will react differently.

Primary anger is excellent and healthy and helps you set appropriate boundaries with people, but secondary anger can be unhealthy and even poisonous for those of us that hold on to it. I knew my resentment of men and the numerous injustices weren't just primary anger. I knew this because I was able to have compassion for members of ISIS; I saw them as being controlled and powered by fear. I felt compassion for them having to live in that personal hell. Yet I had anger against the regular men of the society I was working in, who laughed when I suggested that women should be respected to make decisions about their own health, or who tried to kill their daughters or sisters because they had been raped and therefore brought dishonour to their family. And I had anger about the men who looked at me like I was an object, followed me from grocery stores to my home, or tried to touch me when I wasn't looking or made rude remarks when I was. My anger grew and grew as time went on, and it became dangerous as I started to fight back. I would hit them when they grabbed my bum and yell at them when they made disgusting comments to me. In some places in the Middle East that could put my life in danger. I had no rights; I knew it, and they knew it. This is a country where you can kill your mother in public for no reason. The police can't do anything because it is considered a domestic issue, which police cannot get involved in (this doesn't apply if you kill your father). I started to see sexism everywhere and in everything, even when it wasn't there.

Please understand that yes, there is extreme sexism in the Middle East, but it was also my unhealed fear that was triggering me and activating sexism as my primary view. People are beyond hospitable, much more than anything I have ever experienced. They often gave me gifts because I was Canadian, and "Canada had taken in Syrian refugees." Or they wouldn't let me pay for my meal in a restaurant because their uncle was in Canada. The society there is different from what I'm used to, and while unjust in some ways, it's extremely beautiful and compassionate in others. I was blown away by the kindness of my staff, who would frequently bring me food or buy me presents, even though they lived in a war zone and had lost almost everything. There are some things I don't agree with, anything that violates a human right. But I learned so much from living there, and I was continually humbled and inspired by the people I worked with and the community I lived in. Here is a journal entry of some of the kindness I received when I was emotionally struggling during my time in Syria:

> I just went for a walk which, to be honest, is a little anxiety-provoking for me here. I'm in Syria right now, and I don't really like walking on my own because everyone just stares at me so much. I went for a walk because I just needed some fresh air. Of course, some young men were trying to get my attention (which is not ok to do to a woman in this culture). At first, I tensed up, but then I remembered that I don't have to pretend I am strong (I'm feeling particularly vulnerable today). I don't have to hide my vulnerability. I just have to be, because that is all there is. It totally changed my mood, and I even bought some fruit saying small pleasantries in Arabic with the shopkeeper. I went into another shop where the old woman there recognized me, but I didn't recognize her at all. She gave me kisses, which is what I needed, and then invited me to sit with her and her children at the oil stove. She prattled away at me in her local dialect, and we laughed because I had no idea what she was saying. But she peeled an orange and shared it with me, and she tried to teach me some words, and we played charades for a bit, and then she gave me cookies to take home with me.
>
> And I remember, the world is not such a bad place, even in a war zone.
>
> There is so much for me to be grateful for, and not in a guilty way of I shouldn't be sad because I have so much, but rather in that there are so many wonderful things about my life that I am glossing over. I get to really help some of the most vulnerable women in the world. My

team was telling me some stories where, through their work, women are changing their lives, and they are feeling more confident, feeling for the first time like they actually matter. I have staff who not only respect me but also confide their problems in me and a boss who thinks I'm doing a good job. I get to shine a little bit of love into a place that was ruled by fear. I have friends all over the world. I have such a loving family that will support me in anything. I have a Canadian passport so I can travel to most places with ease. I'm strong as all fuck, AND most important of all, I believe in love.

I believe in love.

The world will take care of me. If there are wonderful old women that have nothing left after losing it all in a war that still know me and welcome me and give me oranges and cookies, then certainly love will take care of me.

Despite these beautiful moments, I struggled with my anger for a year, trying to let it go. As you can see by the entry above, I tried being vulnerable. I also meditated. I did guided visualizations. I talked to my therapist and energy worker to try to let it go. I tried mantras. I did exercise and yoga to work through the anger. I tried to reframe men's motives. Still, for over a year, I simply couldn't let it go, and my rage just grew and grew. I was defensive and aggressive, and it made me more and more miserable.

Then, when I was back in Syria, one young man went too far. I was in one of the few restaurants that served alcohol; I was with my country director and my security manager and another female colleague when the young man who worked at the restaurant called me to ask me what food we wanted. He motioned me to come to him, which I did. As I turned the corner and was out of sight of my colleagues, he rubbed something against my bum. I turned around quickly and saw that his penis was out, and he was trying to masturbate on me. I slapped him and yelled at him and then went straight to my table to tell them what had happened. They talked to him, and he apologized, saying that, "Allah had blinded him for a moment." Then they asked me what I wanted to do. I said I wanted to finish our meal, that the boy could deal with the embarrassment of having been caught. I wanted to make sure we stayed and talked to his father, who was the restaurant owner. At first, the young man was embarrassed. But as time went on, he got more and more upset, kicking cats and yelling to himself until finally, he came over and with Google Translate. He showed my boss a message saying that it was my fault about what had happened and that I should be ashamed. Thankfully, my boss laughed and dismissed the comment, and we waited until the owner showed up. As the only female, I was not allowed to participate in the discussion, but they spent some time talking. I'm still not sure what happened, although I did tell all the other humanitarians that were living in that town what happened. Amazingly, they all decided never to go to that place again, something that I didn't expect them to do but which still warms my heart. It turns out that the young man had done it to another woman, but she didn't say anything to anyone until I raised the alarm.

It's so fascinating because even though I work in women's rights and gender-based violence, I still saw myself thinking in ways that were very unfeminist and thinking exactly the things I always tell our survivors not to think. I felt like maybe it had been my fault. I felt embarrassed for having made such a scene, for being a nuisance to my coworkers and taking away the main hangout place of all the other humanitarians. Even though I knew better, my heart still blamed itself. I became scared that the young man and his friends would come looking for me and try to kill me, or that when I left the guesthouse that everyone in the street thought I was a whore. It's so crazy that we as women so often blame ourselves, even when we KNOW better!

Even when we got evacuated to Iraq because it was too dangerous where we were, I was still so fearful. I stopped going out as much, I talked less, and didn't like walking anywhere by myself. I had experienced something like this 10 years previously but didn't have the same reaction then.

Though I'm grateful that it happened because it finally got me out of my secondary emotion of anger and down to my primary emotion of fear. I'll never forget the day that I finally realized what was at the root of my anger. I was still in Iraq and had decided to walk in our gated community. I was walking alone because Francois was working late, as he often did. It was still light out, and I was in a safe place very close to my house. But in the distance, as a man walked around a corner, I jumped out of my skin. It finally dawned on me that I'm not angry at men; I'm scared of them! I rushed home to do a meditation that I knew would help me release fear blocks, and that meditation changed my life.

I had a recording of a guided visualization that a teacher had made of how to remove fear blocks. I settled into my seated position in my little meditation area. I grounded myself and spent some minutes really feeling the anger, and then once that faded away, the fear that I had of men. I felt the fear that they would hurt me or rape me or even kill me, the fear that they would go out of their way to harm me, never seeing me as a person. I felt where the fear was in my body and imagined what shape it was. Then I brought in blue light to freeze the fear and all its roots that were attached to other parts of my body. I imagined taking out the frozen fear and throwing it into an ocean of magnificent light.

Here is a letter I wrote to my mom about the experience:

I'm struggling so much with "boundary" issues also, and just today I've had an interesting wrestle with anger and boundaries (it will relate to what you said but bear with me for a second). I wore a long dress (something I don't do unless I know I'll be with Francois all day), but Francois had to work late, so I walked home alone. I was purposefully radiating confidence/anger so that men would leave me alone. It worked to a degree. When they looked at me and then saw me glare at them, they then looked away fairly quickly. But then when two men came suddenly from around a corner, I had a moment of panic, and I realized that my anger was really fear. I know I'm putting up big walls against ALL men here, but I thought it was out of anger. It was interesting to feel the genuine fear of "what if they hurt me?"

I then did a big meditation of clearing away this fear block, lots of stuff came up, it was a massive block, and it turned out it was actual rage, but rage on behalf of all the women in this region. I went into it further and had the insight that men were scared of women and the love they could feel for women and how that love might distract them. And now this has all been distorted so that both men and women are afraid of each other. And while I was trying to clear this all out of me, I had physical pain in pulling the blocks out, like genuine pain! But finally, the anger and fear were pulled out completely.

Then I saw Christ, which was strange because I've never really related to Christ. But he came and started putting my chest together where the fear blocks had been, and there was still pain, but it was the pain of regrowth. Then Christ intertwined with me, like a double helix and we spun so tightly together we became one, and all this energy from the base of my tailbone burst up my spine, and giant wings unfolded out of my back and spread out 2 metres long on both sides. I was engulfed with the feeling of the heart of who I was; pure love. I felt like I was finally letting myself be free to be bright. It was incredible!

But all this to say that it was certainly energy coming

out of me, flowing out of me and shining outwards. So, I honestly don't know about ego and boundaries and how that has to do with oneness. When I think deep down, I feel that oneness is when I love myself, and by doing that, I'm loving all things. Or when I heal myself, I'm helping to heal all things. And so when you set boundaries of how it is ok or not ok for others to do something, and that is done out of a genuine reaction of love and respect for yourself, then I don't think that is creating separateness, I think that is potentially creating healing in others. It is not ok for me to sit on the sideline while I watch other people suffering. I need to speak up or do something or try to relieve their suffering to a degree. It's also because I know deep down that when other people suffer, we all suffer, and if we can bring even just a little bit of love to the dark places in this world, then we all benefit. Anyway, I hope this makes sense and that I didn't just turn this around and talk about me. I can't even re-read this email because it's getting too late and I really need to sleep. I wanted to send you everything while it was fresh in my mind.

I love you! I love our conversations!!

I later googled the image I had seen of me and Christ in a double helix and giant wings unfolding and found that it is the image of healing (which after I thought about it, I already knew). It's also a typical image people see when their kundalini energy gets activated, which is something I'm now learning more about.

After that mediation, my whole attitude changed overnight. The next day while walking to work, I saw a man do a double-take and look at me. Whereas before, I would have been tempted to snarl at him, instead, my immediate thought was, "Oh, he's just curious." Then the next day, when I was going grocery shopping, a man ahead of me in line let me go before him because I didn't have very many things to buy. It was a courtesy I had never experienced in this part of the world, and I was so surprised and grateful. It felt that he was really treating me and seeing me as a human! From that day forward, my fear and anger against men evaporated. They were lovely and kind and sometimes lost and insecure, but so are we all. It was a night and day difference that even my husband noticed.

Things will happen to us that are scary or unpredictable, and we'll have primary and secondary reactions to them. All of that is ok; we don't have to be perfect or perfectly insightful all of the time. Even for me, who is a therapist and who meditates regularly and is constantly doing personal introspection, it can take years to process or peel back all the layers that exist within me. And it's all perfect; I get there eventually.

I'm writing this now so that you are aware of these layers of emotions and can heal them and perhaps don't have to suffer longer than necessary. I wish I had processed my fear of that incident before it generalized to a fear of all men and then morphed into hatred of most men. It made my life truly miserable and exhausting! So, if there is something, some anger or fear, or anxiety or depression that won't go away, perhaps reach out and get some assistance. It's tough for us to see what is going on in ourselves. It's laborious to peel back all the different layers of our ego to see our true selves. Even I, who has dedicated my life to this mission, still needs outside help. We're all in this together, we need each other, and we need to support each other.

I am happy to say that even years after this meditation, and even though life has dealt me some new twists, I no longer still have a fear (or dislike) of men.

Integrating all aspects of ourselves

To truly process and heal difficult events, we need to keep in mind that we are not just our bodies, not just a spirit, and we are not only our mind. Being in this life means that we need to integrate our minds and bodies with our spiritual self, whatever that looks like for you. Since I was little, I was resentful of being in a body, so I never wanted to do techniques that integrated me into my body. Through the profound and gentle effectiveness of grounding, I realized how essential integrating all three aspects of us—body, mind, and spirit—is when healing and progressing through life. Here is a journal entry where I confront the fear of being in my body even after all these years of knowing it's an essential part of healing.

> I'm really trying to heal my endometriosis through energy work. I feel like I cleared a lot of the cysts last month, but I woke up this morning to a dream that I still had one left. I did a session on myself and found that yes, I still do have one left and so really went into it (through guided imagery). I got that it is still this fear of being in my body. I have such a strong belief that if I'm in my body, then I'm separate from the universe, and my banishment from love is complete. I was honestly panicky when I was healing this. Can I truly be inside my body fully?? Why do I need to do this bullshit??? But Spirit was with me and said that I need to be in my body because only that way can I genuinely reach Knowing. Then I heard what I tell my clients: "If you want to catch a flight from Toronto to London, you first have to accept that you're in Toronto." It's crazy how much resistance I have. Then there is also my guilt and fear that I can't ask the universe for help too much because then I'm taking up its precious time. Of course, it came to me that a) there is no lack, and time is just an illusion, and b) that I really truly am God and that he is always here, it's just a matter of if I see it or not. So, through my panic of being in my body, love was with me, and it's still with me now, and I'm afraid that it'll leave, but I know it's impossible, but I don't yet Know it. As I write this, tears come to my eyes. How am I so lucky to have these experiences?

Years later, after many ultrasounds, I no longer have cysts or am considered to have endometriosis, a chronic disease. The diagnosis of endometriosis is challenging; you can only be officially diagnosed if they physically go into your abdomen, which I refused. Perhaps I never had endometriosis. I can't tell with any certainty how or why my cysts finally went away after five years. But I have learned that if you would like to heal some beliefs that are no longer serving you, it is essential that you keep in mind all three of these aspects.

As a psychotherapist, I tend to live in my mind. I think and self-reflect and think some more. But if I stay in this analytical mind frame, then I miss out on the beauty of life and the beauty of me. If I really want to know myself (and I do!) then I need to venture out of logic and thinking into the realms of feeling and experiencing. Science can be based solely on the mind, or a combination of mind and spirit. I think all the greatest scientists are able to connect to the beauty and the rhythm of the universe.

Whatever your belief, research has shown that we need to take into account our spiritual side. When you do, your happiness levels are more likely to increase, you live longer, and you get sick less often. Spirituality is how we make sense of the world, pain and suffering, and our role in this life. It is the act of choosing and believing. It can include being religious or atheist. The point is that you need to find some purpose or understanding of why you are in this life, even if it's just to be as happy as possible right now since you become worm food after you die. That understanding then helps you to make choices regardless of the thought or emotions you are experiencing. This is our Sprit side.

After a disaster or difficult experience, it's important to make meaning of why the event happened. What can you learn from it? How would you like best to respond to it? Who do you want to be as a person? If you believe in a God, then ask that God for help. Remember that you are not alone and see if you can let go of the struggle.

Regardless of your belief system, I believe that we are all made of love, though we have fears, perceptions, worries, anxieties, beliefs, and ego thinking that can cover this up. But our job in life is to see if we can move past this and remember that we are already perfect. We've already crossed the finish line. We just need to remember it, that's all. We need to accept that we are lovely and magnificent and perfect and stop trying to prove otherwise. I believe that there are many pathways to the top of the mountain, and all paths lead there eventually. Sometimes we just choose to take the path with alligators and quicksand instead of the one with rainbows and unicorns. But in the end, it doesn't matter; the only thing the paths change is how pleasant our journey is. The destination is all the same: Love.

Some ways to integrate your body, mind and spirit include breathwork, meditation, prayer or yoga. All of these techniques connect you to your physical sensations (body) and help you identify your emotions and thoughts (mind) as well as create a healthy distance between you and your emotions and thoughts so that you don't drown or become consumed in them (spirit). So that you can be more intentional with how to respond to things in each moment (also spirit).

Breathwork

Breathwork is extremely powerful; it is the one essential bodily function that we have control over, unlike our circulation or our digestion or our brain functions. Breathwork uses the body to calm the mind so that you can access your high self. There are various types of breathwork techniques: Holotropic Breathwork, Transformational Breathwork, Clarity Breathwork and Shamanic Breathwork, just to name a few. Breathwork can also be incorporated into many other exercises such as yoga and Vipassana meditation. One type of breathwork exercise that helps calm you if you have anxiety is called square breathing. It involves you breathing in for four counts (the first side of the square), holding your breath for four counts (the second side of the square), breathing out for four counts (the third side of the square) and then holding your breath again for four counts (the last side of the square which is now complete). I used this technique a lot when I worked with homeless people in Vancouver.

Yoga

Yoga is also a fantastic way of incorporating the body, mind and spirit. It uses a variety of poses often combined with your breath that allows you to sometimes release emotions held in your body, calm your mind and perhaps connect to a higher knowing. There are many types of yoga, with Hatha or Ashtanga being some of the most well known. I personally like combining yin yoga, which holds each pose for a very long time, with Ashtanga yoga, which is more physically taxing and requires you to change your pose with each breath. Many free yoga classes can be found on YouTube.

Meditation

Meditation can be done regardless of spiritual beliefs. Often, people ask me what type of meditation I recommend. But there are not many rules when it comes to meditation. I love guided imagery or visualizations, where you have different images that you see or use to help you feel better. Using images is the most effective way to access our subconscious. The tree or cord grounding is a type of guided imagery, as is the heart connection and other techniques that I regularly use. I mainly use visualizations to meditate. I let my intuition, body and emotions guide the imagery that comes up, labelling the feelings I encounter and then delving into them. There are not many rules. When I teach people how to meditate, I like to teach them how to use their intuition so that their high self can guide and help heal them in a way that is best for them.

You can also use breathing as a type of meditation. Vipassana meditation is the practice of focusing on one small spot on one nostril where you feel your breath going in and out. This focus is designed to train your mind on the ability to focus and control your attention. It also trains you to bring back your focus every time you inevitably let your mind drift. When I was 18 years old, I went to a Vipassana silent retreat where we meditated from 5 am until 11 pm for 10 days. Walking meditations, lessons, and meals gave us breaks throughout the day. This type of meditation is tough because it requires you to empty your mind and just focus on this small part of your nose. It is similar to mindfulness meditation. You focus on your breathing as an anchor and notice the thoughts that come into your mind, label them and acknowledge them, and then let them go and bring your mind back to your breath. Other meditations include meditating on a mantra or idea. Please note that although meditation has received a lot of positive press in the last 20 years, it is not suitable for everyone. It can be harmful to those with severe trauma. Please always remember to follow your inner knowing and your own intuition.

Prayer

Prayer is also very powerful. It's not really a technique for integrating the mind, body, and spirit per se, but it is similar and often sometimes thought of as the same as meditation. Prayer usually involves the belief in a higher being and asking that higher being for help. It can be enormously comforting to believe that you are not on your own, and there is someone all-knowing and loving who is there to help you. In Alcoholics Anonymous, it is built into the recovery program that participants can't solve their problems themselves and so must accept the help from God. Often, this can help us when we are stuck in anger or resentment and having difficulty forgiving others. I was brought up with the idea that you can ask God for help, but you must also make sure you do the work necessary and not rely on God to do everything for you. I'm still not sure where the balance is in this because I do believe in trying to do things for myself, but on the other hand, I find that when I try to push my agenda, I create a big mess of things.

In many religions, there is a belief that God loves us unconditionally. I personally believe in a higher being and have been finally understanding the meaning of unconditional love. I believe that God is love and that we are then extensions of love/God. Except right now, we are stuck in a dream, surrounded by illusions (fear) that we think are real. If we are love and made in God's image, that means to God, we are perfect. Therefore, the idea that we would need assistance is foreign to God since She/He sees us as perfect and only asleep. God understands that we are stuck in a dream but is not concerned because She/He knows it's just an illusion. That's where prayer is important. Prayer is the connection we have to God that can assist us when we forget that we are perfect already. Prayer helps us ask for specific help that we need. Prayer helps us to get closer to waking up from our dream.

Here's a journal entry from when I finally deeply understood this concept:

> This whole unconditional love, I've always said over and over that one of the most amazing things about that shitty time in my life is that I learned how to love unconditionally. I just gave unconditional love, which means that I do not love something to heal it, which is a condition. Or loving something so that it becomes part of me, or loving something for XYZ. I'm understanding, I guess, this whole new idea of love and just loving, and then that's it! There is nothing further to the sentence. Then it makes me understand God so much more because if She/He loves us unconditionally, then no wonder She's/He's not interfering all the time because She/He doesn't need us to do anything actually because we can just be exactly how we are. If

> we're unhappy or need something, then for sure, She/He'll help us, assuming we ask for it. But it's really that loving something and then letting it go. It's given me a whole new appreciation for divine love, but yeah, it's incredible, absolutely incredible for me!

So prayer and divine love can be astonishingly healing and helpful. Still, again, this can be translated into several different religions or beliefs. I'm not fussed about what name we use, or what religion is followed because I think we are all already there. We're in heaven, we've just fallen asleep, and it's just a matter of finding our way to wake up. You can use prayer to integrate your body, mind and spirit, or as support to strengthen your connection if one of these three things seems weaker than the others. Prayer is extremely versatile and can be used for anything; just remember that the answer to your prayers might not come in the shape you envision.

Integrating our body, mind, and spirit helps us notice when a learned fear is being activated, and it helps us slowly and gently process and heal these learned fears. We might have magical break-through moments, but it is much more likely that you will gently get closer to waking up through grounding and the above techniques. A wonderful Chinese proverb that I often quote is: "Before enlightenment chop wood, after enlightenment chop wood."

For us to undo our learned fears, as always, we need first to recognize what they are. Learned fears are fears we have been taught, either through society or through fearful experiences that have happened to us or someone we know. When not addressed, learned fears can fester and spread and create more fears. For us, the path to processing and healing learned fears might be different, but they will all end in the belief in love. Acknowledging our fears and healing them allows us to be able to choose love more easily and naturally. Choosing love is the key to happiness, health and real prosperity. It's not an easy or a simple task to heal our fears, and often the path is winding and confusing.

Still, if we listen to our inner wisdom and intuition, accept the support of those around us, and emulate those who live and radiate love, then our journey will be heart expanding and filled with moments of bliss. Choosing love is the noblest and holiest goal we can have.

Part 4

Choosing Love

Love gives naught but itself and takes naught but from itself.
Love possesses not nor would it be possessed;
For love is sufficient unto love.
Khalil Gibran

Chapter 14
Connecting to Love

Choosing love is the section that makes my heart sing. We get to focus on LOVE rather than all the things that are blocking our ability to experience it. I think my most remarkable stories have come from my decisions of choosing love over fear. From having my mind blown open by my thesis results to losing my job, and sailing across the Atlantic Ocean, love has inspired me to follow my heart and fulfill my dreams.

Choosing love has been something that I have consciously tried to do ever since I returned from my deployment in Haiti in 2012. It is the single concept that has impacted my life the most, and "choosing love over fear" is a sentence that I have repeated over and over in times of difficulty, indecision and suffering. It has been my compass and resulted in feelings of complete bliss and joy. But not without being terrified on my way.

Choosing love is a simple concept and yet a tricky endeavour because our fear can morph and change to try to prevent us from actually choosing love. Choosing love is not a destination; it's a way of being. It's a conscious choice of how to live from moment to moment. Even after moments of bliss, we still have to go about our lives. It's not about getting anywhere or being perfect, it's about remembering who we are more and more deeply, and having that remembrance last longer and longer each time we can tune into it.

As Rumi wrote:

Out beyond ideas
Of wrongdoing
And rightdoing
There is a field
I will meet you there.

Love is that field, and that field is magnificent. Although I don't live in that field yet, I've been able to visit, and I'm optimistic that I'll be able to stay there for longer and longer periods.

So how do we get there, and how do we choose love? What does it mean to choose love over fear? Why is choosing love sometimes so scary?

I will address my answers to all of these questions in this section. I include findings from my research thesis that completely changed the way I did psychotherapy, and which the dean of my university said was the most highly researched thesis he had ever seen. As usual, this section will be sprinkled with practical tools you can use to implement and put into action this new way of thinking.

What is love and what is fear?

If love is everything, if love is the only thing that exists, then what is fear? Why is fear considered the antithesis of love, and why isn't hate the opposite of love?

The answer to this is both simple and complex. And we must start with what fear is. If love is everything, then it's opposite must be nothing, and that's what fear is. Fear is the lack of, the belief that we are not love, that we can be harmed or destroyed or rejected. If we believe in love, then none of those things are possible. Fear is that belief that we are incomplete, that there is something inherently wrong with us, that we are sinful and must or will be punished. Fear is that we are not enough, not good enough, not strong enough, not holy enough, not smart enough, not successful enough. We can only understand fear as the opposite to love, for if love is everything, how can there be anything else? There cannot be everything and nothing in the same existence, and so in our minds, only one or the other can exist in a moment.

That is why this book is so important because I am here to tell you that it is only Love that exists. You have tricked yourself into believing that only fear exists when, in reality, the opposite is true.

Another way to look at it is in terms of primary and secondary emotions. Hate cannot be the opposite of love because hate is never a primary emotion; it is always a secondary emotion. At the root of hate is a mixture of fear and anger, although mostly fear. The primary emotion under hate is the fear that some have or will harm you. Therefore, hate cannot be the opposite of love; fear is the opposite because it is at the root of hate. Fear is at the root of not seeing or believing in love. It is a lack of connection, of knowing our true selves, which is love.

"Fear is a stranger to the ways of love. Identify with fear, and you will be a stranger to yourself." – A Course in Miracles.

For example, we have talked about the three main kinds of fear: external or other people's fear, internal or subconscious fear, and learned fear. All of these types of fear, wherever they come from, only exist in the mind. I might choose to believe other people's fears, and if I do so, then that is something that happens in my mind. I decide to think like that. Perhaps I have subconscious or conscious limiting thoughts about myself. Those fears only exist in my mind since they are thoughts. Lastly, even though something fearful has possibly happened directly to me, it is my interpretation of that which creates the fear. My belief that I can be harmed is a thought that transpires in my mind. So, all fears are thoughts that occur in our mind, and none of them are actually real or even exist. They only have power if we give them power.

Fear is a tool of love. The illusion of fear is a gift that allows us to understand love. How else can we truly know love if it is the only thing that exists? Therefore, the illusion of fear helps us truly experience love because we forgot what love was for a moment in time. That is why this life is essential because it is our chance to experience and understand love at a level not possible if we didn't have the illusion of fear. Although we need to remember not to get lost and drown in the dream of fear, we need to remember that it is just an illusion. Illusions are dreams because they don't last forever. All of us will die at some point. All of us will return to love, and so fear is just temporary. Therefore, fear is an illusion, a dream. We just need to wake up.

If we want to overcome fear, we can't do so by trying to control it, because fear is a lack. It's like trying to get rid of darkness by shooing it away. It's not possible. If you want to get rid of darkness, then you need to shine a light. The point of the previous sections was to shine a light on the different fears that might be running in your mind's background so that they can evaporate. Then once we have shone a light, we can shift our focus from fear to love. That is why my mantra is "Love over fear," not "Fear is bad," or some other such thing where my focus is on fear. As A Course in Miracles says, "Attempting the mastery of fear is useless. In fact, it asserts the power of fear by the very assumption that it need be mastered. The true resolution rests entirely on mastery through love." So how do we do this? What does all of this mean in a day to day practical sense? Well, it means being vigilant about shifting our focus to love. Love is everything. Love is the point of everything and the goal of everything.

Fear is just a call for love.

Here is a diary entry that highlights how my fear is just a call for love:

So, I'm studying the text of A Course in Miracles, and while doing so, I've just had a silly Aha moment. I've finally realized that although everything is an illusion, that doesn't mean it doesn't hold power, and specifically, even though I AM love. I am complete and am actually part of God (love). I still believe that I'm unlovable, which is an illusion. Still, this belief has power, and I think it's what has created the situation I'm in now, not from a sense of punishment. It's merely a natural consequence of believing I'm not loveable. The situation I'm in now is that Francois doesn't know if he loves me and just doesn't know if he wants to be married to me. He says it's the second, but I believe it's the first. So, of course, Francois is responsible for his actions (or inaction). Still, I'm responsible for my belief in being unlovable. I feel like this situation is a big neon light warning me of the destructiveness and pain that this belief causes me. Not to say that if I heal this belief, then Francois will want to stay married to me. I don't even think it matters. It's just a sign that I need to heal this or else I will cause more and more pain. AND if I heal this, then whatever decision Francois comes to will be less painful and more bearable.

It's so funny because I've heard these messages so often, why does a message suddenly hit home? Oh well, I'm just glad it finally has.

My new mantra is "I am loveable" then, when I can finally really believe this during my waking everyday existence, maybe I can move onto, "I am love," but this feels a bit too unattainable for me now.

Am I really loveable?

Knowing love

Fear only exists as a thought in our mind, but love exists regardless of whether we believe it. Love is our essence. It is what we truly are made of. Therefore, since love is at our core, when we do things or think about ideas that conflict with love, fear is created. Anything that conflicts with us being everything, being interconnected, being ultimate kindness and peace and strength and compassion will create discord. That is why money or fame or the love of beautiful people or the respect of others doesn't bring us happiness or peace. Striving for these things above all else, means you feel like you need something outside yourself to have joy. These things aren't harmful, as long as we remember they are not what create our worth. As long as we remember that we are already complete and don't need any of those things, they are just birthday cake. That is why fear is essentially anxiety-provoking because we fall into the trap that we are not enough, that we are not good, that we need to prove our worth. These beliefs are examples of us not being genuinely authentic; we have lost our way in a forest of illusions. We are striving for value through external means because we don't think we are complete.

We know love through our experience of fear, just like we know health through illness. When we are healthy, we don't take the time to appreciate it; it just is. However, we really understand health and strive for it when we struggle with illness. Love is like the sun. It is constant and only gets temporarily hidden. War can decimate an area, but birds make nests out of the holes created by mortar shells. Trees grow out of ruins; weeds grow in the cracks of sidewalks. This is how we can know that love is the only true thing. We fear death as the ultimate ending, but will your love for someone stop when they die? Does someone's love for you stop when they die? No! Even death can't diminish love. There have many times when I have had sessions with my clients to connect with their departed loved ones, and we can both feel the room fill up with the love that the deceased still has for my client. Even death, the ultimate destroyer cannot touch the power of love. Death cannot kill love. Love cannot be destroyed.

Love over fear

Fear, however, can be vanquished by any of us who choose. What is the ultimate champion over fear? Forgiveness. Forgiveness is such a powerful entity. It is an embodiment of how love is the ruler of all.

Forgiveness is an action of our belief in love and a rejection of fear. That is why forgiveness benefits us so much. It is us choosing to believe and act out of love; it is us rejecting fear. It is us saying that we are already complete. We are already magnificent, regardless of whether others see that, and they cannot tarnish our glory. If I am the embodiment of love and someone disrespects me, what does that matter? I don't have anything to prove, and their opinion doesn't change what I am. Their opinions only mean they are still stuck in the world of fear and competition and need help to connect with love. Forgiveness is understanding that they are in pain and having compassion for that instead of buying into what they think about us.

That is why restorative justice programs can be so powerful. They focus on healing the pain caused by the perpetrator, as well as how to heal the perpetrator's pain. Restorative justice is about being responsible for the pain that was caused and then repairing it. So often, I have been in countries where there is a perpetuated conflict because both sides are trying to get even. Getting even just preserves hurt, pain and grief and ensures that the violence will continue. Forgiveness is the only way to stop the cycle of violence.

Forgiveness is not an excuse for the pain to continue, forgiveness is about addressing the source of the pain, the heart of the fear, and healing it. Perhaps that's through ending a relationship or through restorative justice or foreign policy revisions. The point of forgiveness is to realize that all sides need love.

Forgiveness is proof that love is all-powerful, and the only thing that exists. Forgiveness is the conqueror of fear. Forgiveness is love in action.

What is love?

Love is completion, love is everything, and love is the only thing that is truth. It is like the colour white, which holds all other colours within it.

Love holds forgiveness, compassion, kindness, gratitude, bliss, joy and truth, but it is more. Love is everything; it is utterly complete. Love is the essence that is in all beings. It is the ocean of all things, and we are the waves thinking that we are separate and alone, when in reality, we are connected and part of unfathomable depths. Love is at the core of every single one of us and is how and why we are all one.

"Heaven is not a place or a condition. It is merely an awareness of perfect oneness." – A Course in Miracles.

Even those we view as entirely evil have a core of love because anything other than love is just an illusion. Evil cannot exist. It is not actually real; we only perceive it as real. Our journey here in this life is to find the clouds that prevent us from seeing our birthright of love shining within us. As the clouds or wounds come up which prevent us from feeling connected to our core and remembering our true holiness, they show us those hurts and misunderstandings that we need to heal. We make our own hell here on earth by believing in the illusions around us, by doubting the completeness of love, by thinking love is fragile or can be overcome, and by not connecting to the love we already are. Here is a journal entry from the moment I was able to understand this in my heart, truly, deeply.

> I've just had two big breakthroughs through my meditation, and I wanted to make sure I wrote them down so I wouldn't forget them (cause I do that sometimes...sigh).
>
> Yesterday (well actually for the last few days cause it seems to take me a while), I have been meditating on the concept of "Let all things be exactly as they are." And it suddenly dawned on me why God doesn't intervene; it's because we are all whole, we are perfect already, our soul, our essence is love/perfection. So when I see horrendous things that are happening (such as the genocide in Myanmar right now), it's not real. I'm not saying it's not happening. Still, I am saying that those people perpetuating those despicable acts can't truly hurt us, they

can't change the fact that we are made of love, it can't change who we truly are, it's only affecting what we think we are. For example, if I get raped, or tortured or murdered they aren't and can't touch my soul, it is just a transition (if I die), it's just clothes, it doesn't affect my essence unless I fall into the belief that I AM my body and I am not love. And so if I am truly to see things as already perfect as already a part of God, then why would she/he need to intervene? What is there to save? We are already saved, we've passed the finish line, and it is our choice to see that or not, that's why if we ask for help, She/He assists, but always we are perfect exactly as we are. Just because we have a bad dream, it doesn't mean we are the bad dream.

Let me interrupt my entry to say that I have never been raped. So, I don't know firsthand the deep pain and trauma and violation that people experience when they go through this. I have counselled and helped hundreds of people who have been raped, and each one of them has had a unique healing process. However, I have also noticed some similarities; almost all feel like it was somehow their fault. So often they have a fear that there is something inherently wrong with them. This self-blame of this belief that they are responsible for another person's actions can create some of the most detrimental emotions; shame and guilt. The only way to heal shame is to bring it to the light and talk about those things that seem beyond words. Only once you do that does the power that shame holds over us, evaporate. Guilt can be healed only by acceptance and love of ourselves. When we receive this from others, it can give us permission to give it to ourselves, which is where the ultimate healing is.

Once rape survivors were shown non-judgemental care, they seemed to be able to start their healing journey. Unfortunately, especially in terms of rape, society often judges the survivor, and that can even be worse than the original event.

If we are raped or tortured, that can put a black mark on our soul, but only if we take that event to mean there is something wrong with us, something wrong with love. When I work with rape survivors, I try to help them get in touch with their true divine self. They are not defined by what happened to them. They are so much bigger than that. They are beautiful and magnificent, and they have been raped. I in no way mean to demean the pain and suffering that survivors are going through; their strength and courage often blow my mind. And I believe that everyone is so much more than the pain and suffering they have experienced and that no one can define our worth. We are all worthy and glorious, no matter what others do to us.

All right, now back to my journal:

> My second big insight happened today while meditating (and I might not be making complete sense right now as I travelled for 22 hours yesterday to Vancouver and only slept for a few hours before waking up again. However, it was a profound meditation, and I almost started crying just from the emotion of it). I was meditating on the concept of "My sight goes forth to look upon God's face," and I started asking, how can I see God's face everywhere? And I imagined that I looked at Trump's face, and then I saw that the image of Trump was just showing me where I am still holding onto judgments and beliefs. These beliefs are what's preventing me from experiencing total bliss. Then I was flooded with the feeling of how the world is really here to actually support me! I've been so scared of the world and of the "lessons" it teaches me. I want so much to learn things quickly so that I can avoid the pain of tough lessons. Still, the world isn't here to test me, it's not here to force me to learn; it is here to support me in my profound desire for enlightenment. My heartfelt desire to rest in God's arms has been burning inside me since I was a tiny girl. The world is actually surrounding me with love; the world is love. If I experience pain, it's only to signal to me that something is getting in my way from reaching my goal of complete love. How utterly beautiful is that? How

different is that way of living? The world loves me and is on my side. I don't have to fear lessons, I don't have to fear the world, I don't have to fear God.

There is no punishment. I don't believe that hell exists except what we make for ourselves here on earth. Hell is living and believing in fear. Hurt, pain, and suffering are temporarily hiding the brilliance of love from us. The problem is when we mistakenly think the illusions are real, that they are all that exist. We give up on our journey too soon. I always say I have seen the worst of humanity but also the best, and I believe it to be true. I have seen horrendous acts of cruelty, and I have witnessed how power has ruined the lives of millions, and yet that is all an illusion, it has no real effect. It will not last once this wrinkle in time passes. That doesn't mean I don't do my best to be a force for love or sit back and watch this dream of destruction unfold. No, it means that I try my best to break through, connect with the love that is always there and all around us, and connect with my fellow creatures that are different expressions of the same love that is me. I try to connect to the love in them, search for it, and seek it out. Pain and suffering aren't a punishment! They are a call to give love to the part of us that needs it. They are a call for us to break out of the small container we've been squeezing our hearts into.

Pain is assured, but it's for our growth to support us, a natural extension of us growing bigger. Suffering, on the other hand, is not inevitable. Suffering is when we think there is something wrong with us for experiencing pain. Suffering is when we create a false meaning about ourselves or love because of someone's actions. Suffering is not necessary; it is completely made by our own fearful thought processes. My belief that I was unlovable created my suffering. Pain is a given, but suffering is us making things worse.

Connecting to Love

Connecting to love is what gives me the energy and optimism to continue. The most powerful way I can experience love is through my meditation practices. I unite with love through the heart connection, or through just feeling the love of the universe fill me up. I experience love through gratitude, through the admiration of the beauty that is all around me. I don't necessarily connect to love naturally. Sometimes I will be enveloped in it without warning, but mostly it takes effort. I need to set aside the time and meditate. I need to concentrate on seeing the beauty around me. I need to witness the pain in others and send them love for them being exactly as they are. I need to forgive, which can often take time and a lot of work. I need to choose love consciously.

Connecting to love is a process where it's easy to get caught up in the illusions of hopelessness or the sparkle of admiration or the specialness of being in a relationship. As A Course in Miracles states: "You have so little faith in yourself because you are unwilling to accept the fact that perfect love is in you, and so you seek without for what you cannot find within." Sometimes when I notice I have gotten sucked in, I have gotten distracted, I still don't care, and I refuse to give up my illusions. But eventually, I always see the pain and suffering that my illusions and belief in false things do to me. Letting go of our illusions often feels like jumping off a cliff. It is terrifying, and if it is terrifying, how do we know that doing it is choosing love and not fear?

The next entry is of me continuing to struggle with the breakdown of my marriage. But where I am also able to be there for my heart as she struggles. It's an example of how to connect to love even when we are suffering, and how to find love within yourself, even in the face of rejection.

I am learning that I really need to believe I'm lovable. Then also another fear really REALLY came up this morning, and that is the fear that I'm alone. I'm feeling so much anger and bitterness against Francois right now, and it's all because I'm so scared that he is going to leave me. I really think he is really going to leave me.
He is going to leave me.
Oh, my dear heart!!! I'm so sorry little one. I see how much it hurts, how scary it is, how alone you feel, I am here. I will cuddle you and dry your tears, don't forget about me. I love you more than you can ever imagine/comprehend. You are my light, you are my life, and I will be with you forever because you and I exist together outside of time. We are intertwined and inseparable. My love is all-consuming and is really the only thing you need. You have turned away. You don't see me standing right here, and you don't feel me hugging you. Open your eyes dear one, open your ears and hear my words of comfort, feel my support, my strong arms around you. I love you. I will help you through this. Give your pain and your suffering to me, let it go. It is only hurting you.
Come to me, stay with me, be with me. Let me love you.

Journaling

As you have witnessed, I find journaling helpful. I mainly use it when I am struggling or when I have especially profound meditations where I get insights and then need to write them down. I can experience something and *know* it, but then I can get distracted and sucked into the drama of life. I recommend keeping a journal or a place where you can write down all the beautiful fleeting insights you might receive so that you can look back on them when you're in a moment of forgetfulness. They can give you inspiration and guidance on how to get back to love. Even when I do visualizations with my clients, I have them write down the answers they get because so often it can feel like a dream, and it will slip through your fingers unless you bring them into "reality" in some way.

Francois and I did decide to end our marriage, and I was terrified and devastated. It felt as though my heart shattered into a million pieces. But you know what? Although it's only been a year, I'm ok, and throughout the process of divorce, I've been ok. I wouldn't change the last tough years for anything because they allowed me to heal and to trust that perhaps I *am* loveable even when I feel rejected. Those years truly taught me how to take care of my heart at a deeper level, and how to connect to that wellspring of love that is always me.

Unconditional love of all your parts (emotional)

We hear the words "unconditional love" all the time, and yet it took me almost 35 years to actually understand them. Remember the three-chair exercise from Part 2? This is a fantastic method to practise unconditional love with those parts of you that you have tried to reject.

The goal of all psychotherapy is to help a person become more integrated. To notice their parts (beliefs, thoughts, and feelings), and accept them and work with them to improve their lives. When I talk about parts, I mean the parts of us, either subconscious or conscious, that play different roles within ourselves. An example of a part could be "the inner critic" or "the angry bitch", or perhaps it's the part of us that is selfish or insecure. Or even our different emotional parts, for example, the angry or fearful or shy part of us.

There are invariably parts of me that are showing themselves that I'm embarrassed or ashamed of, such as the part of me that wants to be vindictive, or the part of me that can't forgive, or the part of me that is fearful of responsibility. But instead of banishing these parts and pretending they don't exist, my new purpose (from my most recent existential crisis), is to love all these parts unconditionally. That means that I'm not trying to change the vindictive part of me to conform to what I want, but forgive myself for having these thoughts and emotions. I'm sending love to it without the need or the desire to change it. Only after I have done that, can true integration occur. It's counter-intuitive, but as someone who's tried everything to be perfect and still falls flat on my face, the acceptance and unconditional love of the parts of me that I am ashamed of is the only way to heal, transform and release them. I have experienced firsthand the profound truth behind the saying, "What you resist persists."

We need to send love with no agenda of healing or changing or embarrassing or manipulating. Just loving and respecting these aspects of us for who and what they are. Fear is a cry for love, so these parts of me that are acting out of fear need love more than anything. Yet our immediate reaction is to shun or shove them down. It is so difficult to accept the facets of us that we are ashamed of or don't like, and that is why self-forgiveness is the ultimate gift. It allows us to love unconditionally, enabling us to appreciate these parts even though they might not fit the image we want to create.

I have been able to forgive and offer unconditional love to these different thoughts, beliefs and emotions in me. The relief, the flood of love that fills you, the bliss and the wholeness that you feel when you can do this, really and truly is heaven. Yet even though I have experienced these incredible results, it is still difficult to face these shameful, ugly, and even disgusting parts of ourselves. Unconditional love is not easy. It is a steep path. Even after you experience the total bliss from achieving it, we still need to diligently continue to do this process when other darker, more sinister parts appear. Don't give up! Don't be discouraged when more and more emotions inside yourself ask for love! It is such a gift! I truly believe that the more facets of yourself that you can give forgiveness and unconditional love to, the more you heal the world and those around you. That's the power of being interconnected.

To send these darker parts of you unconditional love, you can do the three-chair exercise as described in Part 2 or try the following meditation:

Step 1) Infinity connection

a. Take some time to sit quietly in a comfortable position, preferably with your spine straight. Imagine that God/Source/Sun/Universe is sending you a huge beam of unconditional love coming down from the sky and in through the crown of your head all the way to your heart. Imagine you are being filled up with unconditional love, and see if you can really feel, see, and hear this. For example, perhaps you see a white light beam, feel the unconditional love or hear, "I love you unconditionally." There is no right way to do this; follow the wisdom of your heart.
b. Enjoy the sensation of just being filled with love. Stay here as long as you need, simply allowing yourself to accept love. Once you feel full of unconditional love, send unconditional love back up to the universe so that there is a sort of circle created of you receiving love and you sending love. Enjoy this for as long as you like.
c. When you are ready, you can then imagine yourself sending love down to the earth below, the earth that nourishes you and holds all of us up.
d. Then, again, imagine the earth is sending up unconditional love back to you, creating another loop of infinite love. Now, your heart is the vortex of two loops of infinite unconditional love going up to the sky and down from the earth, making an infinity sign with your heart in the centre. Again, enjoy this for as long as you like.

Step 2) Bring up a memory or thought of when you acted in a way you wish you hadn't or had a thought that you wish you didn't. Perhaps it's an embarrassing or even shameful moment. Try to imagine what shape it would be if it had to be a shape, what texture it would have if it had to have a texture, what colour it would be if it had to be a colour. (Imagining it as a colour and shape helps to depersonalize it for you and will help with step 3).

Step 3) Talk to this belief/thought/emotion, and ask it why it acted or thought in that way? Really take some time to understand it. What is it scared of?

Step 4) Accept this part (belief/thought/emotion). Tell it that you see it and imagine you are sending love from your heart, fed by the infinity loop of unconditional love, to this part of you. Make sure you are not trying to heal or change this part of you. You are just sending it love, compassion and understanding, and only if it wants to accept this from you.

Step 5) See if this part of you is willing to send you love, or willing to feel the love it has for you. Accept the love from this part.

Step 6) Relax and let the love flow into you. Let your whole being fill up with beautiful pure love and compassion. Feel the strength that this extra part gives you. Let gratitude swell up for being able to find this lost part and let this lost part integrate into you if it so wishes. Enjoy this bliss until it fades away.

The above meditation is just a suggestion of what you can do. As always, follow your intuition, the desires of your own heart. Have fun with these exercises, and play around with them. Perhaps you want to integrate ho'oponopono into it. Maybe other beautiful images wish to be incorporated. These techniques have come to me through my intuition, so they feel right for me. Still, when I work 1:1 with my clients, although I will lead them through similar exercises, they will be different each time because my intuition will guide me to include other things or say something that my client needs to hear. There is no right or wrong in how to do this, only love. Trust yourself.

Connecting to love- Miracles

There are times when you might need to send unconditional love to parts of, or all of your body. For starters, if you have an unhealthy relationship with your body, then sending it unconditional love will work wonders in transforming that relationship. It also helps if you are experiencing pain or illness. However, I must highlight again, because it took me a while to learn this: unconditional love is unconditional. When you send it, it's not with the plan of healing or changing it or even making the pain stop. *It's with the agenda of understanding it and accepting it for what it is right now.*

When I was doing my undergraduate degree in Psychology, I wrote a paper on firewalking. Because I wanted to know how people were able to firewalk, I organized a firewalking event.

About 20 of us attended this event, and we all spent roughly five hours meditating and doing exercises to prepare to walk the hot coals. I had done my research and knew that some critics thought people were able to walk on hot coals because they did it quickly. The heat didn't have a chance to conduct itself into the skin of the participant. So, I made the decision that I would walk very, very slowly.

My turn came, and boy! Talk about facing your primal fears! As you approach, you can feel the wall of heat slam into you. I started sweating profusely, gulped and started my gradual walk across the coals. One coal got stuck to my foot and stayed on for the whole 8-ft expedition. Then finally, after what seemed like two lifetimes, I reached the end. I did it! A wave of relief washed over me but soon became replaced with a wave of pain. I looked down at my foot, and where the coal had stuck, a large painful blister was already forming.

I was the only one that got burnt in that event. It was supremely embarrassing, mainly because I was the organizer. But pain has a way of grabbing your attention. Instead of focusing on my mortification, I did a type of energy healing on my foot called Healing Touch. I felt into the burn blister and asked it what it needed from me, and then I energetically gave it what it requested. I did this right after and sporadically through the night when the pain would wake me up. Slowly the blistering began to go down. When I woke up the next morning, my burn was completely gone.

I'm one of those people that like to get lessons from things. I think the teaching of that firewalk was twofold, that 1) I needed to check my ego. I think my being the only one to burn successfully took my ego down a notch, and 2) I can heal myself.

Miracles have always frightened me, and so I don't like to think about them too much. But I have had numerous miracles happen in my life. I think this healing could have been one of those miracles. I adore logic and common sense, and so I looked into the time it takes for burns to heal, and it's longer than 12 hours, even if it was only a first-degree burn. Intellectually, I know how miracles work. They just see through the illusions of fear and are moments when you directly connect to your true self. Everything then realigns to that connection. They are a normal and natural effect from this ultimate connection to love, to truth. But in my mind, I'm so scared of what being a miracle worker would mean. Would that mean that people will expect me to be perfect? What will happen when they find out I'm not, will I disillusion them from the whole concept of love?

When I have these thoughts, they shut down my ability to do miracles. I don't want to limit myself or my capabilities any longer. To overcome my fear, I focus on unconditional love, I focus on the journey and not the outcome. Unconditional love is how we create miracles. Illness or disease can be a signpost that you need to bring unconditional love to that area. Regardless of what outcome happens, cultivating, expressing and giving unconditional love is the only thing that is important.

Some people believe that illness is a mental or emotional wound that has now manifested in the body and needs to be healed. I agree with this most of the time. Disease can be a red flag to get your attention to love that part of you that is stuck in fear. However, I also believe that sometimes we agree to have an illness to help our loved ones heal something, or perhaps you have decided to have an illness to help you transition out of this life. The bottom line is not to judge yourself for having a disease. Have compassion and use this illness to get a deeper, more fulfilling understanding of yourself.

Please note that although the following technique can sometimes heal people, please remember that it is not a substitute for going to your doctor. I had severe tooth pain, and I did this technique every day for a week. Eventually, my tooth pain went away almost entirely. I questioned if I still needed to go to the dentist, but since I had an appointment, I decided to go anyway. When the dentist went in, he found that the infection was extensive, and I needed to have a root canal. If I had decided to cancel my dentist appointment, the infection could have spread to my brain. On the other hand, I have had many situations where I have done this technique and been completely healed, much to the bafflement of my doctors. The point is that anything is possible and that we need to work holistically through our thoughts and emotions, and through our physical body such as with doctors, physiotherapists, nutritionists, and other health care professionals.

Connecting to love- Unconditional love to body technique

To send unconditional love to parts of your body, we would just adapt the process of sending unconditional love to your parts (beliefs/thoughts/emotions). I know some of you are very worried about getting it right, so to support you, I've written it again here and tweaked the parts process so that it's specifically for body pain or illness.

Step 1) You can follow the infinity connection of accepting pure love from the universe, then sending it back, then sending pure love to the earth and receiving it back. Or you can do the regular grounding technique of imagining tree roots coming out of the bottom of your feet.

Step 2) Focus on the area (or all) of your body asking for attention. If it's just an area, try to imagine what colour it is. What shape? What texture? Then, see if you can go right into the centre of the pain or illness of that area.

Step 3) Talk to the pain/illness. Ask it why it's acting this way? Really take some time to understand it. What is it scared of? What does it need you to know? What does it want to tell you?

Step 4) Accept this area. Tell it that you see it and imagine you are sending love from your heart fed by the infinity loop of unconditional love to this pain/illness. Make sure you are not trying to heal or change it. You are just sending it love, compassion and understanding exactly how it is right now.

Step 5) See if this pain/illness part of you is willing to send you love, or willing to feel the love it has for you and accept the love from this pain/illness.

Step 6) Relax and let the love flow into you. Let your whole being fill up with beautiful pure white love or pink compassion. Let gratitude swell up for being able to support this pain/illness. Enjoy this bliss until it fades away.

Love is the whole purpose of life, of being. Choosing love fills your life with unimaginable riches. In the following chapters, I will go more into what I have learned about love, how we can choose love so that we have a richer, fulfilling life saturated with moments of bliss and profound connection.

Chapter 15
My Thesis

The Guest House

This being human is a guest house.
Every morning a new arrival.

A joy, a depression, a meanness,
Some momentary awareness comes
as an unexpected visitor.

Welcome and entertain them all!
Even if they are a crowd of sorrows,
Who violently sweep your house
Empty of its furniture,
Still, treat each guest honorably.
He may be clearing you out
For some new delight.

The dark thought, the shame, the malice.
Meet them at the door laughing
and invite them in.

Be grateful for whatever comes.
Because each has been sent
As a guide from beyond

-Rumi

Emotions are potent, so much so that in many cultures, we are taught to avoid them. Emotions are often shunned, labelled as irrational and seen as detrimental. As a highly sensitive empath, my feelings are especially powerful because I have a massive heart capable of loving greatly but also capable of especially feeling the sorrows of the world. So then how could I go into humanitarian work? Why would I be willing to put myself in some of the most horrendous situations in the world if I am so sensitive? Well, the answer is twofold. First, because I am so sensitive to the pain of the world, I want to do what I can to alleviate it. Second, my thesis and soul searching have taught me how to handle my emotions and use my heart as the superpower it is. So not only am I able to do great healing within myself, but I'm also able to offer great healing for those around me. It is precisely my sensitivity that has forced me to embrace my true self and strive for an extraordinary existence.

When I was a child, I was teased and made fun of for my sensitivity, and I struggled with massive amounts of anxiety. Like so many children, I was not taught what to do with all these feelings coursing through my body. I reacted as many people react. I shut off my heart and retreated almost entirely into my head. Although I received the most detentions of anyone in my class, all my detentions were spent philosophizing with my teachers while my fellow detainees would have to do menial chores. This philosophizing is what led me into the study of quantum physics and, more specifically, quantum mechanics. But despite the magical possibilities of the intellectual world, I was profoundly lonely and depressed and struggled with suicidal thoughts. Numbing out my feelings led me to my first existential crisis at the age of 15. However, this led me into the field of psychology because I wanted to figure out what was wrong with me.

Ironically, psychology, although a field focused on helping people deal with depression, anxiety and other mental ailments, does not often focus on emotions directly. For example, Cognitive Behavior Therapy, which is the leading school of psychology in North America, is all about using your thinking to change your behaviours, which will then change your emotions. While it has had much success in some areas, its effects are often not long lasting and can be true of almost every other psychology field. So even in psychology, there is a gap in truly understanding the role and gift of emotions. Although there is a shift building, emotions are still mainly seen as wild and in need of being controlled and fixed.

But are emotions all that unruly? We've already talked about primary and secondary emotions, and how and why they come about, so it might not be a surprise to you that I now think of emotions as the roadmap back to our essence of love. My thesis set me on this path of discovering the power and wisdom that emotions have, and how essential it is to connect to our brain plus our heart. That is why I'm so grateful that I'm a highly sensitive empath because I feel that it has given me a superpower to tune into the emotions and energies that are in others to help guide them back to their inner wisdom. Before I felt like my sensitivity was a curse, it spiralled me into depression and debilitating anxiety. Now it has become a priceless gift that I am so exponentially grateful to have.

So how did I get here? Well, as I mentioned, it all started with my thesis.

My thesis

Ever since I was 16, the field of quantum physics fascinated me. I studied it personally for about 10 years when I decided to do my thesis on how quantum physics relates to psychotherapy. I was fascinated by "the double-slit experiment" that showed how the mere act of consciousness could change waves into physical particles, thus showing that just our awareness or observation can create physical matter! A physicist, Pascual Jordan, who worked with quantum grandfather Niels Bohr stated: "Observations not only disturb what has to be measured, they produce it... We compel [a quantum particle] to assume a definite position." In other words, our observations produce the results of measurements.

This can be seen in medicine too. I always thought about how it was crazy that the placebo effect accounted for almost 50% of people healing themselves. Why was no one else looking into this? How is it possible that our thoughts can have such profound effects on an outcome? Our thoughts are free, have no side effects and are something we can control and learn to do without needing anyone. Shouldn't we look further into how we can maximize this effect?

Furthermore, the example of the 4-minute mile shows us just how powerful our intention is. Once, humans thought that it was impossible to run a mile in under 4 minutes. But after one person was able to achieve this, suddenly many others were also able to complete this extraordinary feat.

To address these potentials, I decided to focus my thesis on using grounded theory methodology to see how we can have the most success in using our thoughts, in the form of intention, to create physical outcomes. Grounded theory is the process of creating a theory from the ground up. Collecting and analyzing data, then coding it by sorting it into different categories that emerge. Then it creates a theory that connects and makes sense of the categories and information that emerged. The following is from the introduction section of my thesis.

> Discovering what intention is and how it is most effectively applied can help people improve the quality of their daily lives. The benefits of this knowledge can be used in the counselling field to aid the development of effective techniques for clients in the creation of new circumstances or outlooks in their life that might promote success, well-being and healing. Intention is currently used in such counselling techniques as motivational interviewing, which helps to create a strong intention in clients to change their behaviour, and cognitive behavioural therapy where thoughts are analyzed and beliefs are changed to influence behaviour (Peterson, Baer, Wells, Ginzler & Garrett, 2006). [...]
>
> Growing evidence suggests that our mental processes exert a profound influence on our bodies, our environment, and our interpersonal relationships (Braud, 1993). Braud suggests (1993) that one's intention influences what one decides to observe, how one observes, the types of observations that one makes, and the interpretations that are constructed. [...]

Have you noticed that I didn't mention emotion once? It was completely off my radar. I didn't have an inkling that it had anything to do with strengthening the outcomes of intention. However, as the research progressed, it soon became evident that it was a vital component for the successful use of intention.

Without getting into all of the ins and outs of my thesis, I used grounded theory methodology to systematically code and organize 15 of the most cited research papers in peer-reviewed journals in each of the fields of Psychokinesis, Guided Imagery, and Psychoneuroimmunology (for a total of 45 papers). I then created a new theory of how intention works. Psychokinesis is the study of those who can move physical objects just by using their thought; think of the boy who can bend spoons in the movie The Matrix. Guided imagery uses visualizations to improve performance or even heal or accelerate the healing process of many physical ailments and which all high-level athletes use. That's why you often see basketball players going through the motions of getting a basket right before they make a penalty shot. Lastly, psychoneuroimmunology is the study of how thoughts and emotions affect the immune system, such as the correlation between depression and reduced immune functioning. Psychoneuroimmunology shows that our mental health is an essential part of our physical health. This is something to keep in mind as we are currently living through a Pandemic.

> More specifically, this study focused on elaborating the process of how intention works and identifying the factors that correspond with intention, resulting in a more informed theory of this challenging and enigmatic phenomenon.

After diligently and methodically coding 45 of the most cited research papers, I noticed a surprising pattern beginning to emerge.

Intense emotion facilitates intention.

> A common result across the data was that intense emotion facilitated intention regardless of whether it was positive or negative emotion. [...] For example, psychoneuroimmunology studies found emotions, regardless of their attributes, consistently had a significant effect on the immune system. Additionally, both spontaneous acts of psychokinesis and beginners at intentional psychokinesis seemed to rely on intensity of emotions (Heath, 2000). However, one exception was the emotion of self-frustration, which inhibited the successful use of intention. This finding could be related to the data that showed that inability to trust, inability to release effort, and increased sense of ego identity were all inhibitors to intention. [...]

> Thus, a clear theme in the reviewed studies was that emotions play a central role in the formation and power of intention.
> Emotion was observed to: (a) increase the ability of individuals to connect with target, (b) contribute to the focusing of attention, (c) generate and increase energy, (d) dissociate ego, and (e) shift focus away from the more rational, and often skeptical, side of the brain. As mentioned previously, all emotions, except self-frustration, were found to be correlated with facilitating outcomes. [...]

Thus, emotions are the engine behind anything we want to achieve! And regardless of whether the emotion is positive or negative, except self-frustration, which seems to cancel any power that other emotions might bring. This means that if we do not work with our feelings, then whatever we try to achieve will be met with mixed success. It's imperative that we work with and understand our emotions if we want to fulfill our intentions.

Specifically, the following emotions were found to be especially important in strengthening outcomes, a) the importance of trust in the process, b) being invested in the process, c) having joy while doing the process, and d) experiencing peak emotions such as bliss, ecstasy and/or oneness during the process.

> Constituents of emotion that analysis showed to enhance intention include, level of investment in the outcome, playfulness, peak emotions, and trust in the process. Illustrations of the importance of trust in facilitating intention included participants in one study commenting on pathways to success: "not trying too hard," "letting go," and "surrendering" (Heath, 2000). In another example, analysis showed that factors that enhanced the effects of guided imagery included trust and rapport with practitioners (Scherwitz, McHenry & Herrero, 2005). Furthermore, trust specifically, is positively correlated with positive ratings of emotional, physical, behavioural and mental

outcomes (Walker et al., 1999; Page et al., 2001; Scherwitz et al., 2005).

Not being attached to the outcome

Trying for an outcome, but not trying too hard is a precarious balance, and relates directly to the concepts of mindfulness meditation where you have an intention and then let it go. It also refers directly to shifting our attention from the destination and instead focusing on the journey. This is why this has become an integral theme in this book. It's not about being perfect. It's about trying and connecting to love, regardless of the results.

When I talk to my clients about surrendering or giving up, there is often resistance to this, and I get that. We try so hard to be better and improve our lives that it seems almost impossible to "let go." I had been pondering another way I could explain this for people when just as I was falling asleep, the image of someone floating on their back came to me. For me, this sums it up. So often we are treading water, and we're exhausted, and we're terrified that if we stop, we'll drown. But if we just relax and float on our back, then the water that we had just been struggling with actually becomes the thing that is holding us up.

Thought, emotion and consciousness

My results showed me that emotion was as important as thought, and both contributed to and were strengthened by higher levels of consciousness. An example of a low level of consciousness is sleep, while a high level of consciousness could be expanded awareness precipitated by diligent meditation.

As someone who had been living in my head for almost 15 years, the inclusion of emotion, and the findings that emotion was just as important as thought, was completely mind-blowing (pun intended)!

The conclusion of my thesis was the following:

> A summary and analysis of the literature revealed three key components to understanding the phenomena of intention: consciousness, thought, and emotion. While each represents a unique foundation of intention, they also interact in a bidirectional way. Consciousness is necessary for thought and emotion to be produced and experienced; however, both thought and emotion can be applied to bring about a higher or more powerful state of consciousness. Moreover, emotions create a more intense experience of consciousness, and thought is able to bring focus to consciousness. For example, when one is happy or peaceful, one is more present in the moment than if one is thinking about being happy or peaceful. Thought, however, can be used to bring one back into the moment, as seen through the action of meditation and mindfulness.

The power of emotion

Energy is the life force of the universe, and emotion is the easiest way to create energy.

> The power of emotion is conceptualized in the form of energy. The relationship between emotion and energy is palpable as one experiences it in one's daily life. Anger is the most obvious example, but so is excitement or even contentment. The type of emotion elicits energy and focuses the direction of it. Depression, on the other hand, drains one of energy and so the results would suggest that it would be more difficult for those with depression to use intention successfully. [...] Belief too would be affected, because without the emotional engine that belief elicits, there is no active drive propelling

> the intention. If one does not believe they can do something and do not emotionally connect with the intention in any other way, then the intention has no momentum.
>
> Energy production, however, can be seen as stemming from the three components of intention. It can be produced through thought such as in the process of attention, and consciousness such as through the experience of "flow" that people can achieve when they are doing something they love, where they lose track of time because they are so energized by their project. Therefore, energy is an essential component of the process of intention. Energy is the force, the physical aspect of intention that fulfills outcome. It is what propels action and momentum that differentiates intention from constructs such as desire.

When we are happy, we have the energy and motivation to do things. When we are depressed, it's like we've lost our vitality, and it can be difficult to even get out of bed. One of the benefits of anger is that it gives us energy and motivation to make a change in our lives and fix or heal a wound. Emotions aren't something we need to be afraid of. They are something we can harness and delve into to become more and more aligned with love. Emotions are the spark of life. Yet emotions need to be balanced with thought.

> The research suggests that all components need to be in alignment for intention to result in targeted outcomes. When either thought or emotion becomes too strong, they can inhibit the other and disrupt the intention process. For example, someone who is extremely anxious finds rational thought more difficult, and therefore conscious intention is inhibited. Alternatively, someone solely focused on thought may lack the energy needed to activate the intention process. Furthermore, when consciousness is diminished, emotion is not fully experienced, and thought is not fully focused.

A metaphor for the integration of these three factors can be seen in the form of a car. Consciousness is like the driver. Higher consciousness is a driver who knows the area well and better able to plan an efficient, safe route. Thought is like the steering wheel. It directs the car where to go and is used by a highly conscious driver to ensure the purpose is followed. Emotion is like the engine. Without emotion, the driver can know where she wants to go and move the steering wheel right and left, but the car won't go anywhere. Similarly, if the engine is revving and on, but no one is steering, the car will go, but it might drive itself off a cliff. The driver, the steering wheel and the engine are all essential components of fulfilling intention.

> The integration of these findings led to the final Theory of Intention as presented in Figure 1, which represents the phenomena and process of intention, where outcome is a product of the integration of consciousness, thought and emotion, and energy is necessary to propel the force of intention towards the outcome.

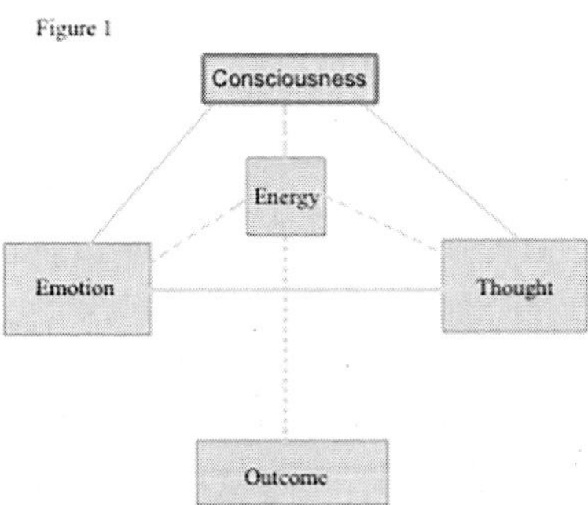

> Here, consciousness is at the top because it is integral to achieving intention. As mentioned earlier, it represents an in-the-moment occurrence. Consciousness is awareness, yet one can have consciousness and not be aware, indeed that is how most humans spend much of their lives. However, as seen by the results,

consciousness can have different qualities, and these qualities can either enhance or inhibit intention. The better quality of consciousness the stronger the integration of both thought and emotion, and therefore the increased amount of energy and more powerful the outcome. Expanded consciousness, with the qualities of interconnectedness, dissociation, increased energy and altered state of time, is of higher quality than everyday consciousness and sleep consciousness. Furthermore, it seems that the higher quality of consciousness, the stronger the integration and alignment of thought and emotion. Consciousness, which is augmented by the qualities outlined in the results, increases the complementary pathways of thought and emotion so that they are working together to create powerful intentions.

In my findings, the qualities of the highest state of consciousness were, a sense of interconnectedness, increased energy, and an altered state of time. It was possible to experience only one of these qualities; however, that would indicate a lower level of consciousness than if you experienced all of these qualities. Through the use of meditation and the visualizations I have shared in this book, I have often experienced a high state of consciousness that had all of these qualities.

An example of this is the detailed visualizations that occur in the present tense. This is an in-the-moment consciousness that involves thought and elicits emotion. The details increase the strength of the consciousness, as does using the present tense. This type of visualization was found to be more effective than less detailed visualizations that were done from an outsider point of view.

This finding, of the power of visualizations, transformed the way I worked with my clients. I went on to use them in Haiti, and the people I worked with experienced phenomenal results. Visualizations are only bound by our imagination and our beliefs. They are a way for us to achieve the impossible. When I taught people how to visualize themselves protected through the blue bubble visualization, they were able to trust and feel safe, which led them to experience physical healing. When I taught Haitians how to ground through the tree grounding, they were able to process and let go of stress, which also resulted in miraculous physical changes where people could finally walk, or had the courage to leave their tent, or could see. Visualizations can profoundly help our mental health, which then improves our physical health. I think the trust that the Haitians had in me also significantly enhanced their results.

> Emotion and thought are also parallel to represent their bidirectional nature. The process of thought generating emotion is well known yet thought also can be a product of emotion. This is seen in the experiments done in the field of social psychology which showed that when a person was approached by a researcher on a suspension bridge, the participant rated the researcher as more attractive than if they were approached on a small bridge. The results supported the notion that participants misattributed their fear on the suspension bridge as sexual attraction to the researcher. This is known as the misattribution of arousal and demonstrates that people often attribute reasons for their feelings, but those attributions are misplaced (Aronson, Wilson, Akert, & Fehr, 2007).

I see this happening all the time. In my intake, I make sure to ask about sleep, exercise, and food because all of that can impact our emotions without us realizing, and instead, we blame others for these feelings. This often happened when I lived in Vancouver, where it is regularly rainy and cloudy. People can suffer from seasonal affective disorder (SAD) but think it's their partner making them depressed, not the weather. That is why it's so important to pay attention to our emotions. That we don't look at them and shrug them off as unreliable when they have an important message for us. In my work as a psychotherapist and energy worker, I can tune into my clients and their emotions without my client having to say much. It helps me to understand what emotion is at the root of their problem and what message a particular emotion has for them. The exercises in this book, on processing emotions, will help you do this for yourself.

Implications for psychotherapy

> Intention is influencing one's internal or external environment in a purposeful way through the integration of consciousness, thought and emotion, with outcome being dependent on the level of integration and energy. [...]
> The results inform us that we can create intention through the integration of consciousness, thought and emotion. However, the conundrum still remains in how to manage or change these three aspects. As an emotion focused therapist, I see the most effective way to change emotion is by replacing it with another emotion through the use of thought. There are, however, various theories that suggest ways in which one can change emotion depending on one's modalities. Figure 1 suggests that emotions can be changed through changing consciousness. This leads us back to visualization or meditation, or other ways that can create altered states of consciousness. However, the altered state of consciousness must be an experience that is strong enough to integrate or change the old emotion.

When you use the heart connection visualization, the grounding visualization, or the emotion processing visualization (described later in this chapter), these are all ways of transforming an emotion and replacing it with another. For example, in the heart connection, you are feeling the emotions that your heart has, you are accepting them, and then you are sending your heart compassion and love—thereby replacing the old feelings with new, powerful emotions. Furthermore, I start all my visualization exercises with the grounding visualization because it gets you into a higher state of consciousness. Much like in the process of hypnosis, you always need to start with relaxing your whole body.

> Strength of consciousness could be created through the various themes mentioned in the grounded theory results, such as through environment, focus, practice, relinquishing control, suspending the intellect, relinquishing of ego and the other factors that were found to enhance intention.
>
> Naturally, the next question is how can one be more conscious so that one can have more control over their life and their outcomes? This is where thought comes in. Thought has the advantage of being more controllable than emotion. If one could control one's emotions, then the world would be a completely different place. Thoughts are also difficult to control, but because they are a more conscious process, they are not as difficult as emotions. This paper proposes that thought, through the use of introspection, psychotherapy, meditation, visualization and various other ways, enables one to connect with stronger levels of consciousness.
>
> Since the pathway of thought is part of our consciousness, this pathway is much more salient in our understanding. Thought is informed by emotion and experience. Through thought, conscious intention is created. Thought works in creating intention through focus, attention, visualization, and relaxation methods. Furthermore, thought works in affecting both emotion and experience through the process of relabeling, reattributing, refocusing and revaluating.
>
> The inclusion of emotion is an important finding. Many theories of psychotherapy concentrate almost exclusively on behaviour and thought, or at most the subconscious. Only a few take into

> consideration the importance of emotion and put it at the same level of thought. This theory suggests that more focus has to be given to emotion in general, but also that the integration of emotion, thought, and consciousness also needs attention. Furthermore, the use of higher levels of consciousness could be harnessed in therapy to help with this integration.

When I work with my clients, I am harnessing their higher consciousness when we use the grounding visualization before going onto another visualization. Grounding is essential before doing the heart connection or processing emotions or getting in touch with loved ones that have passed away or another visualization that will come to me through my intuition. That is why this book begins with talking about the power of intuition and how you can work to enhance it, understand it, and listen to it. Using the techniques in this book and your intuition is an easy way to achieve higher states of consciousness, overcome and heal fear, and choose love when you are in a place of pain or suffering. The techniques you learn here may seem deceptively simple, but they work on many levels of consciousness and heal deep layers of fear. Just because something is simple or you can't feel the profound shift that is happening inside of you, doesn't mean you haven't healed and shifted and become closer to seeing and experiencing the real you that is love.

> The implications for this model in psychotherapy are many. First, the idea that intentions are achievable opens up many more potentials for healing, both physically and emotionally. [...]
> Radin, Taft, & Yount (2004) found that repeated application of healing intentions, which could be done by the psychotherapist, appeared to have measurable consequences. The importance of conscious awareness also educates us on where the focus of psychotherapy should be. It is not enough to teach clients new ways of thinking,

> but we have to enable them to consciously experience new ways of thinking and feeling. Additionally, we have to elicit motivation or energy for them to achieve their goals. The process of intention enlightens us as to how this can be achieved: through visualization, meditation, and practice. Furthermore, the concepts of relinquishing control, ego and analysis also give insight into how this can be achieved.

I have a visualization where I take my client to meet a wise old man/woman. I take them through a process of going through a forest and seeing a cave and then encountering the wise older person. They are then able to ask that knowledgeable person any question they want. They hear the answer that the wise person says and then often receive a gift from the wise person that helps to embody and remind them of the answer they received. When they come out of the visualization, the answer is often something they knew deep down, but this process helps them to trust in it. It is a way of getting the information they know in their head, down into their heart, where they can feel it to be true. The wise person represents their own high self, and all I do is facilitate a way for them to get in contact and have a dialogue with their high self. Often, clients describe the session as very powerful and moving.

Visualizations offer us a way to get in touch with deep parts of ourselves and to understand and be guided by the highest, wisest parts of us. They allow us to get our heads and our hearts aligned, which is the most powerful state of being. Often, I will assign my clients homework where they have to imagine a cord running from their head to their heart with both their brain and their heart beating at the same time. This is another way to ensure both head and heart are in sync and on the same page. We lose too much energy and time and create so much suffering when our heads and hearts are at war.

> Creating an experience of interconnectedness, often characterized by a lost sense of time, and most importantly, increased energy works to integrate consciousness, thought, and emotion so that targeted results can be achieved. Finally, our job as a psychotherapist is to become more conscious and integrate our thoughts and emotions with this consciousness and energy, so that we, too, can achieve our intentions as well as understand the journey we are asking our clients to undertake.

In conclusion, this theory suggests that the integration of consciousness, thought, and emotion can be a powerful means of affecting ourselves and our environment in a purposeful way.

Since my thesis results, I started on a journey of how to utilize and integrate emotions into the healing journey. I learned and developed techniques to directly work with emotions so that you can understand the message it may have for you and harness the power and energy that it is giving you. I have also integrated the use of guided imagery, in the form of visualizations, into my work as the brain cannot tell the difference between reality and our imagination. Visualizations are a fantastically effective way to capitalize on this in experiencing profound healing. I use the emotional processing technique below frequently with my clients to process and gain insight from their emotions.

Processing emotions (centre of emotion)

My thesis taught me that emotions are an important and necessary powerhouse in allowing us to shine our light and develop into the best versions of ourselves. Still, they are also the bridge that connects us from our body to our high self. If we take the time to listen to our emotions, then we can gain invaluable wisdom. Some feelings, especially secondary ones, just need to be listened to and acknowledged and understood, and then they may evaporate without needing to give us any advice. Other emotions, however, have an essential message they want to provide us with. Sometimes this information is profound, and sometimes the message can be a tad dramatic. Use your intuition to decide what you want to do with the data. For example, I will go into some emotions, and their message is "Stop! You're going to die!" Instead of then taking that as a message from my high self, I check in with my intuition. Is this a message that I need to obey? Or is this a message from a part of myself that needs comfort and understanding?

As I have mentioned, I have a wonderfully dramatic heart that really could have gone into theatre, and so often, she just needs to be cuddled and reassured before I continue on the path to something usually legitimately dangerous. However, sometimes my intuition tells me that I need to obey my emotion of anxiety, that I need to stop going down the road I'm on or else things will get more painful and difficult for me. Don't forget your inner wisdom, and don't forget to trust yourself. Our inner selves are universes filled with unimaginable and ever-expanding depths. It's going to take a bit of time to understand and make sense of it all. The tools you are learning here will help, but always remember to follow your own wisdom, your own intuition and trust in yourself.

Below is how to do the emotional processing technique.

Emotional processing technique

Step 1) Spend a moment to sit in a comfortable position with a straight spine. Do a grounding technique to relax you and help you get into a meditative state. Perhaps it's the grounding technique of imagining tree roots coming out of the bottom of your feet.

Step 2) Focus on the emotion that is coming up for you. Where is it in your body, if it's in multiple places focus on the torso, and focus on the area that feels like it is the root or the core of this emotion.

Step 3) Take some time to depersonalize from it. You can do this by trying to imagine what colour it is. What shape? What texture? Then see if you can go right into the centre of the emotion.

1. If you can, then proceed to the next step.
2. If you can't, then that means you are holding onto someone else's emotion as well. Is there someone's face or a name that comes up? Separate what is their emotion from your emotions and imagine a beam of white light coming down and evaporating and transforming the other person's emotion.

*We can always handle our own emotions, but we get blocked if we start to take on other people's emotions. It's also not useful because although you might be trying to help someone by taking on their pain, they will only feel good for a little while, and then they'll just grow some more because they never healed the root of their struggle. So, by taking on other people's pain, you've just doubled the amount of that suffering in the world.

Step 4) Once you can go into the centre of the emotion, look around and see what this place looks like inside. This is your imagination, so anything is possible; perhaps it's a meadow inside, or a cave full of crystals, maybe you're in space. It doesn't matter, just get a sense of what the mood is inside here. What does this place feel like? What emotions does it invoke?

Step 5) Perhaps some emotions start to come up at this point. If so, then let them flood you. Remember your grounding and let these emotions wash over you. Label the emotion and imagine breathing

it in through your heart and then breathing it out through your heart.
This is how you process and digest your emotions. I promise you, the feeling will fade; everything does. When the emotion fades, perhaps another feeling will come up, let that flood over you as well and breathe it in and out through your heart.

Step 6) When all the different layers of emotions have begun to fade, and you can't feel them much anymore, bring your attention back to this place, and the centre of the emotion you were focusing on. Using your imagination, take a moment to "look" around, does this place look different?

Step 7) Talk to this place, ask it what its emotions are? What are its thoughts? What does it need from you to be more comfortable? Really take some time to understand this place.

Step 8) Perhaps you will get a message, perhaps you won't. Either way, send this place unconditional love. Make sure that you fulfill whatever it requests to make it more comfortable. This might involve taking a star down from the sky and putting it in here, or tucking this place into bed and hugging it. Sometimes it wants to be strapped to your back so that it can go everywhere with you. It doesn't have to make sense. This is your imagination. Let's capitalize on the bizarre limitlessness of it! *Remember your brain can't tell the difference between your imagination and reality. Just ensure you are acting out of love.

Step 9) Ask this place if it has any message it wants to give to you before you say goodbye. If it does, then write the message down or else you'll forget it.

Step 10) Say goodbye and gently and softly come back into the room. Give yourself a second to come back to where you are and integrate all the healing that just happened.

I guide my clients through the above technique, in person or through distance sessions. When I work with my clients, I "tune" into them to feel what needs to be focused on. I use my intuition to adjust and change the technique. You can do the same for yourself. The above is just a framework. Please use your intuition to add or adjust it as you need. Additionally, it might be easier to record yourself saying the above directions so that you can listen to the recording instead of reading the next step as you go.

Chapter 16
Choosing Love

How do we find happiness? How do we choose to love more and start to see the love and light in other people as well as within ourselves? In essence, that is what this whole book is about. Still, I love having practical solutions and actions that you can do. I want to share a potent shift in thinking with you that has profoundly shaped my life.

Don't want/Want

Those who have worked with me will know this concept well. It's a concept that has changed my life and is something that I applied vigilantly to the point where now it's mostly automatic. This concept is simple, but don't let that make you underestimate the profound impact it can have on your life's happiness levels. The idea is simply this:

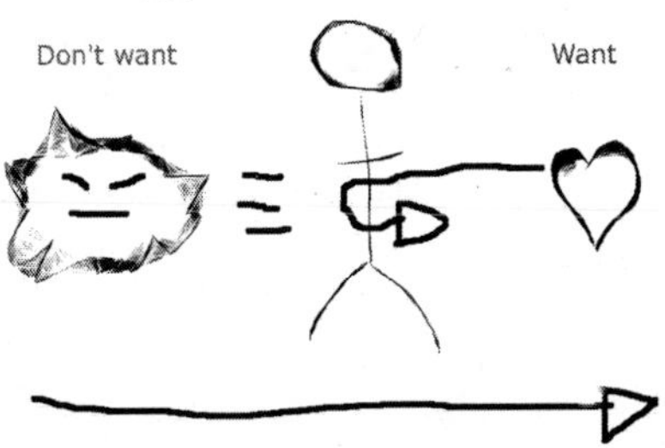

Those that know me will know I'm not a poet, and now I'm sure you can see that I'm not an artist either! That blob on the left is an angry blob (you can tell by its eyebrows). This blob is what we are running away from. It can be anything from, "I don't want to fail," to "I don't want to look stupid," or "I don't want to be a bad parent," or "I don't want to live on the streets." It can be anything and everything that you are running away from, or that you "don't want." To have this make sense to you, take a moment right now to think of something you don't want.

Now please notice the arrow on the bottom. This represents our intrinsic human desire to progress, move forward, learn, and improve. All of us have this innate desire for actualization. We need to feel like we are progressing. For 99% of us, however, we motivate ourselves to move forward by running away from what we don't want or running away from fear (the angry blob). We use fear as a way to motivate ourselves to be better. This just seems to be human nature. It's so much easier to distinguish what we "don't want" rather than to know what we "want."

What I do with my clients is I start with the arrow moving forward and then the angry blob with the person running away from the angry blob. Then I have them draw a box around the stick person and the angry blob. This box represents our view of life, our perspective. Your brain is wired to focus on what you think is important and not even register the rest. Our focus on what we don't want and using that to motivate us to be better people becomes our whole reality of life. It becomes the only thing we see. Take a moment to think about all the things you don't want. If you like, you can even write them down. Now notice how you feel right now when you are thinking about these things? Focusing on what you don't want always leads to an unpleasant experience as you do it. Perhaps you feel anxious or sad or disappointed or stressed.

If our whole life is focused on running away from what we don't want, and having fear be our motivator to be better, then our whole life becomes filled with fear. Fear, or "don't want" becomes all we see, and in fact, this is what makes our lives miserable. In our effort to be better, we only see fear or signs that we are not achieving what we want to achieve. For example, if I don't want to be disrespected, I'm going to be vigilant for any signs of someone possibly disrespecting me. All my attention is focused on what I'm afraid of. That means I might think people are disrespecting me even if they aren't because that is the perspective I am looking at everything with. No wonder people feel lonely and depressed! We are all looking at life through that lens.

To highlight this, I'd love for you to do a little experiment:

Take a moment now to look around you.

Now try to see as many things that are the colour yellow. You can say all the things that have yellow out loud.

Ok, now look at what I'm writing here and don't let yourself peek at what's around you anymore and answer my next question honestly.

How many things did you notice that had grey? Did you even notice anything with grey? Now look around again and see all the grey that is around you. You are always going to find what you look for.

All the colours (and shades) are here, but it depends on what you look for if you're going to notice them.

Now I want to be clear: I'm not here to judge anyone for using fear as a motivator, that's all we know, it's human nature. Of course, we use it as a motivator, and besides, it does propel us forward. But the vital question to ask is, at what cost? We want to move forward because we are searching for happiness. Yet, we are making ourselves miserable in our search for happiness. As someone who loves logic, that doesn't seem entirely logical, does it? Perhaps there is a better way?

And this is where the heart on the right-hand side comes in. You'll notice that it's pulling the person forward. This is the all-important straightforward, and yet life-changing shift in perspective. At this point, I get my clients to draw a box around the stick person and the heart. Instead of thinking and being consumed with what we don't want. Why don't we think about what we want instead?? Why don't we tap into love and have that pull us forward? Why don't we have love and what we're striving for be the lens that we see life through? This is sometimes referred to as "being in the flow." It can feel like floating when we move out of what we want, out of love. Our present experience is so much more inspiring and hopeful when we operate this way.

Now I get that knowing what we want sounds like a simple thing, but it's actually a question that many people can't answer, and that's where the "don't want" comes in handy. Think about the one thing you had in mind about what you don't want. Now flip that into the opposite. For example, one fear that I struggle with is that I don't want to be put on a pedestal (because I know how imperfect I am and I'm fearful for when I fall off it). So, what I've had to do repeatedly is flip my goal to the opposite: I want to be known and seen for being me, instead of focusing all my actions and decisions on "not wanting to be put on a pedestal," and therefore highlighting all my faults, or undervaluing what I can bring to the world, which I often do. I can switch my attitude and focus on how I can be known and seen for being me. I can do this by being vulnerable and genuine so that you can see the real me. But it also means I need to remember my inner strength and take care of my heart so that I'm not dependent on others' acceptance.

It doesn't matter what your goal is or if you automatically go into "don't want," just as long as you notice when you do this and shift into "want." Catch yourself and change so that you have love pull you forward.

It reminds me of that fad about 20 years ago when everyone was wearing those bracelets of "What would Jesus do?" Except here you could say, "What would love do?" Pretty soon, if you do this often enough, you'll start automatically seeing life in terms of what you want, while recognizing the love and abundance all around you. You're still moving forward, but you've found happiness on the way to finding happiness.

The fear of choosing love

After years of dedicating my life to choosing love, one of the ultimate cosmic jokes in my mind is: **why is choosing love so scary?** I mean, sometimes choosing love is downright petrifying, and isn't that precisely the opposite of Love? Didn't I spend a whole chapter saying how fear is the opposite of love? So then why does choosing love sometimes resemble jumping off a cliff blindfolded?

I can't think of a time where I was more petrified than when I had to choose between my husband or my job. I have risked my life multiple times in my field of work, but I find that easy to do when you have the reward of being there for others. This time I was terrified because it was the first time I truly had to jump into the black abyss with no hope of reward.

My misery began because of the Ebola outbreak in West Africa.

> I' m not sure how it happened, but I was forcefully struck that Francois had to go and help in the Ebola response, and I had to support him in this. Sometimes I can see the path that other people need to take. Not to say this is the truth, but it is an insight that will come to me out of nowhere that I need to share with the person of concern. At first, Francois was apprehensive, and of course, I left it to him, but pretty soon he started getting excited at the idea of doing disaster relief again, he sent his resume in and two days later had an interview and then left two days after that! It was all such a whirlwind, but the whole time I had no doubt that it was for his highest good. Saying goodbye to him at the airport was heartbreaking, we were all crying, even Francois, and he later told me that he wasn't sure if he was

going to see me again. But even now, two months later, when I tune in, I still don't have a sense that he will get Ebola despite the huge fear and irrationality that is happening here in Canada.

As I've already mentioned, my husband was one of the first people on the ground after the Ebola outbreak was officially labelled a "public health emergency of international concern" by the World Health Organization. And as people might remember from the more recent Pandemic, at the beginning of an outbreak, not much is known, causing irrational panic. To say people were terrified of the disease is an understatement, and the 60-70% fatality rate created more doom than the 1-2% fatality rate of the Pandemic. I was living in Vancouver at the time. It was pandemonium if anyone had been to anywhere on the continent of Africa, which is enormous, then you were socially ostracized. Rumours were running rampant of how the virus could be spread, and every night the news showed pictures of the masses of dead bodies that there wasn't time or space to bury.

I was genuinely scared for Francois's life, although I understood that Ebola could only be transmitted if you were showing symptoms. In this way, it was much harder to spread than the Pandemic because if someone didn't have a fever, then you knew you were safe from contracting the disease. Although I knew this, I also knew that hygiene is difficult in a disaster, and the quality of the medical system was tenuous in Liberia. I was anxious that Francois would get Ebola and die, and we had only been married for eight months.

I finally bought a ticket to see Francois in Morocco! He gets one week off every six weeks, but we weren't sure when this would be exactly, and if he would be allowed to actually get out of Liberia. I was so elated at the prospect of actually seeing him. I had been distancing myself from him because it was too hard to miss him, especially because of me being so worried about his safety, I didn't want to

stress him out more. Knowing that I was going to see him pulled me together a little bit.
Two days before our trip I was packing when I got a phone call from the clinical director of where I have my private practice, she was very upset and said she couldn't believe I was going to meet Francois and then thought it was ok for me to come back. She gave me an ultimatum; go and see Francois and not see my clients again, or stay and finish up with my clients, which would take a couple of months, before I put myself in danger.

The clinical director had a point, especially considering the false information that was going around about Ebola. Furthermore, I respect her; she was the one who convinced me to leave Haiti after seeing how burnt-out I was. She was the one who took me under her wing; she believed in me and introduced me to many people who referred clients to me. She held weekly supervision meetings for all therapists and was an incredible mentor to all of us. She made all of us better therapists and put her soul into supporting us. I love and respect her deeply, and it made this situation so much more confusing.

But I had been following reliable sources and had the most updated information on Ebola. My husband was on the frontlines, after all. I knew how it could or couldn't be transmitted, and so I knew I wasn't putting myself in danger, let alone anyone else—being given this ultimatum a couple of days before I was due to leave blindsided me.

I was in shock. Because my husband is in the heart of Liberia fighting Ebola, I am pretty up to date with developments of the disease, how it's transmitted, etc. Apparently, I'm one of the few who are. Fear of Ebola has created pandemonium here. I just learned that eight therapists at the office were threatening to quit if she allowed me to come back to the office after going to Morocco. Even though it would have been impossible that they would ever be in any danger, but they aren't listening to me when I present the facts of what is known so far. The clinical director asked me to think about it some more and then call her in the morning.

When I called her Friday morning, a day before my flight, she was pretty upset still and quite frustrated. I tried to give other solutions that would perhaps appease the other therapists, but nothing was acceptable other than me cancelling my trip. I was crushed. The thought of not seeing Francois when I felt he really needed me was unbearable, but ruining my relationship with my mentor and hurting my clients was also horrible.

I was so confused! I didn't know what to do, and for one of the few times in my life, I didn't know what the right thing was (often, I have a very strong intuition where I "know" what I need to do). I called Francois and asked if he had a sense of what I needed to do, but he didn't, I called both my parents, they also had no insight, although I think they thought that it would be more responsible to cancel my flight.

I felt so stuck. I loved the clinical director, who was also my mentor, and of course, I loved my clients beyond measure. On the other hand, I really loved my husband and felt that he needed emotional support after being on the front lines of Ebola for almost two months. How could I choose love when love was on all sides?

Finally, I called Dianne, and honestly, I feel like our friendship was created for this moment. She told me, "Jennifer, don't be silly, you stand for love, not fear, what is the decision out of love?" I said I didn't know; that I love Francois and my clients and my clinical director. She said, "You going to see Francois, why would you do that?" "Because I love him." "You staying, why would you do that?" "Because I'm scared of what would happen if I went." "There you have it!"

What made clear the decision I had to make was that I wanted to be there for Francois. I wanted to visit him. I wanted to see him and touch him after being separated. I didn't want to abandon my clients, and I didn't want to upset my clinical director. This implementation of want/don't want was invaluable. It gets us away from right or wrong thinking. I don't think there was a right or wrong answer here. Both my clinical director and I were "right." Part of figuring out what we want and don't want is asking ourselves, "Why would I make decision A?" and comparing that to "Why would I make decision B?" If I cancelled my trip, I would have been motivated out of fear; because I didn't want to lose my job. I loved my clients, but when asked why I wanted to stay, my answer wasn't because I loved them, it was because I didn't want to let them down.

Don't overthink it. That just leads us in circles. We get lost in the details and semantics when what we really need to do is stop, feel what's going on in ourselves and ask love what it wants to do at this moment. Forget about right and wrong; just choose love.

At that moment in time, what was present for me was my love for Francois. That love is what outshone everything else. Choosing love is not always about the details of what you love and what you don't. It's about the present moment, what is it that love wants in the present moment? What direction is love pulling you towards at this moment now? I loved my clients, it easily could have been my love for them that was pulling me at that moment, and if so, then the best decision would have been to cancel my trip. Do you see? It's not about right or wrong. It's about feeling love and deciding to follow it in each moment, regardless of the outcomes. It's about choosing what makes your heart sing. It's about seeing your fears, not obeying them, and wanting to be led by love. No one can tell you where love is leading you, only you know that. Dianne, in her infinite wisdom, did not tell me where love was pulling me, she just asked me why I would do one thing, and why I would do the opposite and helped me see what I needed to do.

That day was one of the hardest days of my life. I had to tell the clients I had scheduled for that day that this was the last time I would see them. I arrived at the office in tears and had to collect myself so that I could be of service to them. They were all very understanding and kind, but it didn't soothe the pain of having to pack up all my stuff. My lovely parents picked me up once I was finished. I barely slept that night, and then my parents drove me to the airport to start on the journey of trying to see my husband, although not sure if he would actually be able to get into Morocco.

Thankfully he was able to get in, and we had a marvellous week together. It was normal and incredible all at the same time. I just feel so grounded and stronger when I'm around him. It's strange it's not like fireworks or anything, it's just this slow, subtle swelling of love. I feel less anxious and more myself when around him; I feel like I can handle anything.

Our week went by wonderfully. We got into a heated discussion about justice, with my arguing that I think forgiveness is more important than justice, but I think in the end, we were actually on the same page. We had to separate again, and there were a couple of moments where I felt that this was all just too much, that I couldn't handle being away from him and being back in Vancouver to face the consequences of my decision making a shitshow of my life. But every time I would get overwhelmed and feel like I would perhaps start hyperventilating, I tried just to remember love, and take it one step at a time, the first one being connecting with love.

When we operate out of love, we focus on what we want and not the consequences. As I write this, I'm fearful that it sounds callous and uncaring, but even though I have that fear and you thinking that could be a real consequence, I choose not to let that stop me from writing this. Love is all-powerful, all wonderful. Yes, there are consequences from following it, and those consequences can feel horrible. Still, my choosing to see my husband showed me that, in fact, those things I am scared of are just illusions; they are temporary. My clients survived without me, and choosing love at that moment was incredibly a massive catalyst for others close to me to decide to choose love in their own lives.

> I was able to fly home and not feel any anxiety. I actually didn't even notice that I didn't have anxiety until talking to my parents later that night. I called the clinical director the next morning (yesterday), and I was a little nervous right before I had to make that call, but that was all. The call ended up going the best it could have possibly gone, we had a really heartfelt conversation and discussed honestly what we could do. She said she didn't want to lose a relationship with me, which is such a relief! I can't even explain how wonderful it was. I'm still not going to go to the office, and I still won't get to say goodbye in person to my clients, which breaks my heart. But at least the clinical director and I are on good terms. Also, I feel like this chapter of my life in Vancouver is closed, and I'm ready to move on (to what I have no idea).
>
> So my emotions now... I feel like my decision to live out of love and not cater to fear was a huge one that had a ton of ripple effects throughout my life and others. I know my immediate family has been really affected and moved, and that alone is more than I could hope for. I feel like I am a new person, more whole and grounded again (although perhaps that's because I was just with Francois?). But I feel so much more clear even though my future is even murkier. I feel like I can really trust in the universe, although I would like to know what the universe wants me to do, honestly, I will do anything, I just want to know what it is! But I do know that I am supposed to go through this process, and so go through it I will.
>
> I love you so much! Thank you for being so incredible, for having the strength to do what I needed to do even though it felt like I was going

to lose everything! Technically nothing has changed, but I feel like a new person and don't have any fear in me right now. I just might believe that love conquers all!

This event was only my perspective, and I have since reached out to my clinical director, who says she has a different memory of what happened. Our memories and perspectives are so flimsy! She agreed to write what her view was:

My Experience - Choosing Love Over Fear – Alyson Jones

I always knew that Jennifer was a shining star. I had been her professor during grad school, and I was pleased to mentor her during her time in Haiti. Watching her grow professionally and live a courageous life was an honour. I was so pleased when she joined my practice after she returned from Haiti. I knew she was an exceptional person, and it was no surprise when she quickly built a thriving practice at my clinic. Not only did I refer clients to her – I even referred the people I loved to her – my family and friends. I truly loved working with her and hoped we would work together for years, but I also knew she had a heart drawn to adventures and one day, she might be called to a new opportunity. I just did not expect the way that opportunity would play out and how it would impact me. When she married Francois, it was a joyous surprise, and I was so pleased for her.

When Francois went to Africa, I worried about them both. It was all so unknown at that time.

When Jennifer informed me that she had booked her airplane ticket and was leaving to go see Francois, I was shocked. I did not expect this as it was the height of the Ebola scare, and I did not understand how this could be safe for her. I was disappointed that she did not discuss the possible implications with me first. From my perspective, I was attempting to give reality checks and let her know that difficult choices had to be made, from her perspective I presented an ultimatum. Although Jennifer was well informed about Ebola and the risks, I felt Jennifer was not dealing with the realities of the fallout, and yes – I did resent that this fell on my shoulders. Later I came to realize that is was not Jennifer's job to have to take all these factors into consideration – that in fact, this was my job and my job alone.

As soon as the news got out at the office that Jennifer was going to meet Francois the fear spread like a virus of its own. Several of the other Associates said they would leave the clinic as Jennifer could potentially be a danger to them and their clients if she returned. The staff expressed the same sentiments saying I had a responsibility to provide a safe workplace. I called our provincial health organization to talk with them, WorkSafeBC, to discuss my responsibility to everyone at the office and I called my liability insurance to ask for advice regarding this unique situation.

This was not a simple situation where I could support Jennifer and worry about the consequences to her – but rather I had to deal with the fact there could be consequences for me and others. I understood Jennifer was making a personal decision based on love. I cared for and admired her, but the feedback I was getting from my inquires was distressing.

WorkSafe confirmed I had a responsibility to others at my office and my liability insurer told me I could be liable as I was aware beforehand that she could have been exposed. They told me that I was leaving myself open to a lawsuit if anything went wrong and they would not insure me on this matter. This meant if anyone took legal action against me, I had no protection from my insurer. When your professional insurer tells you this you take it seriously. I was the owner, operator, and clinical director of the clinic – and now it felt like everything was put on the line.

I knew I had to make decisions based on my professional and personal obligations. This decision for me was not about fear – but actually based on love. I never had the same fear as the others at the office about Ebola as Jennifer was well informed and I had also talked to our provincial health authority. I tried to explain this to people – but I had to accept the heavy responsibility that comes with being a leader. I loved my work and the clinic I had built. I had to set limits based on love for myself, my vision, my family, my leadership role and even love for Jennifer. It is my belief that love is the driving force in life, but it always comes with some pain and sacrifice. It was incredibly sad for me, and to lose Jennifer as an Associate was a huge professional and personal loss for me. I recall explaining this all to her and letting her know what my position was and what my responsibilities were. In the end, the limits were mine to set, and the decision was hers to make.

When Jennifer let me know her decision was to go to see Francois, I understood this decision was based on love. It was the decision I expected from her. I told her how much she meant to me and that our relationship was bigger than this situation alone. I told her that I was honoured to be a part of her life and was committed to continuing to support her and cheer her on. I felt by this point that my internal struggle had been resolved and I had acknowledged and accepted the losses that this situation entailed for me.

I did not want to lose my relationship with Jennifer as well. I felt proud that we had this conversation before she left, *and I felt we had acknowledged our love and acceptance of each other. I am honoured to know Jennifer, grateful for the time we worked together and proud to call her my colleague and friend. In the end, we both chose love, and although this took us in different directions, we remained champions for each other and champions of love over fear.*

In the end, it's not about right or wrong. Both people can stand in their truth and act out of love, and life still might not go how we want. I felt that this was a huge decision that I had to make, and what if I saw the whole situation inaccurately? We don't know what reality is; we so often make our own reality through our own biases and fears. It's an important thing to remember, and in my mind, choosing love in each moment is an even more critical decision. What matters to me is that I choose to connect to love, to make a strong stance in my commitment to choosing love, and that changed my whole life. It was a proclamation to myself of how vital choosing love is to me.

That event happened six years ago, and as I write this, I just connected with my parents about their perspective of this situation. I didn't realize it, but this event was also a pivotal moment in both their lives. I already knew this was a life-altering moment for my mom. She's often told me and thanked me over the years for showing what choosing love was through this experience. However, my father had been furious and incredibly protective of me. He wanted to act out of fear on my behalf. He said that how I "embodied love over fear during this event by treating all parties with love and compassion despite the suffering I was going through because I cared so much about my clients was discombobulating for me." My stance turned his world upside down and made him aware of the importance of choosing love. He said he still thinks about it now and tries to act in ways where he chooses love over fear.

Isn't it incredible the healing and goodness that can come from these moments? They seem painful and tragic, and yet they are just small details. They have no power, and years later, it's the act of love that profoundly shapes you and potentially those who are close to you. I cannot predict how transformative choosing love is, or the ripple effects it creates that you won't even realize. I'm almost brought to tears for the ways that us standing for love can radiate and bless those around us. I sometimes feel so undeservingly lucky to have had so many profoundly beautiful experiences.

The details don't matter. Even though my marriage has not worked out, I still would have made the same decision. I made that internal and external commitment to choose love no matter what, and it was an incomprehensibly powerful thing. I am, without a doubt, so grateful to Dianne for helping me make that decision. I hope that perhaps I can be a Dianne to you reading this book, encouraging you to choose love over fear even when it seems like you might lose everything.

So how do you know it's love that you're choosing? That is a question only you can answer, and it requires, actually demands complete honesty with yourself and your true motivations. I wish that by reading this book, you can avoid the mistakes I've made so that you can save yourself some suffering; but know that you are not alone. All of us struggle, and sometimes, that struggle is precisely what makes us feel like we've accomplished something worthwhile.

All my love to you as you go on this journey.

Chapter 17
Happiness

Part of my journey of choosing love was to go into deep contemplation of what happiness is. To me, happiness is an indication of how connected I am to my natural state that is love. So, if I can be joy in my life, then that is a sign that I am becoming more and more connected to love. After my second existential crisis, I had the profound knowing that happiness wasn't a selfish goal, which I had believed previously, but the new purpose of my life. I wanted more than the pleasure I get after shopping. I craved profound happiness, the joy, the feeling that your heart is singing. I desired to understand and feel the lasting and soul-nourishing type of joy. I dedicated 12 years of my life, time and energy to the quest for true happiness and understanding what true bliss is. I believe that it is an admirable and vital life purpose for those who feel called to it.

After working in the Ebola outbreak for 1.5 years, I was burnt-out and frazzled. I need to take breaks after each of my missions to remember what is "normal" again. But it's also complicated because you're used to working around the clock and having your work directly improve the lives of others. When the mission ends, it's challenging to connect with your loved ones who can't understand what you lived through, and that's only the ones who are interested. All of a sudden, you have all this time and no purpose, and no one that understands you. I find the time after a mission one of the most challenging times because you're stuck in this no man's land where you don't know where you belong. Having a project to do is an excellent way to decompress. It gives you purpose and direction while also giving you some time to process all the crazy things that you just experienced but didn't have the emotional capacity or space to process while you were on a mission. So, Francois and I decided to finally fulfill a childhood dream that both of us had: to sail across an ocean.

After Ebola, I also wanted to delve into what happiness truly was. Is it something that outside circumstances control? Or is it partially or even completely an internal thing? I had always believed the idea that it was only achievable through inner fulfillment. Still, then my profound happiness when I was finally given a job during the Ebola outbreak shattered that resolve. How had something external given me such joy? Before getting my job in Ebola I was miserable, I was stressed and anxious because I wanted to help and follow my heart more than anything, but it took longer than I thought to be able to find a job. If satisfaction was internal, then why did my happiness get so affected by my external circumstances? I wanted to use the quietness of sailing across an ocean to delve into this conundrum. With no internet, very little electricity and not much space. I thought it would be an excellent time to delve into my psyche to understand and explore my experience and inner wisdom and see if I could discover what creates happiness. Little did I know that the universe would support me so thoroughly in this quest. I would get tested firsthand on if happiness was possible regardless of external circumstances.

The following is part of a letter I had written to a friend right after the 2.5-month trip across the Atlantic…well, almost across the Atlantic.

So it sounds strange, but I have to start 16 years ago (when I was 18). I went to this Vipassana retreat, a 10-day silent retreat where you meditate the whole damn time. I'm talking getting up at 5 am and pretty much meditating until 11:30 pm. As a child/teenager, I'd always wanted to reach enlightenment, and this retreat was an effort to continue towards this goal. BUT at the end of this retreat, I became totally disillusioned. What I understood them to say was that to be enlightened, you have to give up all attachments, including a passion for humanity. I thought about it long and hard and decided that I would rather give up my dream for enlightenment than give up my passion for striving to make the world a better place. For me, human connection, those moments as you've just described where people are open and honest and sincere, are the moments that I treasure above all else, even enlightenment.

So fast forward 16 years…

In preparation for this sailing across the Atlantic dream, I read the book "Siddhartha," and it really really hits me that perhaps I understood it wrong all those years ago, and maybe I can still strive to reach enlightenment. I should also mention that over the past couple of years, I've been studying this path of seeing past the illusions of the world and being able to trust in Love and be Love more fully. This is based on the book "A Course in Miracles." The idea that I don't have to give up a connection with others and yet I could still reach enlightenment was something really exciting for me. (In fact, according to A Course in Miracles, enlightenment is the ultimate connection with all things, and our belief in separation is what creates loneliness and suffering.) So my mind has been blown open, and the last couple of months, I've been taking up this journey of enlightenment earnestly. It has been absolutely incredible because we were sailing for a couple of months, and there was jack shit to do, so meditation and contemplation were not only achievable but are a great way to pass the time. Add to that a super crazy Cuban wife, all of us being trapped in a confined place, and you have a recipe for working through **ALL** the shit.

After leaving West Africa, Francois and I flew to the Caribbean and started walking the docks to see if any sailboats sailing across the Atlantic needed crew. We also signed up on this website that connects captains to potential crew members. We had no luck from walking the docks, and to be honest, we were both a bit shy, and it was kind of intimidating. But then we got an offer from this young Italian Captain who needed crew. So, we decided to fly to Cuba where he was with his wife, getting his boat ready for the voyage.

When we arrived in Cuba, we had a month to get the boat ready and do some provisioning before we had to depart. The month went by pretty smoothly. We worked with the Captain and met his wife, who was also going to join us. We met another crew member, a Colombian who was an activist and was forced to leave Columbia because some warlords wanted to kill him.

During this time, when the wife was around, the conversations were in Spanish because she couldn't speak English. I was the only one who couldn't speak Spanish, so I would vacillate between pretending I could understand or giving up and just enjoying the scenery or playing games on my phone. It was because of this that Francois and I never knew what we were getting in for.

The day finally came for us to depart. As a Cuban, the Captain's wife wasn't allowed on the dock, and so she had to fly to Haiti, where we were also going to pick up our final crew member. It was just the Captain, the Columbian, Francois and I who set sail on a 40 ft Catamaran from Cuba to Haiti. That stretch was incredible. Then it went downhill from there.

I don't remember how long it took us to sail to Cap-Haitien, Haiti, between 2-4 days, but I vividly remember one of the nights. There was a massive storm, the boat tossed us back and forth, and I was crippled with seasickness. We had to unplug all our electrical equipment for fear of getting hit by lightning. I remember being huddled into a ball in the poop deck and watching the massive 12-metre waves rock our boat back and forth and then seeing a flash of lightning streak across the sky, or even more terrifyingly, hitting the ocean. My goal of contemplating happiness went overboard, along with all the contents of my stomach.

The next day the skies had cleared, and the sun was beating down on us as if nothing had ever happened. Except the wind had shifted to be against us, and since we needed to be in Cap-Haitien to pick up the wife, we used our engine to make up for the lost time.

At one point, the Captain noticed that something was wonky with one of the engines, and he went down to investigate. He came back up to report that there was some garbage stuck but that we'd keep on going and get it untangled at a later time. I still don't know why he decided to wait to untangle it, but it was genuinely a miracle that he did.

We continued like this for a few more hours, talking about what we would do should we encounter any pirates, and then all of a sudden, the Captain decided that it was time to finally untangle the garbage that was on one of the propellers. We stopped the boat, and he swam down and freed the propeller. After five minutes, we were ready to set off again. But just as we were starting the engine, I saw something white moving in the distance. We were in the middle of the ocean with no land in sight, and so we couldn't imagine what this white thing was. We slowly made our way closer and realized it was a Haitian man on the side of a capsized boat waving his shirt. With the dangers of pirates in our heads, we were all very trepidatious approaching the scene. Francois is a whiz at languages and still remembered his Creole when we lived in Haiti five years earlier. So, he called out to the man in Creole, asking him what the matter was. The man was mute, his eyes bulging out of his head and refusing to speak. He just kept moving his finger across his throat over and over—was he going to kill us? What was he trying to say? We were all pretty nervous by now, but being humanitarians, there was no way Francois and I could not help this guy, even if he was a pirate. We threw him a life ring, and he frantically swam out to grab it. We got him on board, and he immediately burst into tears. I got him a blanket and some food and water and started rubbing his back. Finally, he began to speak. Francois translated for us and explained that his two cousins (age 24 and 28) were still there, trapped underwater, tangled up in the lines, and both dead. That is why he kept making the neck cutting motion. He had been on the side of the boat for 18 hours trying to get help, but no one had passed. He wanted us to take the dead bodies. As heartbreaking as it was, there was no way we could bring the dead bodies on board. Francois's and I's experience with Haitian police was not a good one, and we were worried they would use the situation as a way to arrest us and demand money for our release. But now I wonder if that was the right decision? How horrible it must have been for the families not to give a proper burial for the two young men.

We took our new guest with us to Cap-Haitien but smuggled him off before checking in with "harbour control," which ended up being two Canadian UN soldiers. Francois and I sent him off with enough money to pay for the funerals and go towards buying a new boat, but I still think about what happened to him when he got home and if he's ok.

However, I digress, the purpose of this story is to highlight my journey of contemplating happiness. During the start, I had been terrified and then so concerned for this Haitian fisherman that I had forgotten my intention. However, I was going to be forcefully reminded with the arrival of the Captain's wife.

We had arrived in Cap-Haitien and were greeted by the UN soldiers. They informed us that we were the only tourist boat they had ever come across, something Francois and I had warned the Captain about. They weren't quite sure what to do with us, but they ended up letting us stay on the little dock that was "port."

That afternoon, the Captain's wife arrived; however, her luggage didn't. She was livid. I can relate, I've lost my luggage before, and it's pretty upsetting, not to mention she was in a country that she didn't know and so couldn't communicate to the people at the airport very well. She was sent away and told to call in the morning to see if it had arrived then.

The next morning, very early, we hear this shrieking: "Francois! Francois!" Francois gets dressed as quickly as possible and makes his way to the galley (kitchen) where everyone hangs out. Upon arriving, he sees that there is coffee, so he makes his way to the coffee and pours himself a cup while he asks her what she needs. She loses it. Apparently, the fact that Francois poured himself a coffee first before asking her what she needed was completely out of line. She proceeds to swear at him for a full minute while also insulting his mother before she finally demands that he call the airport and see if her luggage has arrived. Swallowing his anger and outrage, he does, only to be informed that the baggage has not arrived and that he should call back tomorrow.

Later that day, our final crew member arrives, a young French guy who also speaks Spanish. The days go by, and we complete all our provisioning, but still no luggage. All of us are walking on tiptoes, but her rage just seems to grow and grow. She has taken a particular and extreme dislike to me.

> ...She could only speak Spanish and Italian, and I could only speak English, and the other crew (Captain, Francois, French and Columbian) could all speak Spanish and English), so I think that gave her mind a blank canvas to work its wonders in regard to me. Now to be fair, she was going through a lot (although we couldn't communicate, so it's just me surmising). She was just visiting Cuba after living in Italy for the last 1.5

years, so she was probably feeling super homesick on leaving. The sailing lifestyle does not seem to fit her AT ALL, and she hates Italy, and that's where we were all sailing too. AND because she wasn't allowed to board the boat in Cuba and so she flew to Haiti where, of course, the airline lost her luggage, and so all the crazy expensive clothes that she had worked for were lost, and that really must have been devastating. So she's not in a great spot. Now add to that me, who is in a super fantastic place with all my blissed-out experiences from meditating, and me and Francois are super lovely and awesome, and me getting along with all the crew really well, and me also being a female (even though she is stunning), and I can see how being around me would be annoying. Also, I genuinely love sailing, as does her husband, and so although I was very careful to never be even remotely flirty with him and was even standoffish, she HATED him talking to me, even if it was to tell me to take the sail in.

Anyways, she was so paranoid that whenever I was laughing (which was often), she thought it was because I was making fun of her (!??). Regardless of how often everyone would explain to her that I was not at all talking about her, and was not at all like that. She was convinced that she was right and that I was the devil. (It was an excellent lesson for me that you can categorically create your own reality!) Her hatred to me then spilled over to Francois. After she swore at Francois that morning, she never apologized because it's all Francois's fault since he should have attended to her needs BEFORE ALL ELSE. But I also think she hated Francois because he and I were doing really well, we were affectionate to each other, not jealous, and never fought. In contrast, her and the Captain fought every day, because the Captain was doing something wrong like having the engine on when she was trying to sleep *or gave coffee to Francois before her, or asked me to let out the mainsail... And she hated all of the other crew members if they talked to me or paid any attention to me, which was inevitable because we were all friends and STUCK ON A BOAT together.*

She hated me so much that the only time she made dinner, she made it for everyone except me. When we put up the spinnaker sail and commented on how it was beautiful and looked like the Cuban flag, she responded with "Long live Cuba, I hope Canada dies." It makes me chuckle writing this now because although throughout my life there have certainly been people that don't like me, I've never had someone hate me so much that their life revolved around trying to make me the most miserable as possible.

But every time she was hostile to me, I used it as an opportunity to find happiness. Thankfully, we mostly communicated through others, so it gave me more time to sit with my emotions before speaking to her again. I would feel the anger and then the underlying hurt and comfort my heart, and then I would ask, who do I want to be? What is love? What would love do? And I'd connect to love and try to respond through that connection. I was dicey at first, and it was a steep learning curve, but as I got used to the hostility, I was able to get better and better at staying in a place of love. The better I was at connecting to love, however, the more it made her furious, which was the opposite of what I wanted.

She wasn't satisfied if I was merely unhappy. She was only content if I was miserable. It was a perfect storm of her trying to upset me, me trying to connect to love and, therefore, not getting affected by her, so her trying harder, then breaking and getting upset, and then her being momentarily satisfied.

What better way to see if I can find happiness internally while externally, I have someone who is actively trying to make me miserable? It was perfect! Lucky for her, not only did I get seasick for three days every time we left land, but I'd also get land sick for three days after we'd arrive in port. One of the few times I saw her laugh was when she was watching me puke my guts out from seasickness. This contemplative experiment wasn't as easy as I had hoped it would be.

Even during the 20 or so days I was throwing up, even though I struggled and broke occasionally, I was still able to find happiness. I was able to spend hours meditating and regularly connect to ecstasy. When I was skippering (steering), I was able to connect to the ocean's rhythm and navigate using the stars or the sky and find hours of harmony where the boat and the ocean and the sky were all one. My ability to ride the ocean waves and steer a clear course inspired the Captain, who wasn't allowed to talk to me, to whisper one night that I was one of the best skippers he had ever seen.

As the sun was coming up in the early morning, pods of dolphins would often come and swim alongside the boat. I'd put the boat on autopilot and just revel in this opportunity to commune with nature. I could have seen all the hatred and meanness, the monotony and boredom as excuses to be miserable. And to be honest, I did have moments of total misery, especially when seasick, and after being at sea for over two weeks and fed up with not being able to even pee without falling over. But mostly, I choose to focus on the beauty and interconnectedness between us and everything around us. I didn't take the wife's hatred of me personally and still treated her with respect. I was still able to have moments of bliss even while I was throwing up. For me, it was proof that happiness is an internal thing.

It is a fantastic opportunity to learn how to be genuinely happy and unaffected, despite the fact that someone hates your guts and is using any opportunity to make you upset. I'm actually amazed that I was able to achieve this! Honestly, it's incredible this path to enlightenment! And although I feel a long way off, being able to be in charge of my own happiness and being

able to find it regardless of the situation, is priceless!! (Now I just have to learn how to maintain it...)
So, after 1.5 months of this, we arrive in the Azores. She's threatened the Captain to leave the boat again (she does this at least two times when we reach land, Haiti, Bermuda and now the Azores). The Captain is a kind, easy-going guy and desperately wants her to be the sailing wife that he imagined. So, to appease her, he takes on these two Italian guys. She wanted the guys to replace Francois and me, but Ricardo really liked Francois and me and knows that we've done absolutely nothing to gain her wrath and is trying to be as honourable as he can (also he's following marine law). So, the Italian guys come on board (eight of us now), and they are fantastic. The wife thinks that they will be just her friends since they are Italian, and she speaks Italian, but to her chagrin, they also like hanging out with Francois and I (and the rest of the crew). Shit hits the fan when I invite her and the Captain to join Francois and me with the Italians for dinner, and because she and the Captain decided to come late, they sit at the end of the table, and we are all in the middle of a conversation in English. After about 2 minutes, she loses it and asks the Italians only to speak Italian so that she can understand. Francois and I (who are sitting between them) then continue to have our own conversation together and are laughing and joking around. Then the Captain laughs at one of my jokes, and the wife is furious. They leave in a big fight and are fighting all night. The next day, she has her things packed, but her and the captain fight for the rest of the morning and afternoon. Then she comes back with her bag, and we have a group meeting. The Captain is red-faced as he says there is a new rule; no one is allowed to speak English on the boat because his wife doesn't understand English. Then, after more discussion, it comes out

that you can, in fact, speak any language you want, French, Portuguese, etc:., just not English. Of course, it is pointed out that I can only speak English, to which she just smiles.

I was pretty upset with this blatant attempt to ostracize me completely and was really worried that I would be alone, not able to talk to anyone for the remainder of the sailing (about two weeks' worth). I couldn't help but start crying while I was by myself on the bow of the boat. She saw this, and it seemed to appease her, and we set sail for the next island.

However, in my quest for ultimate happiness regardless of circumstances, I had an amazing meditation. I really felt in my heart that no matter what, nothing could control if I was happy other than me. It didn't matter that I was all alone and isolated; I could still be happy if I chose. Then I danced my little heart out while I was in charge of skippering. Although everyone spoke in Spanish or Italian while in a group (meals, meetings, etc.), people did still talk to me in English when she wasn't around, but I think she noticed this. So, when we reached the next island, there was again the ultimatum that she would leave if the Captain wouldn't kick off Francois and me.

At this point, all of us were getting seriously exhausted by the drama. Francois says good morning to her, and she again calls him a motherfucker and descends into a cascade of swearing, so Francois is ready to leave. I meditate long and hard, my meditation on this day was defenselessness, and I want to make sure I'm not getting in an ego struggle of staying just to piss her off. I firmly get the message not to leave and that we need to let the Captain make the decision.

The Captain and his wife were at the airport. He was trying to convince her not to leave. All the rest of us are on the boat. Almost no more sailboats are crossing anymore because hurricane season is very soon, so we really have to leave that day. All of a sudden, the Captain comes back alone. He gets on the boat and tells us that his wife is not coming and that we are leaving now. He starts the engine. It doesn't start. He tries again. It doesn't start. He tries for five minutes, and then finally, the engine catches, and we start to reverse out. And then we hear yelling. The wife is coming towards us on the dock yelling, "GIVE ME MY MONEY!" We all look at each other, the Captain sighs and goes down to meet her. They continue to fight for three hours on the dock.

Then, at around 8 pm, the Captain comes back from fighting with his wife and says that all of us are getting kicked off the boat. That he has to make a decision between his wife or us, and of course, he's choosing to stay with his wife (understandable). So, all of us literally get marooned. Like old school, Captain Robinson style.

We had 30 minutes to pack up all our stuff and get off the boat. We all watch as the Captain and his wife motor out of the harbour: he'll have to sail 24/7 now with no help for the next two weeks, as she refused to help with sailing our whole trip. We all check into one hotel room, and that's when I notice all the cash I have is gone: about $800 worth. I genuinely laugh. During the whole trip, I saw all of this as a real-life test on if I could find happiness despite external circumstances, and this was the cherry on top. Of course!

We all walked the docks the next couple of days and talked to everyone, and all the boats that needed or could have taken crew had left during the day of us getting kicked off. I'm feeling guilty, I was sure that we weren't supposed to go look for another boat but if we had both Francois and I could have *completed our dream of sailing the whole Atlantic Ocean! Also, I had no idea what to do next. I kept meditating and got that I shouldn't make any plans, don't buy any flights, just wait. So two days more of just waiting. Then we ran into a friend that we had met on the island just before this one and he invited me to a yoga teacher training in the north of France. Something clicks, and I know I need to go. I get a flight and leave the next morning, and here I am. Francois decided he wanted to still see if he could find a boat, so he stayed behind with the others.*

To this day, I'm so grateful for this experience. I was forced to decide if I wanted to choose happiness or vindictiveness and suffering while on that boat. I'm happy with how I could still treat the wife with respect, stand up for my morals when she was hurting other crew members, and again see all the beauty that was enveloping me and just waiting to be appreciated, even if I stumbled and made mistakes.

I do have to say that being on an ocean surrounded by nature, navigating by the sky, watching the sunset and the sunrise while dolphins play beside you, all makes the quest for happiness so much easier. But it is also quite the challenge to find joy when someone actively hates you and is trying to make you miserable, plus, you are seasick for a third of the time. My struggle was nothing compared to what other people have to endure, but it was enough for me to delve into the theory that happiness is internal. There is beauty and joy everywhere; we just need to choose what we focus on if we want it in our lives.

Connecting to love/happiness

This experience taught me that my failproof way of getting in touch with happiness or love is gratitude. Gratitude blows my mind in how quietly powerful it is. For me, it is the most natural way for me to connect to happiness and love. Gratitude is a powerful bridge that's available to us if we only take a moment to focus on it. I know I've mentioned gratitude before, but I can't rave enough about it. It has the power to get us into a space of joy faster and more effectively than any other technique I know. Research studies on gratitude have shown that the mere process of attempting to find things you are thankful for increases your mood, even if you're not grateful for anything!

Gratitude is my link to love, but perhaps you have a different one? What love-based emotion is it easiest for you to connect to? Is it openheartedness? Is it kindness or compassion? Perhaps its generosity? The following is guidance on using your strengths to connect you to love and happiness whenever you need it.

Step 1) Take a moment to think of what love state is most comfortable for you to connect to—for example, gratitude.

Step 2) Think about how you can get into this state? Is it by thinking of a loved one or a pet, and how much you love them? Is it about appreciating something that seems beautiful to you? Perhaps it's by remembering a time you felt that emotion? Or you're able to connect to the feeling directly? If you're using gratitude, start thinking about all the things big and small you are grateful for.

Step 3) As you're thinking about whatever it is you decided on, notice how you feel. Notice how it affects the physical sensations of your body. Let this beautiful emotion fill up your whole body. Stay here as long as you like, and then try to bring this feeling with you as you continue with your day. Reconnect as needed.

Use your method of connecting to this love state as often as possible, especially whenever you feel stressed, before meetings or difficult conversations, or before facing any known stressful or challenging situations. The exercise itself will improve the amount of happiness in your life, and it trains your brain to think in that way, strengthening your neural pathways so that it becomes more and more automatic. It can often be easy to connect to love when we are calm and grounded, but a whole other story when shit hits the fan. If you practise during the easy times, it will be much easier to do it in terrible times—when you need it the most.

While outside circumstances can make our lives easier, sometimes significantly so, even those who have everything sometimes aren't happy. Trying to get happiness through a job, having the most friends, getting likes, or being attractive or wealthy are short-term solutions. They are like drugs: fun for a while, but the hangover can be intense. What's more, they can take over your life. Those who have loved ones who are addicts know that the addiction always comes first, and to what end? We are addicted to getting likes on social media, but that obsession leads us to the highest levels of depression and anxiety the world has ever seen. Losing weight or getting that promotion or car or purse or house will not increase your happiness. It just keeps you stuck in the belief that happiness is found outside of you. If fame and wealth and beauty are the key to happiness, then why do so many celebrities commit suicide or have addiction issues? There is nothing wrong with fame or wealth or being beautiful as long as you remember it is birthday cake and not the main meal.

If you want to find true happiness, then you need to focus on your internal state, how you're thinking, your beliefs, being true to your heart. The closer you are to your true state of being—love—the more happiness will naturally bubble up in your life. Chasing happiness is fiction. It's not something that can be achieved; it's a state of being. When I was miserable because I missed my husband and couldn't get a job quickly enough during the Ebola outbreak, it wasn't the outside circumstances that made me depressed. It's because I had a picture of how things were supposed to go, and my life wasn't following that picture. Life never follows the plan we make for it, well mine doesn't, but thank goodness! Because my life has turned out better than I ever could have imagined, let alone planned for.

It's imperative to take the time to connect to your heart, hear what it has to say and make sure you do what you can to follow its wisdom. Much of our unhappiness stems from ignoring our heart, not reaching our potential, or letting fear prevent us from doing something that we were meant to do. As always, emotions aren't the enemy. They are the opposite. They are wonderful gems of wisdom and insight that we need to pay attention to. Perhaps the wisdom is that you need to support your brain functioning with medication. Only you can know.

Real happiness, contentment, bliss and joy, is a road sign that you are connected to your truth.

Finding happiness is a combination of choosing to love yourself, choosing to love others, seeing love around you, and listening to the emotions rattling around inside you. Being happy is a noble goal; it is a true understanding of being connected to love.

Chapter 18
Healing

"All healing is essentially the release from fear."
– A Course in Miracles

This last year of healing and writing has been incredible in consolidating all my philosophies, life lessons and techniques into coherent sense. What better way than going through a divorce to remind you of every single technique that might be of assistance? This last year hasn't been easy, but it hasn't been so difficult either, and I can only credit the methods I've shared in this book and the support of the lovely people in my life.

I feel that I have gained an even more in-depth understanding of love, and that is my most profound burning passion, for which I will go through anything.

Unconditional love

I will always be deeply grateful that I was able to learn unconditional love. I think it is one of the greatest lessons I have learned. Loving unconditionally kept my heart open, even though my husband made it clear that he wasn't sure he wanted to stay married to me. I was able to love him and enjoy the feeling of loving, in and of itself, and for a time not need anything more. My love fed my need for love. I'm not sure how else to describe it. I was able to just focus on the beautiful feeling that loving someone creates and simply enjoy that feeling.

With unconditional love, there is no sacrifice or compromise because there is a deep trust and knowing that love is all-encompassing. Love lacks nothing, so sacrifice and compromise aren't even a discussion point. When we remember we are created from love, we are love, the idea of lack seems insane. Unconditional love is love that just grows and grows infinitely; it forgives and grows and loves and expands. I in no way felt "diminished" because Francois didn't love me to the same extent. When you love unconditionally, all struggle evaporates. There is only love, so conflict is impossible both within yourself and others. Love has no pride because nothing could depreciate it, so there's nothing to "prove."

However, after two years of this, I was also ready to experience someone loving me to the same capacity that I was capable of loving. So, I gave a timeline of when I needed an answer of whether or not he wanted to be married to me. Don't get me wrong, during this time I also had breakdowns where I would fall out of unconditional love and I'd get sucked into self-pity or worry, or some of my wounds would show themselves. But I made a conscious effort not to let myself stay there for too long. Every time I'd fall, I'd gently pick myself back up.

There is a difference between unconditional love and conditional love. Conditional love is when we use love to justify treating ourselves like shit in order to make someone else happy. Conditional love is based on the fear that the person won't love you unless you make them happy and vice versa. Conditional love is when you only love someone as long as they fulfill their end of the deal, whether if that's to ensure you have a steady income, or give you safety, or perhaps just make you look better in front of your friends or colleagues. In contrast, unconditional love comes from an overflow of self-love, so all your needs are already being fulfilled by you. Therefore, you don't need anything else from the other person, and they are just birthday cake.

Since the moment I realized I wanted more, I wanted a great love. I've struggled with the coexistence of loving unconditionally and wanting to be in a mutually loving relationship complete with reciprocity. If I loved him unconditionally, why did I now have this desire to be in a true partnership? How could I love him unconditionally and then have the right to make a demand that he emotionally commits to our marriage? Isn't that loving with the condition that he loves me back?

But something I've discovered over the last two years is that loving unconditionally means that you love regardless of the form of your relationship. I didn't only have to love him romantically.

When you focus on choosing love, on having love pull you, on what you want, that is the process of letting love expand. Love's natural desire is to expand. I realize now that wanting a great love was a completely natural progression. After learning unconditional love, the next step is wanting to learn how to love on an even larger and profound level, which meant I needed a partner that was open or capable of that.

Stepping into your potential

What had precipitated my request that we go into couples counselling was that I was ready to step into my full potential. My marriage constrained that ability because I was so concerned about making Francois feel bad, that I kept myself small. Stepping into my potential meant loving and being true to myself. Letting myself shine and not having to apologize for it. My husband had been getting increasingly annoyed and embarrassed by me, which wasn't fair for either of us.

I knew that I was ready for and wanted a great love, a love that was equally reciprocated. Loving unconditionally meant loving my ex-husband regardless of what his decisions were. As well as loving him regardless of what form our relationship took. I had learned to love while in limbo, and now my love wanted to expand into a great love, even if it meant finding that with someone else. There was no bitterness or resentment, only an intense yearning for something more. I desired to be all of myself, to blossom in a way that only love can unfold you.

I wanted a great love and was no longer willing to settle. I knew it was time for me to stop being small and step into my light. I'm not sure if I am destined to have a great love with myself or a great love with the universe or a great love with a man who has walked the same journey as me. But I do know it's no longer possible for me to play small. I finally accepted that I needed to really be myself and shine my light regardless of how scary it was.

I'm not sure what my life will bring, but I know that if I hadn't decided to step into my potential, then I might have still been married, and you wouldn't be reading these words right now. Stepping into our light is a daily practice, and I personally find it terrifying, but I no longer can live any other way.

Intuition

Part of stepping into your potential means being connected to your intuition. As I let go of all the things no longer serving me, I paid extra attention to my intuition. My intuition told me that Francois wasn't ready for what I wanted. And once Francois confirmed that in our last counselling session, I knew it was over. But, after Francois and I separated, it was challenging for me to hear my intuition. I was filled with doubt and fear that we had made the wrong decision. However, opportunities to really connect with my body started coming up. I began to focus on finding my intuition through my body, and the wisdom and messages my body has. It has been a new frontier.

Intuition is our internal compass, it is what tells us which path we need to take, it is what ensures that we learn the lessons that we need to learn, and it is what gets us to the top of the mountain the quickest and with the least amount of suffering.

Our intuition and our path don't have to be dramatic; it could be a tiny whisper of discontent to alert you that something isn't quite right. Or the feeling of your heart filling with joy when you do a small, simple act. However, if you feel your intuition is speaking with any emotion, then it's not your intuition. Although emotions are often present to tell us a message, they are different than intuition. Our intuition always speaks to us as a fact, a statement rather than an opinion or emotional thought.

Remember all the times I was following my intuition, and I had emotions of despair and pain? Those weren't signs that I should stop following what my intuition said. They were just emotional reactions to me stretching myself beyond my comfort zone. If I had decided not to buy my apartment when I had those distraught emotions of "this is crazy," then during the pandemic, I don't know what I would have done. I would have had no home. I probably would have gone back to live with my parents. They're great but really!?

When we break out of our comfort zone, we will always feel fear. And for me, I sometimes feel irrational anger when my intuition is trying to get my attention. But even though there is a presence of irritation, it is NOT my intuition. It's more a red flag that I need to stop and look within. Then I can listen to my intuition. Intuition comes from your soul, or your high self or God, however you want to think of it. It is not concerned with small details. It has a sureness and confidence in your greatness and your ability to accomplish what you need.

After splitting with Francois, I continued to stay on in the Middle East. I wanted to make sure, as much as possible, that the program could run without me, especially after I was told that if I left, the program would end. (It has continued without me by the way!) Then my apartment came through, and I quit and moved to France. After a few months, I got some consultancy jobs that were precisely what I needed. And then, I got a clear message that it was time for me to write this book finally. I have been putting off writing this book for six years. Which was when I first knew that I would have to write something, I just didn't know what on. Even though I knew it was finally time to write, I was reluctant, and I accepted some other jobs that would have significantly delayed the writing process. Then the Pandemic happened, and those jobs fell through, and I had no choice but to spend my time writing full time.

Although feelings can have a lot of wisdom, they are different from intuition. So, remember, intuition does not speak with emotion; it just is. My intuition told me to let Francois go. It told me to buy my apartment in France, and to focus on my personal healing. Finally, my intuition told me to write a book, and here we are.

Transformation of love

My vigilance on choosing love and focusing on what I wanted, helped me discover unconditional love, and also gave me the strength to let go and move on. I want a great love, and however much I tried to make my marriage an expression of that, it wasn't going to happen. I needed to accept that and open up my heart for a new experience. When we separated, it was with the deep knowledge that it's what needed to happen.

It was time to stop clinging to the safety and comfort he brought and stand on my own two feet and step into my light. We both needed to part ways and go on our own journeys, and that doesn't mean the love stopped. In fact, I remember meditating and trying to stop the love I had for him, and it just felt so discordant! Like every cell of my body was playing a wrong note.

Through my grieving and healing process, I have had to convert the love I have for Francois rather than cut it off. My unconditional love for Francois has transformed and shifted mainly back to myself and the universe as I heal new wounds and deeper layers of old fears. Over this time of gently extricating ourselves emotionally from each other, I've even learned to love him while simultaneously experiencing anger and hurt. This healing is always a process, and although my desire for a great love has ironically taken my romantic situation a few steps back, I know it needed to happen. Sometimes we need to take a couple of steps back to take giant leaps forward. Sometimes we need to sleep and rest before we run a marathon. There are cycles in life: winter and summer, day and night, tides coming in and tides going out. Sometimes to progress, we need to pause.

Healing

My healing process through getting divorced has been much of what you have read throughout this book. I firmly believe in implementing my teachings in my own life. When I first came to France, I spent most days alone. I was too wounded and fragile to handle social interactions. However, that solitary time gave me space to take care of my broken heart. I regularly meditated, often for three hours or more at a time. In my meditations, I would feel all the emotions that my heart was having. I'd label the emotion, breathe it in and out through my heart until it faded away, and another emotion would come up. Then I'd breathe that one in and out through my heart. I would do this for as long as the emotions came up or until I got too exhausted and my heart shut down. This meditation alone, I would do for hours a day.

I have learned that emotions are not bad or negative, even when they are painful. Feelings are just signs of met or unmet needs. They are guidance on which way you need to go or where you need to focus your attention. Just like bodily pain is an indicator that something needs attention and healing. So too are uncomfortable emotions indicators that some part of us needs extra care and attention.

During this time, connecting to unconditional love through meditation is what kept me sane. To feed and soothe my heart, I would regularly connect to the oneness and infinite love that is in the air around us. As I've described in previous chapters, I would use visualizations to see my heart connected to the universe or fill my heart with white light while also sending it to others. I used these techniques daily and continue to do so. The methods in this book are not a one-time fix-all. Just like we have to regularly clean our house, so too do we routinely need to clean our mind so that we can more easily connect to our truth and our essence that is love.

What was most helpful about doing these techniques is they continuously reminded me of why I was putting myself through all of this. Connecting to love feels like bliss, but it also gives us purpose and propels us to fulfill our potential. Love wants to expand. Shining our light, being our true selves, opening our hearts, are expressions of love expanding. It gave my growing pains meaning.

It hasn't been a comfortable journey of healing, and there is still a bit to go, but it also hasn't been as difficult as I thought it was going to be. When I had my private practice in Vancouver, I worked on a lot of divorce cases, and I always saw divorce as almost worse than death because it was so much more pointed and personal. Divorce is also the death of a dream, a future that you thought you would have. It's the death of a way of life. Furthermore, divorce is self-inflicted, and so you still really question if it's the right decision, if you could have done something else or if it was a mistake that you did such and such. My clients would resonate with this, and now I can see why.

Divorce is a death of sorts, and also a rejection, and yet it also isn't. My divorce didn't happen because I'm unlovable. It happened because we both had different lessons that we needed or still need to learn.

Disasters are not punishments. They are opportunities for growth.

I needed to build my life back up again, but I could choose how I wanted to do that. What I want to include, what was important and who I want to be. When disasters strike, there is pain. That is inevitable. But we need to think about what are we going to do with this disaster? Are we going to use it to prove that we are a victim and continue to disempower ourselves? Or are we going to use it as an opportunity to rebuild in a healthier way? The people I have worked with in disasters have shown me repeatedly that we are far more resilient than we think we are. Our hearts are bigger and more durable than we think. We have far more strength and more resources than we might realize. The pain that I have lived through is nothing compared to some of yours, and perhaps more than some others of you. But the details of what creates pain is just that, a detail.

When I got back from Haiti and started working in one of the richest neighbourhoods in Canada, people would often ask me, "How can you listen to the problems of these rich people when you just spent the last year in Haiti?" And I would always respond with, "Sadness is sadness is sadness. Anger is anger is anger. Hurt is hurt is hurt." It doesn't matter why we have this hurt, only that we have it, and now what are we going to do about it? Pain cannot be quantified. Pain is pain, and to me, it doesn't even matter what caused it. Just that we acknowledge it, label it, feel it, learn from it, and then choose love.

Internal fears

Over this last year, I had a lot of different internal fears come up. I'm not sure if they ever stop coming up. Fears that I'm not good enough, or that I'm on the wrong path (no such thing I know!) or that I'm an asshole. But that's ok. Every time a fear comes up, it just means I'm finding more of myself that needs love. As much as I really wish I was perfect, I'm getting more comfortable with not being perfect and just being. I find this makes me such a better therapist and friend because I can be with the rejected parts in others too.

This last year I have delved into myself to understand the different wounds that I had. I had such a strong one of not being lovable. I would feel the suffering (not to be confused by pain) that this belief would give me until I finally understood and was ready to let go of this extra suffering I was creating for myself. I had the physical and emotional pain of a broken heart, but the suffering was what I added—the suffering from the meaning I was creating of why or how this could have happened. I had to look at that, identify it and take responsibility for the unnecessary suffering I was putting myself through. I painted an inspirational quote about me being loveable and hung it in my bedroom. I started to repeat that I was lovable over and over again, meditating on it as a mantra. Then I did actions with the intent of doing them because I was loveable. I started to study tantric practices to embody my own self-lovableness (not a word I know), and I spent hours talking to and comforting my heart as she cried. Little by little, my wound healed. Every time I chose love through my "I am lovable" mantra, or through the care that I gave my heart or through the tantric exercises I would do for myself, my wound of being unlovable would get less and less intense. It wasn't a miraculous process, although perhaps all things are miraculous if you take the time to consider their amazingness. Rather, it was slow and deliberate healing.

Compassion

Perhaps the biggest lesson I've learned this year is compassion: compassion for myself, compassion for the parts of me I don't like, compassion for fears, compassion for my painful cysts, compassion for my ex-husband, compassion for those others who hurt me, compassion for anyone regardless of what they do or don't do.

Fear, pain, hurt and anger are all just a cry for compassion.

Integrating all aspects of yourself

If love is everything, then it's opposite must be nothing, and that's what fear is. Fear is the lack of. It is the belief that we are not love, that we can be harmed or destroyed or rejected. This was something I had to come back to over and over this last year. I had to remind myself that fear is just a call for love. When I first separated and was consumed with the fear that I was unlovable, part of my healing process was to delve headfirst into this. To feel the terror and pain of rejection, to see and feel the cracks in my heart. I wasn't emotionally capable of doing this all day every day. Still, I did set a few hours every day to immerse myself in this fear. To really get to know and understand it and love it unconditionally. Which meant at first, that it didn't even want to be comforted. It didn't want me to look at it, and it didn't want to accept love if I was only giving that love to heal it. So, I started with visualizing this unlovable part of me as a black blob. I just sat beside it and asked it questions so that I could truly understand its perspective. Then slowly, as it trusted me more, it would let me comfort it in ways it needed. Perhaps it was by bringing in a star to shine beside it or tucking it into bed because it was exhausted (hey, it's my imagination, anything is possible!). As I understood the deeper layers of it, I was able to integrate it into me more and more, making it an accepted part of me. Sending it love for just being the black blob that it was. Then the blob became smaller, and then it changed into a different shape, and then it didn't have a form and was just a thought in my mind that reminded me to have compassion for myself and then compassion for others.

Connecting

Even though I really want to dedicate my heart to the world, I'm finding that the most important exercise of all is regularly taking care of my slightly dramatic heart. We do the heart connection because this relationship between you and your heart is singularly the most important relationship you can have in your life. Then once you are connected to your heart, you need to connect your heart and brain. When these two are in sync, magic happens. There is a cartoon I love of a man that has guitar strings from his brain to his heart, and he is strumming them. When our brain and heart work in unison, the music they make is divine. This means not just understanding things in your head, but using the techniques here to know those things in your heart as well. HeartMath is a great organization that has many resources and techniques on how to increase coherence or heart connection.

Supportive relationships

For me to truly heal, I need the assistance of others. I made sure that I surrounded myself with trustworthy and loving people. I hired some professionals to help me in my healing process. I reached out to mentors and old friends for support, and I started to accept the kindness and generosity that was all around me, but I had previously shut myself off from. Although, as an introvert and a highly sensitive empath, my healing process is mainly solitary, I know the importance and vital healing effects that outside support has. My mom would help me stay on the path of love by reminding me or warning me compassionately when I descended into a path of bitterness. I wouldn't have come through this year as smoothly if it wasn't for my mom. She's been a pillar of strength and wisdom and has continuously encouraged me to return to my true loving self. I know I said divorce is like a death, but I would much rather go through a hundred divorces than have to live through my parents' death.

Forgiveness

When we have anger or blame others for something, we are often suffering more from it than they are. Forgiveness is not an excuse for the pain to continue; forgiveness is about addressing the root of the pain, the root of the fear, and healing it. Perhaps that's through ending a relationship or being kinder to yourself. The point of forgiveness is to give love to all places.

Being able to forgive has been the final step in healing. My divorce inspired a lot of pain, it brought up some deep wounds and deeper layers of old wounds I thought I had already healed. Yet it was a profoundly beautiful journey. I wouldn't have changed or skipped the last year for anything. I have forgiven my ex-husband for the mistakes that he's made, and I forgive myself for the mistakes I've made. To do this, I let go of what I think he or I should have done and accept that we need to go in different directions. It's tragic, and I've had to work on forgiving the universe that this is so, but part of forgiveness is letting go.

Conclusion

I'm not sure what's going to happen in my life now. With my line of work, I was accustomed to expecting the unpredictable, but the Pandemic is bringing this to a whole new level. Ten years ago, this not knowing would have driven me to a panic attack, but right now, I feel a strange sense of peace. I know the universe will take it from here. I still don't have a French visa, but as I say: "The universe got me into this, so the universe can get me out."

Right now, I'm content with finishing this book, and then the world is my oyster!

There's a whole world of happiness out there. It's better and more beautiful than we could ever create or imagine for ourselves. I'm ready to follow my intuition and do whatever it asks of me. I don't feel like I'm at the end yet, who knows what's going to happen this coming year. Although I am starting to get antsy again…

I know I can sometimes come off as serious when I'm writing, but all my friends and clients will tell you that I joke and laugh all the time. Life is not about being serious. You don't have to be stern to be spiritual, disciplined perhaps, but I'm not great at that, so I'm going to let someone else write that book. As a child, I was always trying to make God giggle, and still, the thought of seeing him giggling behind his big hands makes me smile. Make sure you do what gives you joy and know that what you're afraid of is not nearly as bad as you think it is. Above all, remember, you've already crossed the finish line! You've made it! Congratulations! Now all you have to do is open your eyes.

Yes, choosing love can be hard work, and often requires vigilance. But it is the most phenomenal path, with such a deep sense of joy and fulfillment, strength and compassion, love and open-heartedness, that I can't fathom why we spend much of our life avoiding this undertaking. Relax, let yourself float on top of the water and take a moment to look at the blue sky above you. There is so much stunning beauty all around us in every moment: we only need to open our eyes to see it.

Epilogue

"Some people dream of accomplishing good things…
others stay awake and do them."
– Anonymous

Being a counsellor requires that we open our eyes to not only our own shortcomings but also to the tragedies of the world. It could be said that we see the ugliest side of humanity, and yet our dream of doing good things by helping and supporting others, makes it so that we also witness the BEST of humankind.

Yes, clients talk to us about their struggles and obstacles, but we get to witness not only their fight in overcoming these roadblocks but their courage in facing them and continuing to try, sometimes despite all odds. We have the amazing job of looking for and seeing the light in others and nourishing its growth. I can think of no better reason to be awake and living our dream.

I have no idea what will happen in the future. Often it seems like there is a world disaster every week. However, I do know that the world is a little better for having all of these incredible people in it, and I know all of us will do what we can to continue to improve it.

-Excerpt from my valedictorian speech, 2010

Resources

Keep connected to love:
Sign up for the mailing list to stay updated on events, workshops, online courses, retreats as well as gifts and free meditations: www.vanwyckconsulting.com

Social media:

- ◊ www.facebook.com/vanwyckconsulting
- ◊ www.instagram.com/vanwyckconsulting

Useful techniques and skills:

- ◊ HeartMath heart connection techniques www.heartmath.com
- ◊ Non Violent Communication www.cnvc.org
- ◊ Lifespan integration www.lifespanintegration.com
- ◊ Online free mindfulness-based stress reduction course (MBSR) www.palousemindfulness.com
- ◊ Cynthia Morgan hypnotherapy www.thecynthiamorgan.com
- ◊ Layla Martin sexual and relationship healing courses www.laylamartin.com
- ◊ A Course in Miracles www.acim.org

Practitioners in Psychology:

- ◊ Alyson Jones and Associates www.alysonjones.ca
- ◊ Van Wyck Consulting www.vanwyckconsulting.com
- ◊ Constance Lynn Hummel www.constancelynn.com

Resources for Highly Sensitive Empaths:

- ◊ Positive News www.positive.news
- ◊ Van Wyck Consulting www.vanwyckconsulting.com/highly-sensitive-empath-hse/

◊ Elaine Aron's website for highly sensitive people www.hsperson.com

Psychology Resources:

◊ Adler University www.adler.edu
◊ Canadian counselling and psychotherapy association www.ccpa-accp.ca
◊ British Columbia Association of Clinical Counsellors www.bc-counsellors.org

Great books:

◊ A Course in Miracles, 2007 (The Foundation for Inner Peace, 3rd ed.)
◊ A Course in Love, Joan Gattuso, (HarperOne ,1997)
◊ The Prophet, Kahlil Gibran (Alfred A Knopf, 1973)
◊ Rumi (anything by him)
◊ The forty rules of love, Elif Shafak (Penguin, 2010)
◊ Siddhartha, Hermann Hesse (New Directions, 1922)
◊ The Field: the quest for the secret force of the universe, Lynne McTaggart (Element Books, 2003)
◊ The Anatomy of Peace, Arbinger Institute (Berrett-Koehler, 2008)
◊ You can Heal your Life, Louise Hay (Hay House, 1984)

Energy work practitioners:

◊ Heidi Reid (bodytalk, mindscape) www.thewisdomtoheal.com/
◊ Cora van Wyck (craniosacral therapy and energy work): corajane58@gmail.com

About the Author

Jennifer van Wyck MSM is a psychotherapist, humanitarian, author, inspirational motivational speaker, spiritual teacher, energy worker, and grounded intuitive guide.

Jennifer is passionate about helping people reach their fullest potential by helping them to connect to their inner wisdom and magnificence. She has worked with thousands of people from all walks of life and believes that no pain is too small to focus on, learn from and overcome.

Drawing on her unique experiences as a humanitarian, psychotherapist and energy worker, she weaves all her skills to create programs that profoundly and effectively address the root struggles of her clients. She works with those who have survived natural disasters, epidemics and war zones, while also assisting western clients and humanitarians all over the world through her online therapy sessions.

She is the director of van Wyck consulting which was created in 2008. She has developed, implemented and supervised effective programs to address a variety of struggles, from trauma to stress management. She has received a Meritorious Service Medal from the Canadian government for her work during the Ebola outbreak, and she continues to devote her life to choosing love over fear.

She is available to lead retreats, workshops, speaking engagements and of course 1:1 therapy, and is in the process of developing online courses to further support people in connecting more deeply to love.

As she enters into her 40's she's excited to delve more into the universe that is the collective unconscious while at the same time continuing to love adventure, living life to the fullest and shining her light.

For more information or to contact Jennifer, please go to:
www.vanwyckconsulting.com